BEYOND
HUMAN
UNDERSTANDING

RACHEL TUGUTU

Copyright © 2025 Rachel Tugutu.

All rights reserved.

ISBN: 9783264641400.

BOOK 1

CONTENTS

Front Matter..............................5

Chapter 1: The Limits of Human Perception..............................11

Chapter 2: Exploring Consciousness..............................40

Chapter 3: The Nature of Reality..............................68

Chapter 4: Spiritual Perspectives..............................97

Chapter 5: The Search for Meaning and Purpose..............................127

Chapter 6: Time and Space..............................157

Chapter 7: The Anthropic Principle..............................188

Chapter 8: The Search for Extraterrestrial Life..............................217

Chapter 9: The Big Bang and the Origin of the Universe..............................245

Chapter 10: Quantum Mechanics and its Interpretations..............................274

Chapter 11: Black Holes and Wormholes..............................303

Chapter 12: The Nature of Reality..............................332

Chapter 13: Ethics and the Future of Technology....................362

Chapter 14: The Role of Science in Understanding Existence....................390

Chapter 15: Conclusion....................420

Back Matter....................446

FRONT MATTER

DEDICATION

To the tireless seekers of truth, those who dare to question, to explore, and to embrace the humbling vastness of the unknown. This book is dedicated to every individual who has ever gazed at the stars and felt a profound sense of wonder, a yearning to understand the universe's intricate tapestry. It is for those who acknowledge the limitations of human understanding, yet remain steadfast in their pursuit of knowledge, however elusive it may be. To the brave souls who navigate the labyrinth of perception, acknowledging the inherent biases that shape our reality, and who strive for a more nuanced, objective understanding of existence. May this work serve as a testament to the enduring human spirit's insatiable curiosity and its relentless quest to unravel the mysteries that lie beyond the grasp of our current comprehension. To those who find solace and inspiration in the mysteries of the cosmos, and who find the courage to confront the unknown with open hearts and minds. This is for you, the explorers of the unseen, the architects of understanding in a universe that perpetually exceeds our grasp.

PREFACE

This book, *Beyond Human Understanding*, is not a definitive answer to the universe's grand mysteries. It is, instead, an invitation to contemplate the vastness of existence that lies beyond our current comprehension. Our journey begins by acknowledging the inherent limitations of our sensory apparatus and cognitive processes. The information we receive about the world is constantly filtered and shaped by our biology, our biases, and our preconceived notions. This inherent imperfection, however, does not diminish the profound significance of our quest for understanding. It simply shifts the focus from seeking absolute truths to embracing the ongoing process of inquiry. We'll delve into the profound implications of confirmation bias, the availability heuristic, and other cognitive biases that subtly, and often unconsciously, shape our perceptions. We will explore the intricate dance between scientific observation and the philosophical implications of what we observe. We will consider how these limitations influence not only our personal understanding of reality but also the way we conduct scientific research, engage in political discourse, and even participate in the administration of justice. This exploration is not intended to instill skepticism or cynicism, but rather to foster a deeper appreciation for the complexities of knowledge and the limitations of human perception. It's a journey of intellectual humility, a recognition that there are depths of reality beyond our grasp, and that the process of discovery itself is a profound and enriching experience. The book intends to inspire a thoughtful consideration of our place in the cosmos and the endless possibilities that lie beyond our current understanding. It is an exploration of the boundary between what we know and what we don't, and an acknowledgement of the beauty and mystery that reside within that space.

INTRODUCTION

The human quest for understanding is a timeless endeavor, a journey driven by an innate curiosity about the universe and our place within it. However, this quest is fundamentally constrained by the limitations of our own being. Our sensory organs, though remarkably sophisticated, provide only a filtered glimpse of reality, omitting an immeasurable amount of information that lies beyond their capacity to perceive. Furthermore, the very structure of our minds, shaped by evolution and experience, introduces systematic biases that distort our interpretation of the information we do receive. This book delves into the fascinating interplay between these limitations and our pursuit of knowledge, exploring the profound implications of what we do and don't know. We will discuss how cognitive biases such as the anchoring effect, the framing effect, and the confirmation bias subtly shape our beliefs and judgments, influencing everything from everyday decisions to scientific breakthroughs. We will investigate the implications of these biases on scientific methodologies, political discussions, and even legal systems, highlighting the need for critical thinking and rigorous self-reflection. Beyond this, the book explores the humbling realization that our current scientific understanding, however impressive, only scratches the surface of reality. We'll look at the tantalizing possibilities presented by fields like quantum physics and consciousness studies, and how these fields push the boundaries of our conventional understanding. The overarching theme is one of intellectual humility, a recognition that the universe's vastness and complexity vastly exceeds our capacity to fully comprehend it. The journey we embark on is not one of arriving at definitive answers, but of exploring the questions themselves, embracing the wonder and mystery that define the unknown, and acknowledging the ever-evolving nature of our understanding of existence. This book is a testament to the ongoing human quest, an acknowledgment of our limitations, and a celebration of our unwavering curiosity.

CHAPTER 1

The Limits of Human Perception

Sensory Perception and its Constraints

Our understanding of the universe, of reality itself, begins with our senses. These five gateways – sight, sound, touch, taste, and smell – are the conduits through which we experience the world. Yet, to believe that these senses offer a complete or even accurate representation of reality is a profound misconception. The truth is far more nuanced and intricate. Our sensory experience is not a passive recording of the external world, but rather an active construction, a subjective interpretation shaped by the limitations and biases of our biological apparatus and cognitive processes.

Neuroscience reveals the intricate mechanisms through which our brains process sensory input. The process isn't simply one of direct transmission; it's a complex interplay of filtering, interpretation, and construction. Our brains actively select, amplify, and suppress sensory information based on a multitude of factors, including prior experiences, expectations, and emotional states. What we perceive is not a raw, unfiltered representation of the external world, but a carefully curated version, tailored to our individual biological and cognitive frameworks.

Consider the limitations of our visual perception. Our eyes detect only a fraction of the electromagnetic spectrum, leaving us blind to the vast ranges of infrared and ultraviolet radiation that permeate our environment. The colors we see are not objective properties of the world, but rather our brain's interpretation of specific wavelengths of light. Even within the visible spectrum, our perception is prone to illusions and biases. Optical illusions, such as the Müller-Lyer illusion or the Ebbinghaus illusion, demonstrate how our brain can be easily misled into misinterpreting the size or shape of objects based on contextual cues. These illusions highlight the active, constructive nature of our visual perception, revealing that what we see is not always what is truly there.

Auditory perception, similarly, is far from a perfect representation of reality. Auditory illusions, like the Shepard tone or the Tritone paradox, exemplify the subjective nature of sound perception. The Shepard tone, a continuously ascending or descending melody, creates the illusion of an unending rise or fall in pitch, even though it's a carefully constructed auditory trick. The Tritone paradox, involving a dissonant interval between two notes, demonstrates how our perception of consonance and dissonance is culturally influenced and learned. These and many other auditory illusions showcase the active role our brains play in interpreting and constructing our auditory experiences.

Our sense of touch, too, is susceptible to distortion and misinterpretation. The same temperature can feel different depending on the context; a lukewarm bath can feel cool after being in a hot shower, while it might feel warm after being in a cold environment. The perceived texture of an object can also vary depending on factors like moisture, temperature, and the force of touch. The complexity of our tactile sensory system, with its diverse receptors and neural pathways, ensures a rich and varied experience, but also one open to subjective interpretation and bias.

Our senses of taste and smell, closely intertwined, add further layers to the complexity of sensory perception. Taste is influenced by a combination of chemical receptors on our tongue and our prior experiences. The same food can taste differently depending on our mood, our level of hunger, or even the environment in which it's consumed. Smell, an even more subjective sense, is capable of triggering powerful memories and emotions, highlighting the intricate relationship between sensory input and our internal psychological states.

Beyond the limitations of individual senses, our sensory systems work in coordination to construct a holistic perception of reality. Yet, even this integrated perception is imperfect and prone to error. Our brains constantly integrate and interpret information from multiple senses, but this integration is not always seamless or accurate. Sensory conflicts, such as those seen in the McGurk effect (where visual information contradicts auditory information, leading to a different perceived sound), illustrate the complexities of sensory integration and the vulnerability of our perceptual systems to biases and distortions.

The biases inherent in our sensory processing further complicate the picture. Confirmation bias, for instance, leads us to favor information that confirms our pre-existing beliefs while ignoring or dismissing contradictory evidence. This bias, deeply rooted in our cognitive architecture, affects all aspects of our perception, influencing what we see, hear, and feel. Other cognitive biases, such as anchoring bias, availability heuristic, and halo effect, similarly distort our perception and understanding of reality. These biases, though often unconscious, profoundly shape our worldview and influence our judgments and decisions.

The subjective nature of sensory perception underscores the limitations of relying solely on our senses to understand the nature of reality. Our sensory apparatus provides a window into the world, but it's a window with inherent limitations and distortions. What we perceive is not necessarily what exists; our subjective experiences are but one interpretation among many possible ones. This realization, however humbling, lays the foundation for considering realities that exist beyond the confines of our sensory grasp, realities that may lie beyond the reach of our current cognitive and technological capabilities. This realization necessitates a shift towards intellectual humility, a recognition of the inherent limits of human perception, and an acceptance that there are depths of existence that remain, and perhaps will always remain, elusive to us. The journey into the unknown, beyond the limits of our immediate sensory experience, is a journey that demands both courage and a willingness to accept the limits of our understanding. This sets the stage for exploring the broader realms of existence, realms that challenge the very foundations of our perceived reality. The next section will delve into the ways our cognitive biases further limit and shape our perceptions, adding another layer to the intricate puzzle of human understanding.

Cognitive Biases and Illusions

Our sensory experience, as previously discussed, is a far cry from a neutral, objective recording of reality. It's a dynamic construction, filtered and shaped by the intricate workings of our brains and the inherent limitations of our biological apparatus. However, the story doesn't end with the imperfections of our senses. Even when information successfully navigates the hurdles of sensory perception, it encounters another layer of distortion: the pervasive influence of cognitive biases. These ingrained mental shortcuts, while often serving us well in the everyday navigation of life, can systematically skew our understanding of the world, leading to flawed conclusions and distorted perceptions.

Confirmation bias, perhaps the most well-known of these biases, represents a potent force shaping our beliefs. It's the tendency to favor information that aligns with our pre-existing beliefs, while simultaneously downplaying or dismissing contradictory evidence. This bias is not merely a passive preference; it actively influences how we search for, interpret, and remember information. For example, someone who believes climate change is a hoax is more likely to seek out and readily accept information supporting this belief, while dismissing or reinterpreting evidence that points to the contrary. This isn't necessarily a conscious act of deception; rather, it's a deeply ingrained cognitive process that operates below the level of conscious awareness. The result, however, is a skewed perception of reality, where evidence confirming pre-existing beliefs is disproportionately weighted, leading to an incomplete and potentially inaccurate understanding. The scientific method, with its emphasis on rigorous testing and the acceptance of falsifiable hypotheses, is a direct response to the powerful influence of confirmation bias.

The availability heuristic is another significant cognitive bias that impacts our perception and judgment. This bias reflects our tendency to overestimate the likelihood of events that are easily recalled, often due to their vividness or recent occurrence. For example, after seeing news reports about a plane crash, individuals might overestimate the risk of air travel, even though statistically, it remains incredibly safe. Similarly, the fear of shark attacks is often disproportionate to the actual risk, fuelled by the media's tendency to sensationalize such events. The ease with which these events are recalled, often due to their dramatic nature, distorts our perception of probability, leading to irrational fears and misinformed decisions. This bias highlights the importance of distinguishing between anecdotal evidence and statistically significant data.

Anchoring bias, a pervasive influence in decision-making, demonstrates the significant impact of initial information on subsequent judgments. This bias involves placing disproportionate weight on the first piece of information received, even if that information is irrelevant or arbitrary.

Negotiations provide a clear illustration of this bias. The initial offer often serves as an anchor, influencing the subsequent counter-offers and the final agreement. For example, a real estate agent presenting a high initial asking price will typically achieve a higher final selling price than if they had started with a lower offer. This demonstrates how an arbitrary initial value can disproportionately influence final judgments, highlighting the vulnerability of our cognitive processes to manipulation. Awareness of anchoring bias is crucial in various contexts, from negotiating salaries to evaluating investment opportunities.

Beyond these common biases, a multitude of others significantly impact our perception of reality. The halo effect, for example, causes us to let one positive trait unduly influence our overall judgment of a person or thing. If someone is perceived as attractive, we might unconsciously attribute other positive qualities to them, such as intelligence or kindness, even in the absence of supporting evidence. Conversely, the horns effect leads to the opposite bias, where a single negative trait overshadows other positive characteristics. These biases illustrate the interconnectedness of our judgments and the potential for one aspect of perception to significantly influence other unrelated aspects.

The framing effect, another critical bias, illustrates how the way information is presented can dramatically influence our interpretation and decision-making. For example, a medical treatment described with a 90% success rate will likely be perceived more favorably than the same treatment described with a 10% failure rate, even though the underlying information is identical. This emphasizes the importance of considering the context and framing of information when evaluating its validity and implications.

The impact of these cognitive biases extends beyond the realm of personal decision-making. They play a significant role in shaping scientific inquiry, political discourse, and even legal proceedings. Confirmation bias, for example, can lead to researchers selectively interpreting data to support their pre-existing hypotheses, potentially hindering the advancement of scientific knowledge. Political polarization, often fuelled by confirmation bias and the availability heuristic, can create echo chambers where individuals are predominantly exposed to information reinforcing their existing beliefs, leading to increased division and decreased understanding. The legal system, despite efforts to remain objective, is susceptible to these biases as well. Jurors, for example, might be unduly influenced by emotionally charged testimony or the way evidence is presented, leading to potentially flawed verdicts.

Overcoming the pervasive influence of cognitive biases requires a conscious and sustained effort. This involves developing critical thinking skills, which entails questioning assumptions, seeking out diverse perspectives, and rigorously evaluating evidence. Cultivating self-awareness is crucial in recognizing the inherent biases that shape our perception. While it's impossible to completely eliminate these biases, understanding their influence is the first step towards mitigating their impact. The scientific method, with its emphasis on replication, peer review, and rigorous testing, represents a robust framework for combating bias in scientific inquiry. Similarly, in daily life, seeking out diverse sources of information, actively seeking out contradictory evidence, and engaging in thoughtful reflection are essential steps in navigating the complexities of information and forming well-informed conclusions.

Numerous psychological experiments have demonstrated the pervasive influence of these biases. The Wason Selection Task, for example, highlights our tendency to confirm rather than falsify hypotheses. In this experiment, participants are presented with cards displaying letters and numbers and asked to determine which cards need to be turned over to test a specific rule. Results consistently demonstrate that participants are more likely to select cards confirming the rule than those that could potentially falsify it. Similarly, numerous studies have explored the anchoring bias, consistently demonstrating the profound influence of initial information on subsequent judgments. The effectiveness of techniques such as blind testing in scientific research underscores the importance of minimizing bias to achieve objective results.

In conclusion, while our senses offer a crucial window to the world, they are fundamentally limited and prone to distortion. Adding to this complexity are cognitive biases, pervasive mental shortcuts that systematically distort our understanding of reality. These biases, often unconscious, impact our decision-making, our understanding of the world, and even the pursuit of scientific knowledge. Developing critical thinking skills, cultivating self-awareness, and utilizing rigorous methodologies are crucial steps in navigating the complexities of information and forming accurate and well-informed conclusions. Recognizing the inherent limits of human perception, both sensory and cognitive, is not a sign of weakness; it is a necessary foundation for a more nuanced and objective understanding of existence. The journey beyond human understanding demands a commitment to intellectual humility and a willingness to confront the inherent biases that shape our perceptions.

The Role of Language in Shaping Reality

Our exploration of the limits of human perception has thus far focused on the inherent constraints of our sensory apparatus and the pervasive influence of cognitive biases. However, the story doesn't end there. A further layer of complexity arises from the very tool we use to understand and articulate our experiences: language. Language, far from being a neutral medium for transmitting information, actively shapes our perception of reality, influencing not only how we describe the world but also how we experience it.

The Sapir-Whorf hypothesis, also known as the linguistic relativity hypothesis, posits a profound connection between language and thought. This hypothesis, in its strongest form, suggests that the structure of a language determines the structure of thought and perception. In other words, the language we speak fundamentally shapes how we perceive the world and conceptualize reality. While the strongest version of this hypothesis has been subject to significant debate and refinement, a weaker version, suggesting that language influences thought and perception, is widely accepted within linguistic and cognitive science.

The core argument of the weaker version of the Sapir-Whorf hypothesis rests on the observation that different languages categorize and conceptualize the world in distinct ways. These differences are not merely superficial variations in vocabulary; they extend to fundamental aspects of our understanding of time, space, color, and even causality. Consider, for example, the Hopi language, which lacks grammatical tenses in the same way as Indo-European languages. This grammatical structure doesn't simply mean that Hopi speakers lack words for "past," "present," and "future"; it suggests that their conceptualization of time itself differs fundamentally from that of English speakers. Instead of viewing time as a linear progression, Hopi speakers may perceive time in a more holistic or cyclical manner, integrating aspects of past, present, and future within a single, unified experience.

Similarly, different languages categorize colors in distinct ways. While English distinguishes between blue and green, some languages group these colors under a single category, highlighting the cultural and linguistic relativity of color perception. This doesn't imply that speakers of these languages cannot distinguish between blue and green visually; rather, their linguistic system doesn't necessitate separate categories for these colors, influencing how they conceptualize and categorize the visual spectrum. These differences in linguistic categorization extend to other aspects of perception, including spatial relationships and the conceptualization of causality.

The implications of linguistic relativity are far-reaching, extending beyond simple vocabulary differences. They suggest that our understanding of the world is not a purely objective, universal experience, but rather a culturally and linguistically shaped construction. What we perceive as fundamental aspects of reality, such as time, space, or color, are not necessarily universal constants but rather constructs shaped by our linguistic and cultural backgrounds. This perspective challenges the notion of a single, objective reality accessible to all, suggesting instead a multiplicity of realities shaped by the diverse languages and cultures of humankind.

However, the Sapir-Whorf hypothesis also raises important questions about the limits of language itself. Even within a single language, the capacity to fully articulate experiences and ideas is often limited. Many experiences, particularly those that are deeply emotional or spiritual in nature, defy simple verbal description. The ineffable aspects of consciousness, the profound sense of awe inspired by a natural landscape, or the overwhelming power of love – these are experiences that often resist easy translation into language. This inherent limitation of language doesn't diminish the validity of these experiences; rather, it highlights the richness and complexity of human experience that extends beyond the boundaries of linguistic expression.

The challenge, then, lies in recognizing both the shaping power of language and its limitations. While language provides a crucial framework for understanding and communicating our experiences, it's essential to acknowledge that it's only one lens through which we perceive the world. Our understanding of reality is not simply a matter of translating sensory input into words; it involves a complex interplay of perception, cognition, language, and culture.

Furthermore, the very act of naming something – the act of assigning a label to a phenomenon – can significantly influence how we perceive and interact with it. By categorizing and defining aspects of reality, language simultaneously creates boundaries and limits our understanding of the interconnectedness of things. The scientific endeavor, while seeking to describe reality objectively, relies heavily on language to articulate its findings, and this reliance can introduce its own set of limitations and biases. The very act of measurement, a seemingly objective process, involves choices of units, scales, and definitions that reflect underlying linguistic and conceptual frameworks.

The evolution of scientific language itself serves as a testament to the dynamic interaction between language and understanding. As our scientific understanding advances, so too does our linguistic capacity to articulate those advancements. New concepts and theories necessitate the creation of new terms and frameworks, constantly pushing the boundaries of language to encompass increasingly complex phenomena. This ongoing evolution underscores the fluid and dynamic relationship between language and our comprehension of the universe.

Consider the challenges faced by scientists attempting to describe phenomena at the quantum level. The counterintuitive nature of quantum mechanics requires the development of new linguistic frameworks to grapple with concepts such as superposition, entanglement, and wave-particle duality. These concepts challenge our everyday intuitions, demanding the creation of new linguistic tools to effectively communicate and understand these realities. The development of these new linguistic tools is not simply a matter of finding suitable words; it involves the creation of new conceptual models that reshape our understanding of the fundamental nature of reality.

The limitations of language are not confined to the realm of science; they extend to all aspects of human experience. Attempts to articulate complex philosophical concepts, emotional states, or spiritual experiences often encounter the same challenges. The richness and nuance of human experience often resist straightforward verbalization, leaving us with a sense of incompleteness and inadequacy in our attempts to express ourselves fully. However, this inadequacy should not be viewed as a failure of language; rather, it serves as a reminder of the vastness and complexity of human experience, which often transcends the boundaries of linguistic expression.

The creative arts, in their various forms, offer an alternative approach to grappling with the limitations of language. Music, painting, sculpture, and literature provide alternative means of expressing ideas, emotions, and experiences that resist easy verbal articulation. These forms of expression utilize sensory modalities beyond language, allowing for a more nuanced and evocative communication of complex realities.

In conclusion, the exploration of the limits of human perception necessitates a critical examination of the role of language in shaping our understanding of reality. While language provides a crucial framework for communication and thought, its inherent limitations and biases should be acknowledged. Understanding the interaction between language, thought, and perception is crucial in navigating the complexities of existence and pursuing a more nuanced and objective understanding of the universe. The journey beyond human understanding demands a recognition of the power and limitations of language, coupled with an appreciation for the richness of human experience that transcends the boundaries of linguistic expression.

The Unknowable and the Limits of Scientific Inquiry

Our preceding discussion highlighted the profound influence of language on perception, revealing how the very tools we employ to understand the world shape our understanding of it. However, the limitations we face extend beyond the constraints of language itself; they penetrate the very core of our scientific endeavors, revealing inherent boundaries to our ability to comprehend the universe's fundamental nature. This section delves into the unknowable, exploring the inherent limits of scientific inquiry and the humbling realization that certain aspects of reality may forever remain beyond our grasp.

One potent metaphor for these limitations comes from the realm of mathematics, specifically Kurt Gödel's incompleteness theorems. These theorems, proved in the 1930s, demonstrated that within any sufficiently complex formal system – a system of axioms and rules of inference – there will always exist true statements that cannot be proven within the system itself. In simpler terms, there will always be truths that lie beyond the reach of the system's logical framework. This has profound implications for our understanding of the universe, suggesting that even the most rigorous and comprehensive scientific theories may ultimately be incomplete, incapable of encompassing all truths about reality.

The incompleteness theorems are not merely a technical detail within mathematical logic; they represent a fundamental limitation on our ability to achieve complete knowledge. They serve as a powerful reminder of the inherent limitations of formal systems in capturing the richness and complexity of the universe. Just as a formal system can contain true but unprovable statements, our scientific models may struggle to explain certain phenomena, not due to flaws in the models themselves, but due to inherent limitations in our capacity to construct a complete and encompassing framework for understanding. This is not to say that scientific inquiry is futile; rather, it underscores the need for intellectual humility and a recognition that certain aspects of reality may forever remain beyond our complete understanding.

The limitations of scientific inquiry extend beyond the abstract realm of mathematical logic and into the concrete world of observation and measurement. The very act of observation inevitably alters the system being observed, a principle vividly illustrated in quantum mechanics. The Heisenberg uncertainty principle, a cornerstone of quantum theory, states that there is a fundamental limit to the precision with which certain pairs of physical properties of a particle, such as position and momentum, can be known simultaneously. This is not simply a matter of technological limitations; it is a fundamental constraint imposed by the nature of reality at the quantum level. The act of measuring a particle's position inevitably disturbs its momentum, and vice versa. This implies that our attempts to gain complete knowledge about the quantum world are inherently constrained by the very act of observation.

Further complicating matters, quantum phenomena exhibit a degree of randomness and indeterminacy that challenges our classical understanding of causality. The behavior of quantum systems cannot always be predicted with certainty, even with complete knowledge of the initial conditions. This inherent probabilistic nature of quantum mechanics introduces a fundamental limit to our ability to make precise predictions about the universe at its most fundamental level. The apparent randomness in quantum events isn't necessarily a sign of our incomplete understanding; rather, it might reflect an underlying reality that intrinsically defies deterministic descriptions. This challenges our intuitive expectation of a universe governed by predictable, causal laws and forces us to confront the possibility of inherent indeterminacy in the fundamental building blocks of reality.

The challenges are not restricted to the quantum realm. Even in seemingly well-understood areas of classical physics, limitations in observation and measurement remain. For instance, the vastness of the universe and the limitations of our observational tools restrict our ability to observe all celestial objects and phenomena. The distant reaches of space remain largely unexplored, and our understanding of the universe's evolution and structure is limited by the information we can currently gather. Furthermore, even within our observable universe, there are limitations imposed by the speed of light and the finite age of the universe itself. We can only observe events that have had time to reach us, meaning a significant portion of the universe's history and evolution remains beyond our observational reach.

These limitations, however, should not be viewed as failures of science, but rather as opportunities for deeper reflection on the nature of knowledge and the limits of our understanding. The pursuit of scientific knowledge is not about achieving ultimate explanations; it is a continuous process of refinement, of building ever-more sophisticated models and theories that better describe and explain the universe as we perceive it. The incompleteness theorems, the uncertainty principle, and the limitations of observation are not obstacles to be overcome but rather intrinsic features of the landscape of knowledge, shaping the contours of our understanding.

The recognition of these limitations calls for a fundamental shift in perspective, a move away from the aspiration of complete and definitive knowledge towards a more nuanced and intellectually humble approach. Instead of striving for ultimate explanations, we should embrace the unknown as an inherent part of the universe's nature. Scientific inquiry becomes, in this perspective, a journey of exploration rather than a quest for absolute certainty. The focus shifts from finding definitive answers to asking more profound questions, acknowledging the inherent limits of our understanding and accepting the existence of mysteries that may never be fully solved.

This intellectual humility is not a sign of defeat but a vital component of the scientific spirit. The ability to acknowledge the limitations of our knowledge and to approach the universe with a sense of wonder and curiosity is essential for fostering genuine scientific progress. It allows us to approach scientific challenges with a more open mind, recognizing that our current understanding is always incomplete and subject to revision in light of new evidence and insights.

Moreover, embracing the unknown fosters a more profound appreciation for the mysteries of existence. The realization that certain aspects of reality may forever remain beyond our complete comprehension doesn't diminish the value of scientific inquiry; instead, it enhances its significance. It allows us to appreciate the profound depths of the universe and the limitations of our human intellect, reminding us of the vastness of the unknown that surrounds us. The awe and wonder inspired by confronting the unknowable are powerful motivators for scientific exploration, driving us to push the boundaries of our knowledge while acknowledging the inevitable limits of our understanding.

In conclusion, the unknowable represents not an end to scientific inquiry, but rather a defining characteristic of it. The limitations of our sensory apparatus, the inherent biases in our cognitive processes, the constraints of language, and the fundamental limitations of scientific methods themselves all contribute to the vast realm of the unknown. Embracing these limitations with intellectual humility, acknowledging the incompleteness of our understanding, and appreciating the inherent mysteries of existence are not signs of failure, but rather essential elements of a truly profound scientific worldview. The pursuit of knowledge, in this context, becomes a lifelong journey of exploration, discovery, and acceptance – a journey where the unknown serves not as an obstacle but as a constant source of inspiration and wonder.

Embracing the Mystery

The previous sections explored the concrete limits of human perception, highlighting the constraints imposed by our sensory apparatus, the biases inherent in our cognitive processes, and the fundamental limitations of our scientific methods. These limitations, however, shouldn't be interpreted as a failure of the human endeavor to understand the universe. Instead, they point to a profound truth: the universe, in its vastness and complexity, contains an inherent element of mystery that will likely always elude complete comprehension. This mystery, far from being a source of despair or intellectual frustration, can be embraced as a source of wonder, inspiration, and even profound spiritual insight.

Many philosophical traditions have actively celebrated the mysterious and the unknowable. Mystical traditions, spanning diverse cultures and spanning millennia, often emphasize the limitations of rational understanding in grasping ultimate reality. The pursuit of knowledge, in these traditions, isn't solely a matter of intellectual analysis; it involves direct experience, intuition, and a willingness to surrender to the awe-inspiring power of the cosmos. Eastern philosophies, for example, often describe reality as ultimately beyond conceptualization. The concept of "Brahman" in Hinduism, or the "Tao" in Taoism, represent ultimate realities that are ineffable, transcending the limitations of human language and thought. Understanding these concepts doesn't involve a purely intellectual process, but a transformative experience that alters one's perception of reality.

The writings of Meister Eckhart, a 14th-century German mystic, beautifully illustrate this point. Eckhart emphasized the importance of "Gelassenheit," often translated as "detachment" or "resignation," but more accurately encompassing a state of willing surrender to the divine mystery. This wasn't a passive resignation to ignorance, but an active embrace of the unknowable, a recognition that true understanding comes not through intellectual striving, but through a

transformative encounter with the divine. His paradoxical pronouncements, often defying logical analysis, aimed precisely to shatter the rigid frameworks of rational thought and open the mind to the boundless depths of spiritual reality.

Similarly, the Kabbalah, a system of Jewish mysticism, emphasizes the inherent mystery at the heart of existence. The Kabbalistic worldview portrays the divine as infinitely transcendent, beyond human comprehension. The process of understanding, therefore, involves not merely intellectual inquiry but a profound journey of spiritual self-discovery, a gradual unveiling of hidden dimensions of reality through contemplation, prayer, and ritual.

The scientific pursuit of knowledge, despite its emphasis on empirical evidence and rational analysis, also encounters its own limits. The inherent uncertainties of quantum mechanics, as previously discussed, reveal a profound randomness at the heart of physical reality, challenging the deterministic worldview of classical physics. The existence of dark matter and dark energy, representing the vast majority of the universe's mass-energy content, further underscores our limited understanding of the cosmos. While scientific inquiry strives to unravel these mysteries, it simultaneously confronts the inherent limitations of its methods, recognizing the existence of truths that may forever lie beyond our grasp.

This recognition of the limits of scientific understanding doesn't imply the abandonment of scientific inquiry; rather, it encourages a more nuanced and humble approach. It fosters a recognition that our current models and theories are always provisional, subject to revision and refinement in light of new evidence and insights. This intellectual humility, essential to genuine scientific progress, allows for a more open and receptive attitude toward the unknown, recognizing that even our most advanced theories are but partial glimpses into the vast expanse of reality.

But embracing the mystery extends beyond the realm of science and spirituality. It pervades the realm of art, literature, and music. The greatest works of art often evoke a sense of awe and wonder, capturing something that transcends the purely rational or the easily definable. They resonate with a profound sense of mystery, inviting us to contemplate the vastness of human experience and the limits of our own understanding. The same can be said for great literature and music, which often explore themes of love, loss, hope, and despair, touching upon the fundamental mysteries of human existence.

The capacity for wonder, for awe, is a uniquely human trait, a source of inspiration and motivation. It is this sense of wonder that propelled early explorers to chart unknown seas and conquer seemingly insurmountable mountains. The same spirit drives
scientists to explore the farthest reaches of the universe, delving into the intricacies of the subatomic world. This inherent human desire to explore, to understand, is inextricably linked to our capacity for wonder, for awe in the face of the unknown.

The embrace of mystery, therefore, is not a surrender to ignorance; it's a recognition of the limitations of human understanding, combined with a profound appreciation for the richness and depth of existence. It's an invitation to engage with the world with a sense of openness and curiosity, to approach the unknown not with fear or rejection, but with a sense of wonder and humility. This perspective doesn't negate the value of scientific inquiry or rational thought; rather, it complements them, offering a framework for understanding the limits of human knowledge and the inherent mystery at the heart of reality.

The role of intuition and creative imagination becomes particularly crucial when dealing with the incomprehensible.

While scientific inquiry relies heavily on empirical evidence and logical reasoning, the exploration of the unknown often requires a leap of faith, a willingness to entertain possibilities that lie beyond the confines of current knowledge. Creative imagination allows us to formulate new hypotheses, to envision alternative perspectives, and to generate innovative solutions to complex problems. It is the bridge that connects the known to the unknown, facilitating
the exploration of uncharted territories of thought and experience.

In conclusion, the mystery of existence is not a problem to be solved, but a reality to be embraced. It's a profound invitation to engage with the world with open hearts and minds, to approach the unknown with humility and wonder. The limits of human perception, far from being a constraint, are an opportunity to cultivate a deeper understanding of ourselves, our place in the universe, and the boundless depths of the unknown that surrounds us. The journey of discovery is not a quest for ultimate certainty, but a continuous exploration, a lifelong immersion in the awe-inspiring mystery of existence. The unknown, far from being an obstacle, becomes a source of unending inspiration and a powerful reminder of the vast and wondrous universe in which we find ourselves. This acceptance of the unknown fosters a profound sense of peace and acceptance, freeing us from the relentless pursuit of definitive answers and allowing us to appreciate the beauty and complexity of existence in all its mysterious glory.

CHAPTER 2

Exploring Consciousness

The Hard Problem of Consciousness

Having explored the inherent limitations of human perception and the embrace of the unknown, we now turn to a particularly challenging enigma: consciousness. The very nature of subjective experience—the "what it's like" aspect of consciousness—presents a profound philosophical puzzle, often referred to as the "hard problem" of consciousness. This problem isn't simply a matter of scientific ignorance; it challenges the very foundations of our understanding of the relationship between mind and matter.

Materialism, a dominant perspective in contemporary science, posits that the universe is fundamentally composed of matter and energy, and that all phenomena, including consciousness, can ultimately be explained in terms of physical processes. This view, while seemingly straightforward, encounters significant difficulties when attempting to account for subjective experience. How can the purely physical processes of the brain give rise to the qualitative feel of sensations, emotions, and thoughts? The redness of red, the pain of a headache, the joy of love—these subjective qualities, or qualia, seem irreducible to purely physical descriptions. A complete neurobiological account of the brain's activity during a sensory experience might explain the firing patterns of neurons, the release of neurotransmitters, and the electrical signals traversing the brain, but it doesn't inherently explain the subjective experience itself. This is the core of the hard problem.

Consider the example of visual perception. We can meticulously map the neural pathways involved in processing visual information, from the retina to the visual cortex. We can identify the specific neurons that respond to different colors, shapes, and movements. But this detailed neurological description, however comprehensive, doesn't explain the subjective experience of seeing—the "what it's like" aspect of seeing red, green, or blue. Similarly, we can analyze the brain activity associated with feelings of pain, but this doesn't explain the qualia of pain itself—that unpleasant, intensely subjective feeling.

This gap between objective, physical descriptions of brain activity and subjective, qualitative experience is the central challenge of materialism when it comes to consciousness. While materialism successfully explains many aspects of human behavior and cognition, it struggles to provide a satisfactory account of the subjective, experiential aspect of consciousness. Some materialists attempt to circumvent this problem by arguing that qualia are ultimately epiphenomenal—byproducts of brain activity with no causal influence on behavior. This view, however, seems counterintuitive, as our subjective experiences clearly shape our thoughts, actions, and decisions.

Idealism, in contrast to materialism, proposes that reality is fundamentally mental, that consciousness is primary and that the physical world is a manifestation of mind. In this view, the subjective experience isn't a mysterious byproduct of the physical world; it's the foundation of reality itself.

While idealism provides a seemingly elegant solution to the hard problem by placing consciousness at the forefront, it encounters difficulties in explaining the apparent objectivity and regularity of the physical world. If reality is fundamentally mental, how can we account for the consistent and predictable laws of physics that govern the universe? The challenge for idealism lies in bridging the gap between subjective experience and the objective, seemingly independent physical world we observe.

Dualism, another influential perspective, proposes a fundamental distinction between mind and matter, suggesting that consciousness is not reducible to physical processes. In this view, the mind and the brain are distinct entities that interact in some way, although the nature of this interaction remains a subject of considerable debate. Dualism offers a straightforward explanation for the existence of subjective experience; it simply postulates that consciousness is a non-physical substance that interacts with the physical brain. However, this approach raises significant challenges regarding the causal relationship between mind and matter. If the mind is non-physical, how can it causally influence the physical world? And how can we empirically investigate a non-physical entity? The interaction problem, central to dualism, remains a major obstacle in establishing its scientific plausibility.

The hard problem of consciousness also underscores the limitations of reductionist approaches in science. Reductionism, a common strategy in scientific inquiry, aims to explain complex phenomena by reducing them to their simpler constituent parts. While reductionism has been remarkably successful in many scientific domains, its application to consciousness presents significant challenges. The subjective nature of experience seems resistant to reductionist analysis, as the whole seems to be more than the sum of its parts. The complex interactions of neurons in the brain, while necessary for consciousness, do not fully account for the subjective quality of experience.

Many attempts to solve the hard problem have focused on integrating scientific and philosophical perspectives. Integrated Information Theory (IIT), for example, attempts to quantify consciousness using information-theoretic concepts. It proposes that consciousness is a fundamental property of systems with high levels of integrated information. While IIT provides a potentially measurable framework for studying consciousness, it still faces challenges in fully explaining the subjective quality of experience. Other approaches, such as global workspace theory, suggest that consciousness arises from the integration and broadcasting of information across different brain regions. These theories, while offering valuable insights, haven't fully resolved the hard problem.

The persistent difficulty in addressing the hard problem highlights the inherent limitations of our current understanding of consciousness. It suggests that our existing scientific and philosophical frameworks may be inadequate to fully comprehend this fundamental aspect of existence. The quest for a comprehensive explanation of consciousness remains an open and exciting frontier of inquiry, requiring a creative integration of scientific, philosophical, and potentially even spiritual perspectives. The mystery of consciousness, far from being a source of discouragement, should be embraced as an opportunity to expand our understanding of the universe and our place within it. The journey towards understanding consciousness is not a quest for definitive answers, but a continuous exploration, a humbling reminder of the profound mysteries that still lie before us, beckoning us towards a deeper and richer understanding of ourselves and the universe we inhabit. This ongoing exploration will require a combination of rigorous scientific inquiry, insightful philosophical analysis, and an open mind capable of acknowledging the limitations of our current understanding. The hard problem, in its very difficulty, points to a realm of reality that surpasses our current grasp, challenging us to expand our conceptual frameworks and to appreciate the profound mystery at the heart of existence. And perhaps, in embracing this mystery, we may find a deeper understanding of what it means to be conscious, to exist, and to experience the wonders of this universe.

NearDeath Experiences and Altered States

Near-death experiences (NDEs) represent a compelling area of inquiry into the nature of consciousness, pushing the boundaries of conventional scientific and philosophical understanding. These experiences, often reported by individuals who have come close to death due to cardiac arrest, severe trauma, or other life-threatening situations, share striking commonalities. Many describe a sensation of leaving their body, a feeling of peace and tranquility, and encounters with deceased loved ones or spiritual entities. Some recount traversing a tunnel towards a bright light, a perception often interpreted as a transition to another realm.

The universality of certain elements within NDE accounts has led some to consider them evidence for a non-physical aspect of consciousness, capable of existing independently of the body. The detailed and vivid memories reported by individuals, despite experiencing profound physiological distress, often defy simple explanations based solely on brain malfunctioning or hypoxia. While critics point to possible physiological explanations like endorphin release or cerebral anoxia affecting brain function, these accounts remain a powerful challenge to materialistic views of consciousness. The subjective intensity of these experiences, their emotional impact, and the profound shift in perspective they often trigger in survivors cannot be easily dismissed.

One prominent interpretation of NDEs aligns with dualist perspectives on consciousness. If consciousness is not solely a product of brain activity, but possesses an independent existence, it might be able to persist even when the brain ceases to function normally. The reported out-of-body experiences, vivid perceptions of deceased loved ones, and journeys through seemingly non-physical landscapes, all challenge the notion that consciousness is entirely confined to the physical realm. However, this interpretation faces the significant challenge of explaining the mechanics of interaction between this supposed non-physical consciousness and the physical world. How would such a non-physical entity acquire information, perceive sensory details, and interact with the environment? These questions remain central challenges for dualist explanations of NDEs.

Another avenue of interpretation approaches NDEs from a neurobiological perspective. While not denying the profoundly subjective and transformative nature of these experiences, this approach seeks to explain them entirely within the framework of brain function. Research exploring the effects of oxygen deprivation on the brain has suggested possible neurological correlates for some aspects of NDEs. The release of endorphins during stressful situations could explain feelings of euphoria and peace, while disruptions in visual processing might account for the tunnel and bright light imagery. However, this approach faces difficulties in fully explaining the detail and coherence of some NDE accounts, as well as their transformative effects on the survivors' beliefs and values. The subjective richness of these experiences often transcends simple neurological explanations.

The study of NDEs is fraught with methodological challenges. The inherently subjective nature of these experiences makes rigorous scientific investigation difficult. The lack of standardized protocols for collecting data, potential biases in recall, and the influence of cultural beliefs all complicate the interpretation of reported accounts. Furthermore, the very nature of these events—occurring during life-threatening circumstances—limits the possibility of controlled experiments. Ethical considerations regarding the intervention and study of such critical events further restrict research avenues.

The exploration of altered states of consciousness, beyond NDEs, expands this inquiry further. Practices like meditation, psychedelic experiences, and sensory deprivation all induce altered states that challenge our understanding of consciousness and its boundaries. Meditation, for instance, can produce profound shifts in awareness, with reports of heightened self-awareness, altered perceptions of time, and feelings of oneness with the universe. These experiences, while deeply personal and subjective, suggest the potential for consciousness to operate in ways that differ significantly from our ordinary waking state. Psychedelic experiences, induced by substances like psilocybin or LSD, often involve vivid hallucinations, altered perception of reality, and profound emotional experiences. While these experiences can be unpredictable and potentially challenging, they offer further insights into the plasticity and flexibility of consciousness.

Sensory deprivation environments, similarly, can lead to altered states characterized by vivid hallucinations and distorted perceptions of time and space. These conditions underscore the crucial role of sensory input in shaping our conscious experience. When sensory input is minimized, the brain appears to generate its own internal experience, highlighting the active and creative nature of consciousness. Across these various altered states, common themes emerge—a sense of transcendence, altered perceptions of time and space, and heightened awareness or altered sense of self.

The exploration of NDEs and other altered states of consciousness underscores the limitations of reductionist approaches to understanding the mind. Attempting to reduce these complex experiences solely to their physiological or neurological correlates risks overlooking the richness and complexity of subjective experience. A more holistic approach, integrating scientific, philosophical, and even spiritual perspectives, appears more appropriate. This integration might allow for a more nuanced and comprehensive understanding of consciousness, acknowledging both the physical and potential non-physical dimensions of this fundamental aspect of existence.

It is crucial to acknowledge the limitations inherent in studying subjective experiences. The very act of verbalizing or describing a deeply personal and transformative experience inevitably involves a degree of interpretation and subjective filtering. The inherent difficulty in accessing the raw, unmediated experience complicates the process of scientific investigation. Researchers must be mindful of potential biases in both the reporting of experiences and their interpretation. A balanced approach necessitates both rigorous scientific investigation and a respectful acknowledgement of the profound subjective nature of these phenomena.

The study of NDEs and altered states, while challenging, provides valuable insights into the nature of consciousness and the possibility that our understanding of reality may be more limited than previously assumed. By cautiously exploring these experiences, integrating diverse perspectives, and maintaining a rigorous scientific approach while acknowledging the limitations of current methods, we can gradually deepen our comprehension of this fundamental aspect of human existence. The ongoing investigation holds immense potential for redefining our understanding of consciousness, self, and the universe itself. The quest remains a journey of exploration and intellectual humility, acknowledging the limitations of current knowledge and embracing the awe-inspiring mysteries that continue to reside at the heart of human consciousness.

Quantum Physics and Consciousness

The exploration of near-death experiences and altered states of consciousness naturally leads us to consider the profound implications of quantum physics. While seemingly disparate fields, the study of consciousness and the intricacies of the quantum realm surprisingly share intriguing commonalities that challenge our classical understanding of reality. Quantum mechanics, the theoretical framework governing the behavior of matter and energy at the atomic and subatomic levels, introduces concepts radically different from the deterministic laws governing the macroscopic world. Instead of predictable trajectories and definite properties, quantum mechanics presents a world of probabilities, superpositions, and entangled states. This inherent uncertainty and the seemingly paradoxical nature of quantum phenomena have prompted several interpretations, some of which suggest a role for consciousness in the very fabric of reality.

One of the most debated aspects of quantum mechanics is the measurement problem. In the quantum world, particles exist in a superposition of states until measured. This means that a particle, for instance, can simultaneously exist in multiple locations or possess multiple properties until an observation is made. The act of measurement, however, appears to "collapse" the wave function, forcing the particle to assume a definite state. The question that arises is: what constitutes a "measurement," and what role does the observer play in this collapse?

Some interpretations of quantum mechanics suggest that consciousness is intrinsically linked to this measurement process. The von Neumann-Wigner interpretation, for example, proposes that consciousness is essential for the collapse of the wave function. This perspective suggests that the observer's consciousness actively influences the outcome of a quantum measurement, implying a direct interaction between consciousness and the quantum world. This idea challenges the objective, observer-independent view of reality that has underpinned classical physics for centuries. It suggests that the very act of observing a quantum system fundamentally alters its state, blurring the line between observer and observed.

However, this interpretation is far from universally accepted. The Copenhagen interpretation, a more widely held perspective, avoids explicitly assigning a role to consciousness. Instead, it focuses on the mathematical formalism of quantum mechanics, emphasizing the probabilistic nature of quantum phenomena without directly addressing the role of the observer. Many physicists find the von Neumann-Wigner interpretation too subjective and lacking in empirical evidence. The challenge lies in finding a way to experimentally test the role of consciousness in quantum measurement, a task that remains exceptionally difficult, if not impossible, given the current state of our technology and understanding.

The concept of quantum entanglement further complicates our understanding of the relationship between the observer and the observed. Entanglement describes a phenomenon where two or more particles become linked in such a way that they share the same fate, regardless of the distance separating them. Measuring the properties of one entangled particle instantaneously determines the properties of the other, even if they are light-years apart. This instantaneous correlation defies classical notions of locality and causality, leading to speculations about non-local correlations and the potential for faster-than-light communication. While the phenomenon of entanglement is experimentally well-established, its implications for our understanding of reality and the potential role of consciousness remain highly speculative.

Some proponents of a connection between quantum physics and consciousness argue that entanglement could provide a mechanism for non-local correlations between conscious minds. This perspective suggests that consciousness may not be confined to individual brains but could potentially exist as a interconnected network, influencing events across vast distances. This hypothesis, while fascinating, lacks empirical support and treads into realms of pure speculation. It is vital to distinguish between scientifically testable hypotheses and philosophical speculations, particularly in areas as complex and challenging as the interplay between quantum mechanics and consciousness.

The exploration of quantum physics and consciousness also intersects with the field of quantum biology. This emerging field explores the potential role of quantum phenomena in biological systems, questioning whether quantum effects contribute to the functions of living organisms. Some researchers have suggested that quantum processes, such as superposition and entanglement, could play a role in photosynthesis, enzymatic reactions, and even the functioning of the brain. If verified, these discoveries could have profound implications for our understanding of life itself, offering potential bridges between the quantum world and the biological realm.

However, it's crucial to maintain a critical and rigorous approach to these ideas. The complex nature of biological systems and the delicate environment required for quantum coherence poses significant challenges to experimental verification. Many proposed quantum effects in biology remain highly debated, and it is important to distinguish between well-substantiated experimental results and speculative hypotheses. Overreaching claims can undermine the credibility of the field, and a cautious, evidence-based approach is vital.

The inherent difficulties in studying consciousness further complicate the exploration of its connection to quantum physics. Consciousness itself remains a mystery, defying simple definitions and straightforward measurement. Subjective experiences, personal interpretations, and the limitations of our current scientific tools make it challenging to establish robust links between quantum events and conscious experience. Moreover, the very act of measuring or observing a conscious system might inherently alter the system being studied, introducing observer bias and complicating the interpretation of results.

Therefore, a balanced approach is essential. While the parallels between quantum physics and consciousness are intriguing and warrant further investigation, it is crucial to separate scientifically testable hypotheses from speculative interpretations. The allure of connecting consciousness to the quantum world should not overshadow the need for rigorous experimentation and critical evaluation of data. The lack of strong empirical evidence for many claims connecting quantum physics and consciousness requires us to exercise caution in our conclusions. Future research, perhaps focusing on more precisely defined experimental frameworks, may shed more light on the relationship between these two profound mysteries. But currently, the connection remains largely a stimulating area of philosophical inquiry rather than a well-established scientific fact. Further research is required to bridge the gap between the fascinating theoretical possibilities and the robust experimental data required to validate or refute these proposed relationships.

The potential connection between consciousness and quantum mechanics, therefore, is a captivating frontier. It compels us to reconsider the fundamental nature of reality, the role of the observer, and the very essence of consciousness itself. This journey necessitates a multidisciplinary
approach, integrating insights from physics, neuroscience, philosophy, and even spirituality, to foster a more comprehensive understanding of these seemingly disparate, yet potentially interconnected, realms. The exploration is

ongoing, and while definite answers remain elusive, the very pursuit of understanding pushes the boundaries of human knowledge and challenges our deeply held assumptions about the universe and our place within it. The intellectual journey, fraught with uncertainty and replete with potential breakthroughs, is itself a testament to the boundless curiosity of the human spirit. The cautious, rigorous, and multi-faceted approach to this area of investigation will ultimately serve to unravel the mysteries surrounding the link, if any, between these two fundamentally important aspects of our existence.

The Nature of Self and Identity

The preceding discussion of quantum mechanics and consciousness naturally leads us to ponder a more fundamental question: what is the nature of self, and how does our understanding of self influence, and perhaps even shape, our experience of consciousness? The concept of "self" – this seemingly stable entity that experiences the world, makes decisions, and carries a sense of continuity across time – is a cornerstone of human experience. However, the
philosophical exploration of self reveals a surprising complexity, challenging our intuitive notions of personal

identity and prompting us to reconsider the relationship between consciousness and the wider universe.

One prominent perspective on the self stems from Buddhist philosophy, specifically the concept of "anatman," or no-self. This doctrine asserts that there is no permanent, unchanging self or soul residing within us. Instead, the self is viewed as a constantly shifting collection of physical and mental processes, a temporary aggregation of sensations, perceptions, thoughts, and emotions. This impermanent nature of the self is not to be interpreted as nihilism or a denial of personal existence; rather, it is a profound recognition of the dynamic and fluid nature of reality. From this perspective, clinging to a fixed, permanent sense of self is the root of suffering, as this clinging prevents us from fully experiencing the ever-changing flux of life. The illusion of a stable self, therefore, obscures the interconnectedness and interdependence of all things.

This Buddhist perspective stands in contrast to many Western philosophical traditions which posit a more substantial and enduring self. The Cartesian "cogito, ergo sum" ("I think, therefore I am") epitomizes this tradition, emphasizing the inhe"en" self-awareness of the conscious mind as the foundation of existence. This viewpoint sees the self as a unified, coherent entity capable of independent thought and action, a subject distinct from the objects of its experience. This concept of a continuous, enduring self has influenced Western psychology and our prevalent understanding of personal identity. Yet, even within the Western tradition, a spectrum of views exists regarding the nature of the self, ranging from the purely rational and independent self of Descartes to more socially constructed and fluid notions of self.

The implications of these different perspectives on the self for our understanding of consciousness are significant. If the self is indeed a constantly changing aggregation of mental processes, as suggested by anatman, then the nature of consciousness itself might be less fixed and more fluid than we often assume. Consciousness, in this view, may not be tied to a permanent, unchanging self, but rather emerges from the dynamic interplay of various mental processes. This perspective suggests that the boundaries of the self might be more porous and permeable than we typically imagine, perhaps extending beyond the confines of the individual body and mind to encompass the wider environment.

Conversely, if we adhere to the concept of a stable, continuous self, then consciousness might be seen as a property of this enduring entity, a capacity inherent to the self. This view could potentially support the idea of a soul or a non-physical aspect of the self that persists after physical death. While the evidence supporting this view is largely anecdotal and speculative, the enduring influence of this perspective highlights its profound impact on our beliefs about the nature of consciousness and our place in the universe.

Culture and personal experience profoundly shape our sense of self. Individuals raised in collectivist cultures often have a more fluid and interdependent sense of self, emphasizing their connections to family, community, and society. Their sense of identity is often more fluid and less separate from their social context than individuals raised in individualistic cultures, where the emphasis is placed on personal autonomy and achievement. Even within the same culture, individual experiences and life events influence the development of our self-concept. Trauma, loss, and significant life changes can dramatically alter our perception of who we are, highlighting the dynamic and malleable nature of the self.

Furthermore, the exploration of altered states of consciousness reveals the multifaceted and elusive nature of self. Near-death experiences, deep meditation, and psychedelic experiences can temporarily dissolve the sense of a fixed, separate self, leading to feelings of oneness, unity, and interconnectedness. These experiences suggest that our ordinary understanding of the self, though deeply ingrained, may be merely one perspective among many, and that other, less limited forms of awareness are possible. These experiences challenge our inherent bias towards a self-centered perspective, prompting us to reconsider our assumptions about selfhood and consciousness.

The influence of neuroscientific research further complicates the issue. While neuroscience has made significant strides in mapping the brain and its functions, it has not yet fully elucidated the neural correlates of consciousness or self-awareness. The "hard problem of consciousness," as philosopher David Chalmers has termed it, remains a significant challenge. This difficulty stems from the subjective and qualitative nature of conscious experience, which resists reduction to purely physical or neural descriptions. While the neural processes underlying consciousness can be studied, the subjective "what it's like" aspect of conscious experience remains an enigma.

Moreover, the integration of insights from quantum physics suggests that even our physical reality might be more fluid and interdependent than the classical model suggests. The implications of quantum entanglement, for instance, invite consideration regarding non-local interactions, questioning the traditional boundaries of individual systems. Could this interconnectedness at a fundamental level suggest a similar interconnectedness of consciousness itself? This remains a highly speculative question, but it underscores the need for interdisciplinary approaches in addressing the complex relationship between the nature of self, consciousness, and the universe.

The question of self and identity, therefore, is not simply a philosophical puzzle; it has profound implications for our understanding of consciousness, our relationship with others, and our place in the universe. The exploration of the self necessitates a multidisciplinary approach, integrating insights from philosophy, psychology, neuroscience, and potentially even quantum physics, to gain a more comprehensive understanding of this fundamental aspect of human existence. The journey towards a clearer understanding of self continues, challenging our assumptions and prompting us to reconsider the very fabric of reality, consciousness, and our place within the cosmos. The ongoing exploration of this profound mystery reflects the enduring curiosity of the human spirit in its quest to understand itself and its relationship with the universe.

Consciousness and the Cosmos

The preceding exploration of self and consciousness naturally leads us to contemplate the vast expanse of the cosmos and the possibility of consciousness existing beyond the human realm. While the nature of human consciousness remains a profound mystery, the sheer scale of the universe prompts us to question whether consciousness is a uniquely human phenomenon or a more fundamental aspect of reality, perhaps even woven into the fabric of the cosmos itself. This possibility, often termed "cosmic consciousness," suggests that consciousness is not limited to biological organisms but permeates the universe in various forms and expressions.

The concept of cosmic consciousness is deeply speculative, and its exploration necessarily treads into realms beyond the reach of current scientific methodologies. However, its consideration opens up fertile ground for philosophical and spiritual inquiry, challenging our anthropocentric worldview and prompting us to reconsider our place within the vast tapestry of existence. One might imagine cosmic consciousness as a universal, interconnected field of awareness, a cosmic mind, or a universal energy field that underlies and informs all of reality. This doesn't necessarily imply a sentient, anthropomorphic entity, but rather a fundamental principle of organization and awareness inherent to the universe.

Several lines of inquiry suggest the plausibility, albeit indirectly, of a cosmic consciousness. Quantum physics, with its emphasis on interconnectedness and non-locality, challenges the classical Newtonian model of a universe composed of isolated, independent objects. Quantum entanglement, for instance, demonstrates a correlation between particles even when separated by vast distances.

This non-local interaction suggests a deeper interconnectedness of reality, a subtle interconnectedness that could potentially extend to the realm of consciousness. If fundamental particles are interconnected in this way, could this same interconnectedness extend to the consciousness that emerges from these particles?

Furthermore, the ongoing search for extraterrestrial life fuels the contemplation of cosmic consciousness. The sheer vastness of the universe and the discovery of exoplanets suggest that life, in its various forms, may be far more prevalent than previously imagined. If life exists elsewhere, might it also be accompanied by consciousness, perhaps in forms far beyond our human comprehension? The potential diversity of consciousness across different planetary systems challenges our anthropocentric biases and opens up the exciting possibility of multiple forms of sentience existing across the cosmos. This possibility naturally leads us to question the nature of those consciousnesses, whether they are connected, and whether they might even interact.

The concept of cosmic consciousness also touches upon the profound questions surrounding life, death, and the nature of reality. If consciousness is not limited to the individual body or even to biological life, then the traditional understanding of death might be challenged. Instead of viewing death as the complete cessation of consciousness, one might consider the possibility of consciousness continuing in some form, perhaps reintegrating into the cosmic consciousness. This perspective aligns with certain spiritual traditions that emphasize the interconnectedness of all things and the continuity of consciousness beyond the physical body. This perspective, while speculative, offers a unique framework for understanding the cyclical nature of existence and offers a potential solace in the face of mortality.

However, the speculative nature of cosmic consciousness should not be understated. It is crucial to acknowledge that there is currently no definitive scientific evidence to support the existence of cosmic consciousness. While quantum physics and the search for extraterrestrial life provide suggestive avenues for exploration, they do not definitively prove the existence of a universal consciousness. The vast majority of evidence for cosmic consciousness stems from spiritual experiences, mystical encounters, and anecdotal evidence. While valuable in informing our philosophical inquiry, these sources require a critical approach, acknowledging their limitations and the potential for subjective interpretation.

Nevertheless, the exploration of cosmic consciousness is a valuable intellectual pursuit. By venturing beyond the confines of our current understanding, we can challenge our anthropocentric biases and deepen our appreciation for the complexity and mystery of the universe. This exploration encourages interdisciplinary dialogue between science, philosophy, and spirituality, fostering a more holistic understanding of consciousness and our place within the cosmos. This approach enables us to appreciate how various perspectives—scientific, philosophical, and spiritual—can enrich our understanding of this fundamental aspect of existence, even in the absence of definitive proof.

Furthermore, the exploration of cosmic consciousness can have practical implications. By considering the interconnectedness of all things, we may develop a more profound sense of responsibility towards the environment and other living beings. Recognizing our place within a larger cosmic context can promote empathy, compassion, and a deeper appreciation for the intrinsic value of life. The idea of a shared cosmic consciousness might even inspire a renewed commitment to global cooperation and a more harmonious coexistence amongst people and nations.

In conclusion, the contemplation of cosmic consciousness opens up a fascinating realm of possibilities. While the current scientific understanding does not offer conclusive evidence, the philosophical and spiritual implications of this concept are profound and compelling. The exploration of cosmic consciousness invites us to embrace the mystery of existence, to challenge our assumptions about the nature of reality, and to approach the vast expanse of the cosmos with a sense of wonder and humility. Through the ongoing dialogue between science, philosophy, and spirituality, we can gradually deepen our understanding of consciousness, both human and cosmic, and gain a richer appreciation for our place within the grand scheme of the universe. The journey of exploration will continue, driven by human curiosity and the enduring quest to comprehend the fundamental nature of our existence and our relationship with the cosmos. This ongoing exploration serves as a testament to the boundless capacity of human consciousness, the very consciousness we seek to understand. It is in this continuous pursuit of understanding that we truly find our connection to the cosmos and to the enigmatic possibility of cosmic consciousness itself.

CHAPTER 3

The Nature of Reality

Different Models of Reality

The contemplation of cosmic consciousness naturally leads us to a deeper investigation into the very nature of reality. What is "real"? Is the universe as we perceive it the complete picture, or is there a deeper, more fundamental layer of existence underlying our sensory experience? This question has occupied philosophers and scientists for millennia, giving rise to numerous models of reality, each with its strengths and weaknesses. Understanding these different models is crucial for navigating the complex landscape of our cosmic inquiry and for making sense of the profound implications of cosmic consciousness.

One prominent model is **realism**, which posits that reality exists independently of our perception of it. In this view, the universe possesses an objective existence, whether or not we are there to observe it. This aligns with the classical Newtonian view of the universe as a predictable, deterministic system governed by immutable laws. Objects exist with inherent properties, and these properties are independent of the observer. The apple is red regardless of whether anyone is looking at it; its redness is an inherent property. This model provides a straightforward and intuitive framework for understanding the physical world, and it has been remarkably successful in explaining many aspects of our macroscopic experience. The efficacy of classical physics in explaining everyday phenomena is a testament to the apparent accuracy of realism in many contexts.

However, the advent of quantum mechanics has significantly challenged the realist perspective. The famous double-slit experiment, for example, demonstrates that the act of observation fundamentally alters the behavior of subatomic particles. In this experiment, electrons behave as waves when not observed, but as particles when measured. This suggests that the observer plays an active role in shaping reality, contradicting the realist notion of an objective, observer-independent universe. Quantum entanglement further complicates the picture, showcasing non-local correlations between particles, even when separated by vast distances. This "spooky action at a distance," as Einstein called it, suggests a deeper interconnectedness of reality than is captured by classical realism. These quantum phenomena raise profound questions about the nature of objectivity and the role of consciousness in shaping reality.

In contrast to realism, **idealism** proposes that reality is fundamentally mental or spiritual in nature. In this view, reality is a construction of the mind, a product of consciousness, or perhaps a manifestation of a universal mind. Idealism doesn't necessarily imply that the physical world is an illusion, but rather that its existence and properties are dependent on consciousness. The universe, in this perspective, is essentially a projection of consciousness. This view finds resonance with certain spiritual traditions that emphasize the interconnectedness of all things and the power of intention. The act of creation, in this framework, is an act of consciousness giving form to potential.

While idealism offers a compelling explanation for the observer effect in quantum mechanics, it faces challenges in accounting for the apparent objectivity of the physical world.

If reality is entirely a mental construct, how do we explain the consistency and predictability of the natural world? How can we account for the agreement between multiple observers regarding physical phenomena? These questions highlight the difficulties inherent in basing a complete model of reality solely on subjective experience.

A third model, **pluralism**, attempts to synthesize aspects of both realism and idealism. It acknowledges the existence of an objective physical reality while also recognizing the significant role of consciousness in shaping our experience of that reality. Pluralism argues that neither realism nor idealism alone provides a complete picture. Reality is multifaceted, encompassing both physical and mental aspects, neither of which can be fully understood in isolation. The physical world exists independently, but our understanding and interpretation of it are shaped by our consciousness and our cognitive frameworks.

This perspective helps to bridge the gap between scientific objectivity and subjective experience. It allows for the objective existence of the physical universe while also acknowledging the crucial role of consciousness in our perception and understanding of it. The intricate dance between observer and observed, between the physical and the mental, becomes a central aspect of this multifaceted reality. This model can accommodate quantum phenomena more readily than strict realism, as it allows for the influence of observation on the behavior of subatomic particles.

Furthermore, pluralism offers a framework for understanding the potential interplay between cosmic consciousness and the physical universe. If cosmic consciousness is a fundamental aspect of reality, as suggested earlier, then it could be understood as an organizing principle that both underpins and interacts with the physical world. This interaction might be subtle and indirect, yet profoundly significant in shaping the evolution and nature of the universe. Such an interaction could provide a compelling explanation for the seemingly fine-tuned nature of the universe that allows for the emergence of life and consciousness.

Beyond these three major models, many other frameworks exist, each with its unique strengths and limitations. Some models explore the possibility of multiple realities, existing simultaneously or sequentially. Others posit the existence of hidden dimensions or underlying structures that influence the reality we experience. The debate about the nature of reality is far from settled; it continues to be a rich area of inquiry for physicists, philosophers, and spiritual seekers alike.

Choosing one model over another is a complex process, often influenced by one's personal beliefs, philosophical orientation, and the specific aspects of reality being considered. No single model perfectly captures the totality of experience. The most fruitful approach might involve integrating insights from various models, recognizing the limitations of each while appreciating their contributions to a more holistic understanding.

The exploration of these models of reality is not merely an academic exercise. It has profound implications for our understanding of our place in the universe, the nature of consciousness, and the meaning of existence. If reality is ultimately mental, as idealism suggests, then the power of consciousness to shape reality becomes enormously significant. If reality is fundamentally interconnected, as quantum physics suggests, then the implications for ethical responsibility and global cooperation are far-reaching.

Therefore, the ongoing investigation into the nature of reality is not just a quest for intellectual understanding, but a journey of self-discovery. By engaging with these different models, we deepen our understanding not only of the cosmos, but also of ourselves and our intricate relationship with the universe. The pursuit of knowledge, in this context, becomes a spiritual journey as much as a scientific endeavor, a continuous process of refining our understanding of the multifaceted nature of existence, and our place within it. The open-ended nature of this inquiry is a testament to the profound mystery of reality itself, a mystery that is both intellectually stimulating and spiritually enriching. The journey of exploration continues, and it is in this continued pursuit that we begin to glimpse the vast and wondrous landscape of reality itself. It is within this unfolding exploration that we find a deeper appreciation for the mystery, the beauty, and the profound interconnectedness of all things.

Simulations and Virtual Realities

The exploration of cosmic consciousness and the nature of reality naturally leads us to consider a particularly intriguing and increasingly popular hypothesis: that our reality is, in fact, a sophisticated simulation. This concept, often explored in science fiction, has gained traction in recent years, prompting serious consideration from philosophers, scientists, and technologists alike. The idea hinges on the exponential advancement of computing power and the potential for creating increasingly realistic virtual worlds indistinguishable from our own. If we, as a species, are on the cusp of creating such simulations, is it not plausible that we ourselves are already inhabiting one?

The philosophical arguments for a simulated reality often center on the sheer improbability of our existence. Consider the vastness of the cosmos, the precise conditions necessary for life to emerge, and the seemingly fine-tuned constants of physics. Some argue that such a confluence of improbable events is statistically improbable to the point of suggesting an alternative explanation. A simulation, with its inherent ability to control and manipulate parameters, might offer a more plausible explanation for the apparent fine-tuning of the universe. If a sufficiently advanced civilization possesses the technological capability to create a realistic simulation, the sheer number of such simulations that could potentially exist far surpasses the likelihood of our universe arising randomly through natural processes. This argument is often framed as the "simulation argument," suggesting that we are more likely to be simulated beings than inhabitants of a "base" reality.

However, this argument relies heavily on certain assumptions, notably the future technological capabilities of advanced civilizations. We can only speculate on the technological prowess of such civilizations, and projecting our current understanding of physics and computation into the distant future may be a significant oversimplification. Our understanding of physics, especially at the quantum level, remains incomplete. The limitations of our current understanding might obscure unknown physical principles that make the creation of a universe-scale simulation far more difficult, or perhaps even impossible, than currently imagined. There may be fundamental physical constraints that we are yet to discover that prevent the creation of such a comprehensive and realistic simulation.

Beyond the technological hurdles, the philosophical implications of a simulated reality are profound. If our reality is a simulation, what does this mean for our free will? Are our choices pre-determined by the parameters of the simulation, or do we possess genuine agency? This question touches upon some of the most fundamental debates in philosophy and neuroscience. If our actions and thoughts are merely the outputs of a complex algorithm, then the notion of free will becomes questionable. The very concept of consciousness would need to be re-evaluated within the context of a simulated environment. Is consciousness an emergent property of complex computation, or is it something fundamentally different, something that transcends the physical or computational framework of the simulation? These questions challenge our fundamental understanding of ourselves and our place within the universe.

Furthermore, the simulation hypothesis raises questions about the nature of reality itself. If our reality is a simulation, then what lies beyond it? Is there a "base" reality, a fundamental level of existence from which the simulation is generated? And if so, what are the characteristics of this base reality? The simulation hypothesis could potentially lead to an infinite regress of simulations within simulations, raising further metaphysical questions about the ultimate nature of reality.

The arguments against a simulated reality are equally compelling. Some critics point to the lack of empirical evidence supporting the hypothesis. While there have been attempts to identify potential glitches or anomalies in our reality that might indicate its artificial nature, none of these have been conclusively proven. Furthermore, there are significant philosophical and scientific challenges to the hypothesis. The amount of processing power and data storage required to simulate a universe as vast and complex as ours seems to surpass our current understanding of physics and computing.

Moreover, simulating consciousness presents a particularly thorny problem. We do not fully understand the nature of consciousness, even within our own brains. Creating a truly conscious entity within a simulation might require a level of computational complexity far beyond our current capabilities. Even if we could simulate the behavior of a conscious entity, it is unclear whether this would constitute true consciousness. This raises the question of whether a simulated being could experience qualia, the subjective, qualitative aspects of experience, such as the redness of red or the feeling of pain. Without a deeper understanding of consciousness, the simulation hypothesis remains largely speculative.

Even if we could overcome the technological and philosophical challenges, the very concept of distinguishing between a simulation and true reality becomes incredibly problematic. If a simulation is perfectly realistic, indistinguishable from reality itself, then there is no operational difference between the two. Any experiment designed to prove or disprove the simulation hypothesis would necessarily be conducted within the simulation, making it impossible to obtain objective, external validation. This suggests that the question of whether we live in a simulation might ultimately be unanswerable, a fundamentally unknowable aspect of existence.

The simulation hypothesis, however, is not merely a philosophical thought experiment; it also has practical implications. Understanding the potential for creating increasingly realistic simulations is crucial for addressing ethical considerations surrounding artificial intelligence, virtual reality, and the creation of synthetic minds. As our technological capabilities advance, we need to carefully consider the long-term implications of creating virtual worlds and their potential impact on our understanding of reality, consciousness, and the human condition.

In conclusion, the question of whether our reality is a simulation remains a captivating and profoundly complex inquiry. While the arguments for and against are both compelling, the very act of considering this hypothesis forces us to confront fundamental questions about the nature of existence, consciousness, and our place in the universe. Even without definitive answers, the exploration of this hypothesis pushes the boundaries of our scientific and philosophical understanding, leading to deeper insights into the nature of reality itself and encouraging a more nuanced and critical perspective on our place within the cosmos. The pursuit of knowledge, in this case, is a continual process of questioning, refining our models, and confronting the inherent limitations of our understanding. The mystery remains, but the journey of inquiry is itself a testament to the human spirit's relentless pursuit of understanding.

The Multiverse Hypothesis

The exploration of simulated realities naturally leads us to contemplate an even grander, perhaps more unsettling, hypothesis: the multiverse. This concept, far from being the exclusive domain of science fiction, occupies a significant space within theoretical physics and cosmology, offering a potential explanation for some of the most perplexing aspects of our universe. The multiverse hypothesis posits the existence of not one, but many universes, potentially infinite in number and vastly diverse in their physical laws and constants. These universes, often described as separate bubbles or branches within a larger cosmic landscape, might coexist alongside our own, unseen and perhaps forever unreachable.

One of the most prominent frameworks for understanding the multiverse comes from the many-worlds interpretation (MWI) of quantum mechanics. This controversial interpretation, proposed by Hugh Everett III in the mid-20th century, suggests that every quantum measurement causes the universe to split into multiple branches, each representing a different possible outcome. In other words, every time a quantum event occurs – an electron taking one path versus another, for example – the universe branches into two or more parallel universes, each embodying a different result. In this framework, the infamous Schrödinger's cat is not merely in a superposition of states, alive and dead simultaneously; instead, the universe splits, with one universe containing a living cat and another containing a dead cat. These universes then continue to evolve independently, each following its own unique path.

The implications of the MWI are far-reaching. If true, it implies that every conceivable quantum possibility, however improbable, is realized in some universe within the multiverse. This includes universes with slightly different physical constants, universes where life evolved in radically different ways, and perhaps even universes with fundamentally different laws of physics. The sheer scale and variety of these universes are almost beyond human comprehension. While elegant in its explanation of quantum mechanics, the MWI is notoriously difficult to test experimentally. The lack of direct observational evidence makes it remain a matter of ongoing debate among physicists.

Another compelling framework supporting the multiverse concept is inflationary cosmology. This theory, which attempts to explain the early universe's rapid expansion, suggests that the inflationary period might not have been a unique event but rather a continuous process, leading to the formation of numerous "bubble universes," each with its own set of physical parameters. These universes could be vastly different from our own, possessing different dimensions, different fundamental forces, and possibly even different constants of nature. Some models of inflationary cosmology even predict the existence of universes with entirely different physical laws, defying our current understanding of physics.

The evidence for the multiverse, unlike the simulation hypothesis, is largely indirect. Observations such as the flatness and uniformity of the cosmic microwave background radiation have been interpreted by some as supporting evidence for inflation, which in turn suggests the possibility of a multiverse. However, these observations are also compatible with other cosmological models, making it challenging to establish the multiverse as a definitive conclusion. Furthermore, the sheer vastness and inaccessibility of other universes pose considerable challenges to direct observational verification.

The philosophical implications of a multiverse are profound and challenge our deeply ingrained intuitions about uniqueness and purpose. If our universe is merely one of countless others, does this diminish the significance of our existence? Does it render our individual lives and achievements inconsequential in the grand cosmic scheme? Some argue that the multiverse reinforces the uniqueness of our universe, highlighting the extraordinary conditions necessary for the emergence of life and consciousness within our specific physical parameters. Others, however, might find the idea of an infinite number of universes, many of which may be similar or even identical to our own, somewhat disconcerting. The uniqueness of our own experiences may be called into question.

The multiverse concept also raises questions about the nature of physical laws and constants. If different universes possess different physical laws, this would suggest that these laws are not fundamental or immutable but rather contingent features of a larger cosmic landscape. This challenges the traditional view of physics as a search for universal, unchanging laws that govern the entire universe. Instead, it implies a more complex and fluid reality, where the laws of physics themselves may vary from one universe to another.

Furthermore, the existence of a multiverse would have significant implications for our understanding of the fine-tuning of the universe. The argument for fine-tuning rests on the idea that the universe's fundamental constants are precisely adjusted to allow for the emergence of life. Some have interpreted this as evidence of a divine creator or some other form of intelligent design. However, in a multiverse context, fine-tuning can be seen as a natural consequence of the vast number of universes with varying physical constants. Our universe may simply be one of the few where life is possible. The seemingly miraculous fine-tuning of our universe may be simply a matter of cosmic luck within an ensemble of universes.

The multiverse hypothesis remains a highly speculative area of scientific inquiry. While many theoretical frameworks lend credence to its plausibility, definitive observational evidence is lacking. However, its implications for our understanding of reality, uniqueness, purpose, and the very nature of physical laws are too significant to ignore. The exploration of the multiverse continues to challenge our assumptions about the universe and our place within it, pushing the boundaries of both scientific understanding and philosophical contemplation. The debate over the multiverse's existence is not merely a scientific endeavor; it is a profound philosophical journey that compels us to question the very foundations of our reality. It is a testament to humanity's relentless pursuit of understanding, even in the face of cosmic scales and potentially infinite possibilities. The question of whether we inhabit one universe among many, however, remains a central challenge and a captivating area of future investigation. As our observational capabilities and theoretical understanding advance, we may one day come closer to unraveling this cosmic mystery. Even if we never attain definitive proof, the exploration itself enhances our appreciation of the universe's complexity and our own remarkable existence.

The Role of Observation in Shaping Reality

The exploration of the multiverse naturally leads us to a deeper consideration of the observer's role in shaping reality. This is particularly pertinent when considering the bizarre and counter-intuitive world of quantum mechanics. While the multiverse hypothesis deals with the vast expanse of potentially countless universes, the observer effect operates on a much smaller, yet equally profound, scale – the quantum level. This section delves into the intricacies of the observer effect and its implications for our understanding of the nature of reality.

The observer effect, a cornerstone of quantum mechanics, posits that the act of observation fundamentally alters the system being observed. This isn't simply a matter of disturbing a delicate experiment; it's a more fundamental interaction where the very act of measurement forces a quantum system to "choose" a specific state from a superposition of possibilities. Before measurement, a quantum particle, for instance, exists in a superposition – simultaneously occupying multiple states or locations. This is famously illustrated by Schrödinger's cat, a thought experiment where a cat is placed in a box with a radioactive atom; the atom's decay (or non-decay) determines whether the cat is alive or dead. Before observation, according to quantum mechanics, the cat is both alive *and* dead simultaneously. It's only when we open the box and observe the cat that its state collapses into either alive or dead.

This seemingly paradoxical behavior raises fundamental questions about the nature of reality. Does the cat's state truly exist in a superposition before observation, or is the superposition simply a reflection of our incomplete knowledge of the system? If the act of observation determines the outcome, does this imply that consciousness, the observer, plays a crucial role in shaping reality at the quantum level? These are questions that have fueled decades of debate among physicists and philosophers.

Different interpretations of quantum mechanics offer varying perspectives on the observer's role. The Copenhagen interpretation, one of the most widely accepted, suggests that the act of measurement causes the wave function to collapse, forcing the quantum system to choose a definite state. While it doesn't explicitly define the nature of the "measurement" or the observer, it implicitly acknowledges the observer's critical role in determining the outcome. This interpretation, however, leaves many physicists uneasy because it seems to introduce a subjective element into the fundamentally objective realm of physics.

The many-worlds interpretation (MWI), as discussed earlier, offers an alternative explanation. Instead of the wave function collapsing, MWI suggests that every possible outcome of a quantum measurement creates a separate branch of the universe. In the Schrödinger's cat example, the act of opening the box doesn't cause the cat to become either alive or dead; instead, the universe splits into two parallel universes: one where the cat is alive, and one where it is dead. The observer then experiences one particular branch of this reality. While elegant in its avoidance of wave function collapse, MWI introduces the far-reaching concept of the multiverse. It sidesteps the problem of the observer's subjective role by eliminating it; the observer simply exists within one of many realities.

Another interpretation, the de Broglie-Bohm theory (also known as pilot-wave theory), proposes that particles always have definite positions and trajectories, even when not being observed. The wave function doesn't represent the particle's probability of being in various locations, but rather guides its motion. In this interpretation, the observer's role is minimized; observation doesn't fundamentally change the particle's state, only reveals its pre-existing reality. However, this interpretation requires the acceptance of "hidden variables," influencing particles' motion that we are yet unable to detect.

These differing interpretations highlight the deep philosophical questions at the heart of the observer effect. The issue is not merely a technical detail within quantum mechanics; it touches upon the very nature of reality, knowledge, and consciousness. If the act of observation truly shapes reality, then our understanding of the universe is inextricably linked to our act of observing it.

The scientific challenges in understanding the observer effect are significant. The difficulties arise in part from the inherently probabilistic nature of quantum mechanics. Unlike classical physics, which deals with deterministic systems, quantum mechanics inherently deals with probabilities and uncertainties. Even with precise measurements, we can only predict the probability of a particular outcome, not the outcome itself. This fundamental uncertainty makes it challenging to separate the effect of observation from the inherent randomness of quantum systems.

Furthermore, the act of observation itself is difficult to define precisely. Does observation require a conscious observer? Could a sophisticated measuring instrument alone suffice? Experiments involving entangled particles, where two particles are linked in such a way that their fates are intertwined, even when spatially separated, have been used to explore these questions. However, the results remain open to different interpretations, highlighting the complexities involved.

The philosophical implications are no less profound. If consciousness does play a role in shaping reality, then it raises questions about the nature of consciousness itself. Is consciousness a fundamental aspect of the universe, inextricably intertwined with its physical laws? Or is it a more emergent property, arising from the complex interactions of physical systems? These are questions that have been debated by philosophers and scientists for centuries, and the observer effect in quantum mechanics provides a new and compelling context for exploring them.

The concept of the observer effect and its interpretations have far-reaching consequences for our understanding of the universe. It challenges the traditional view of a detached, objective reality, independent of the observer. It suggests instead a more interactive and dynamic reality where the observer and the observed are inextricably intertwined. The universe, viewed through this lens, is not simply something to be passively observed; it is something we actively participate in shaping, at least at the quantum level.

This raises further questions concerning the limitations of our knowledge. If observation shapes reality, does this imply that our understanding of the universe is inherently incomplete? Our observations are limited by our tools, our senses, and our very consciousness. We can only observe the universe through a limited perspective, possibly missing a broader, richer reality that lies beyond our current grasp.

The observer effect is not merely a scientific curiosity; it represents a fundamental shift in our understanding of the relationship between the observer and the observed. It forces us to grapple with the limitations of our knowledge and the profound implications of our own consciousness in the tapestry of existence. It challenges us to redefine our relationship with reality, encouraging a deeper examination of the interplay between the subjective and the objective, the conscious and the unconscious, in the ongoing quest to understand the nature of the universe and our place within it. As our understanding of quantum mechanics advances, so too will our understanding of the observer effect's significance. This journey remains a continuous process of exploration and refinement, promising further surprises and deeper insights into the fundamental nature of reality. The ongoing debate and exploration are integral to the evolution of our scientific and philosophical understanding, underscoring the boundless nature of inquiry itself. Indeed, the universe, in its quantum complexity, continues to challenge and reward our relentless pursuit of knowledge.

The Limits of Scientific Explanation

The preceding discussion of the observer effect in quantum mechanics highlights a crucial limitation of scientific explanation: the inherent difficulty in predicting and understanding the behavior of complex systems solely based on the properties of their individual components. This limitation stems from the concept of emergence, a phenomenon where complex systems exhibit properties not readily predictable from their constituent parts. A flock of birds, for instance, demonstrates emergent behavior in its coordinated flight patterns, patterns not inherent in any single bird but arising from the interactions between them. Similarly, the human brain, a complex network of neurons, generates consciousness, a property that cannot be explained simply by understanding the behavior of individual neurons.

This emergent behavior presents a significant challenge to reductionist approaches to science, approaches that seek to understand complex phenomena by breaking them down into their simpler components. While reductionism has been remarkably successful in explaining many aspects of the physical world, its limitations become apparent when applied to systems with a high degree of complexity and interconnectedness. In these systems, the interactions between components become so intricate and numerous that predicting the overall behavior based on an understanding of individual components becomes practically impossible, even with the aid of powerful computers. The sheer number of variables and the complex feedback loops involved render a purely reductionist approach insufficient.

Consider the human genome, for example. While significant progress has been made in mapping the human genome and identifying individual genes associated with specific traits, our ability to predict an individual's characteristics solely based on their genetic code remains limited. This is because the expression of genes is highly complex and influenced by a multitude of factors, including environmental influences and epigenetic modifications. The interaction between genes and the environment generates a complex emergent phenomenon: the individual human being, whose characteristics are far more than simply the sum of its individual genetic components.

The limits of scientific explanation are also evident in the study of consciousness. Despite significant advances in neuroscience, we still lack a complete understanding of how consciousness arises from the complex interactions of neurons in the brain. While we can identify brain regions associated with specific cognitive functions, the subjective experience of consciousness—qualia, the raw feeling of what it's like to experience something—remains a mystery. Reducing consciousness to purely physical processes, while providing partial explanations of brain function, does not fully capture the subjective and qualitative aspects of conscious experience. The emergent nature of consciousness transcends the simplistic analysis of its neural underpinnings.

The challenge of understanding emergent properties is further complicated by the concept of complexity. Complex systems are characterized by a high degree of interconnectedness and feedback loops, making it difficult to isolate the influence of individual components. Small changes in one part of the system can have unpredictable and far-reaching consequences throughout the system, exhibiting what is known as sensitive dependence on initial conditions, popularly described as the "butterfly effect." This makes predicting the long-term behavior of complex systems extremely difficult, if not impossible. The weather, for instance, is a classic example of a complex system. Even with sophisticated computer models and vast amounts of data, accurate long-term weather forecasting remains a significant challenge because of the system's intricate interactions and sensitive dependence on initial conditions.

These limitations of reductionist approaches necessitate a shift towards more holistic and interdisciplinary approaches to understanding reality. Instead of focusing solely on the individual components of a system, interdisciplinary approaches emphasize the importance of understanding the interactions and relationships between those components, as well as the emergent properties that arise from these interactions. This requires collaboration between scientists from various disciplines, including physics, chemistry, biology, mathematics, and computer science, to provide a more comprehensive understanding of complex phenomena. The study of climate change, for instance, requires a multidisciplinary approach incorporating insights from atmospheric science, oceanography, ecology, and social sciences to address the intricate interactions within the earth's climate system.

The shift towards interdisciplinary approaches also emphasizes the importance of systems thinking, a way of thinking that views phenomena as interconnected systems rather than isolated entities. Systems thinking recognizes that complex systems are characterized by feedback loops, emergent behavior, and adaptive capacity. It provides a framework for understanding the dynamic interactions within complex systems and their adaptation to changing circumstances. This approach is particularly important in addressing complex global challenges, such as climate change, where the interactions between human activities and the environment are highly complex and interconnected.

Moreover, understanding the limits of scientific explanation requires acknowledging the role of subjective experience and human consciousness in shaping our understanding of reality. Our perception of reality is filtered through our senses and our cognitive frameworks, which are themselves products of biological and cultural evolution. While scientific methods provide powerful tools for investigating the physical world, they are not inherently equipped to capture the full spectrum of human experience. The emphasis on quantitative measures and objective observations can neglect the qualitative and subjective aspects of human experience that play a significant role in our understanding of the world.

Integrating subjective experience and consciousness into our understanding of reality requires a critical engagement with philosophy and humanities. Philosophy provides a framework for examining the foundations of knowledge, the nature of reality, and the relationship between the observer and the observed. The humanities offer insights into human culture, values, and beliefs, and provide context for understanding how our perceptions of reality are shaped by our cultural and social environment. This interdisciplinary approach is crucial for developing a more comprehensive and nuanced understanding of reality, one that acknowledges the limitations of purely scientific approaches.

In conclusion, the limits of scientific explanation are not indicative of a failure of the scientific method but rather a recognition of the inherent complexity of the universe. Emergence and complexity pose fundamental challenges to reductionist approaches, highlighting the need for more holistic and interdisciplinary strategies that embrace systems thinking and incorporate insights from various fields of inquiry. Furthermore, acknowledging the role of subjective experience and consciousness in shaping our understanding of reality is crucial for developing a more complete and nuanced picture of the universe and our place within it. The journey to understand the nature of reality is an ongoing one, requiring continuous exploration and a willingness to engage with both scientific rigor and philosophical reflection. The pursuit of knowledge remains a boundless endeavor, and the limitations we encounter often unveil further avenues for deeper insight and a more complete understanding of our existence. The universe, in its intricate tapestry of complexity and emergence, continues to inspire our relentless quest for understanding, urging us to embrace the richness of interdisciplinary collaboration and the profound mysteries that still lie ahead.

CHAPTER 4

Spiritual Perspectives

Mystical Experiences and Altered

The preceding exploration of the limitations of reductionist science naturally leads us to consider experiences that lie beyond the readily quantifiable and measurable—mystical experiences and altered states of consciousness. These experiences, often characterized by profound shifts in perception, emotion, and sense of self, challenge the boundaries of conventional scientific understanding and offer compelling perspectives on the nature of reality and spiritual understanding. Their investigation requires a departure from purely reductionist approaches, demanding instead a more holistic and nuanced perspective that integrates phenomenological analysis with insights from both religious traditions and psychological research.

The phenomenology of mystical experiences is remarkably diverse, varying greatly across individuals and cultures. Yet, common threads weave through these seemingly disparate accounts. A frequent motif is the experience of unity, a transcendence of the ordinary sense of separation between self and other, between subject and object. This sense of unity can manifest as a feeling of connection to nature, to humanity as a whole, or even to a transcendent reality beyond the material world. Descriptions often include feelings of boundless love, profound peace, and an overwhelming sense of awe and wonder. Time and space may lose their conventional significance, replaced by a timeless, spaceless experience of pure presence.

The altered states of consciousness accompanying mystical experiences frequently involve changes in sensory perception. Visual hallucinations, auditory distortions, and altered body sensations are commonly reported. These altered perceptions, however, are not typically experienced as pathological or frightening, but rather as deeply meaningful and revelatory. The subjective experience is often one of heightened awareness, clarity, and insight, a feeling of accessing a deeper layer of reality beyond the grasp of ordinary consciousness. These profound shifts in perception can lead to profound changes in worldview, fundamentally altering the individual's understanding of their place in the cosmos.

Religious traditions across the globe have long attributed significance to these experiences, often interpreting them as encounters with the divine, or as glimpses into ultimate reality. In many mystical traditions, these experiences are considered essential to spiritual growth and liberation. Practices such as meditation, prayer, fasting, and ritual are often employed to cultivate these states of consciousness, viewed as pathways to spiritual awakening. The interpretation of these experiences, however, varies widely depending on the specific religious framework. Some traditions emphasize the absolute transcendence of the divine, while others focus on the immanence of the divine within the created world.

Psychological perspectives on mystical experiences provide alternative interpretations, often framing them within the context of altered brain states or psychological processes. Neurobiological research has explored the correlation between specific brain regions and activities during mystical experiences, shedding light on the neurological underpinnings of these states. The release of endorphins, the activity of the prefrontal cortex, and changes in neurotransmitter levels have all been associated with altered states, offering potential biological mechanisms underlying the reported phenomena. However, these correlations do not necessarily negate the spiritual significance that many individuals ascribe to such experiences. The neurological substrates may provide a framework for understanding *how* these experiences arise, but they do not necessarily explain *what* they mean or imply.

The psychological perspective also examines the role of expectation, suggestion, and cultural context in shaping the interpretation of these experiences. The cultural narratives and beliefs surrounding mystical traditions can profoundly influence an individual's interpretation of their altered states. What one culture may interpret as a divine encounter, another may explain as a psychological anomaly. This highlights the crucial role of cultural relativism in understanding the meaning and interpretation of mystical experiences. It does not, however, diminish the subjective reality and profound impact these experiences can have on individuals.

A balanced approach acknowledges both the subjective reality of mystical experiences and the potential for psychological and neurological explanations. The subjective nature of the experience cannot be discounted—the profound transformations in consciousness reported by individuals who have undergone these experiences are deeply meaningful and transformative regardless of scientific explanations. However, scientific inquiry can provide valuable context and understanding, illuminating the underlying mechanisms and processes that contribute to these extraordinary states.

The integration of scientific and spiritual perspectives requires a nuanced approach that avoids reductionism on the one hand and naive acceptance of subjective experience without critical scrutiny on the other. A true understanding demands a critical examination of both the objective and subjective dimensions, embracing both the scientific method and phenomenological analysis. This interdisciplinary approach can lead to a richer, more comprehensive understanding of consciousness, spirituality, and the nature of reality.

Furthermore, the study of mystical experiences forces us to confront the limitations of language itself. The ineffable nature of these encounters often defies adequate verbal description. The very attempt to articulate the experience often falls short, failing to capture the richness and depth of the subjective reality. This limitation highlights the crucial role of non-verbal modes of communication, such as art, music, and poetry, in expressing the inexpressible. These forms of expression can convey the emotional and spiritual resonance of mystical experiences more effectively than language alone.

The exploration of mystical experiences and altered states challenges the traditional boundaries of science and religion, compelling us to reconsider the relationship between mind, body, and spirit. It requires a humility that acknowledges the vastness of the unknown and the limitations of our current understanding. These experiences underscore the depth and complexity of human consciousness, suggesting that our understanding of reality might be far more limited than we commonly assume.

The quest for understanding mystical experiences should not be solely a pursuit of scientific explanation, nor merely a matter of religious dogma. It should be a holistic inquiry that embraces multiple perspectives, drawing from science, religion, psychology, philosophy, and the humanities. Such an interdisciplinary approach allows for a more nuanced and comprehensive understanding of these powerful experiences, enriching our comprehension of human consciousness and our place in the universe. This exploration is an invitation to confront the limits of our own preconceptions and to embrace the mystery at the heart of existence. In doing so, we may find a deeper appreciation for the richness and complexity of human experience and the boundless potential of consciousness itself. The path forward involves not dismissing the unknown, but engaging with it with a spirit of open-minded inquiry, recognizing that the journey of understanding may be as significant as the destination itself. The pursuit of such knowledge compels us to integrate scientific rigour with spiritual insight, creating a richer tapestry of understanding than either approach can achieve alone. The universe, in all its enigmatic

splendor, continues to invite us into the depths of its mysteries.

NearDeath Experiences and the Afterlife

Near-death experiences (NDEs) represent a particularly compelling intersection of science, psychology, and spirituality. These profound events, often occurring during periods of clinical death or extreme physiological stress, involve a constellation of subjective experiences that have challenged conventional understandings of consciousness and the afterlife for centuries. Characteristically, NDEs include a sense of peace and detachment from the body, out-of-body experiences (OBEs) where individuals report viewing their own bodies from a detached perspective, encounters with deceased loved ones, and journeys through tunnels of light towards a blissful realm. These experiences frequently leave individuals with a profound alteration in their worldview, a deepened sense of spirituality, and a diminished fear of death.

The sheer volume of documented NDEs, reported across diverse cultures and throughout history, demands serious consideration. While anecdotal accounts alone cannot provide definitive proof of an afterlife, the consistency and emotional intensity of these narratives are undeniable. Many accounts describe a vivid sense of entering a realm of profound peace, love, and understanding, often characterized as profoundly transcendent and unlike anything experienced in ordinary life. The commonality of these themes, despite differences in cultural backgrounds and personal beliefs, raises questions about the potential universality of the underlying experience.

One of the key challenges in understanding NDEs lies in distinguishing between genuinely transcendental experiences and the effects of physiological processes. During clinical death or extreme stress, the brain undergoes significant changes in blood flow, oxygen levels, and neurotransmitter activity. These alterations can potentially induce altered states of consciousness that mimic aspects of NDEs. For example, oxygen deprivation can lead to hallucinations and distortions of perception, which might explain some of the visual and auditory elements reported in NDEs, such as the perception of bright lights or hearing voices.

The role of endorphins and other neurochemicals released during periods of stress also warrants investigation. These naturally occurring opioids can induce feelings of euphoria, peace, and altered states of consciousness, potentially accounting for the sense of tranquility and bliss commonly reported in NDEs. Furthermore, the brain's limbic system, associated with emotions and memory, may play a critical role in shaping the narrative and emotional intensity of the experience. The brain's attempt to synthesize and process extreme physiological stress, perhaps through the generation of vivid imagery and emotional responses, could be a significant factor contributing to the experience.

However, reducing NDEs to purely physiological explanations remains a reductionist approach that fails to fully account for the depth and transformative effects reported by many individuals. Many individuals report profound spiritual insights and personal transformations that extend far beyond the immediate physiological experience. The reported encounters with deceased loved ones, often described in minute detail and with emotional realism, challenge purely physiological explanations, implying a level of cognition and interaction beyond the limitations of the physical brain.

Furthermore, some NDEs involve verifiable information acquired during the period of clinical death, suggesting the potential for consciousness to exist independently of the physical body. Accounts of individuals accurately describing events that occurred outside their field of vision during their period of unconsciousness, known as "veridical perception," are particularly compelling. These instances suggest the possibility of consciousness existing and functioning beyond the constraints of the physical body, raising profound questions about the nature of consciousness itself.

The spiritual perspective on NDEs views these experiences as genuine glimpses into the afterlife or as evidence of a non-physical aspect of consciousness. Many religious and spiritual traditions interpret NDEs as supporting the existence of a soul or spirit that continues to exist after the death of the physical body. These accounts are frequently integrated into existing theological frameworks, providing further evidence for their core beliefs regarding the nature of life, death, and the continuity of consciousness.

However, this perspective acknowledges the complexities of interpreting such profoundly subjective experiences. The challenge lies in balancing a respectful appreciation for the profound spiritual meaning these experiences hold for individuals with the need for rigorous scientific and psychological scrutiny. The aim is not to dismiss or deny the transformative effects of these experiences but to provide a nuanced understanding that acknowledges both their subjective power and the potential contribution of physiological and psychological factors.

The careful investigation of NDEs requires a multidisciplinary approach integrating perspectives from medicine, neurology, psychology, and religious studies. This integrative approach recognizes the limitations of any single explanatory framework and embraces the complexity and ambiguity inherent in the phenomenon. It acknowledges the possibility of multiple contributing factors, ranging from physiological changes in the brain to profound spiritual insights, without necessarily reducing the experience to a single, simplistic explanation.

The ultimate interpretation of NDEs remains a matter of personal belief and philosophical reflection. However, the widespread nature of these accounts, their profoundly transformative effects on individuals, and the challenges they pose to our conventional understanding of consciousness and death warrant continued and rigorous investigation. The ongoing study of NDEs pushes the boundaries of our scientific understanding and our understanding of the very nature of reality, inviting us to embrace a deeper sense of humility and wonder in the face of the unknown.

The exploration of NDEs invites us to confront the limitations of our current scientific paradigms and to consider the possibility of experiences transcending the boundaries of our established knowledge. While scientific inquiry continues to shed light on the physiological and psychological aspects of NDEs, their spiritual significance cannot be disregarded. The reported encounters with a transcendent reality, the profound sense of peace, love, and unity with the universe, and the transformative impact on individuals' lives suggest a dimension of human experience that remains largely unexplored.

It is important to note that the interpretation of NDEs can be highly subjective. The cultural background, religious beliefs, and personal experiences of the individual undergoing the NDE will inevitably influence how the experience is interpreted and remembered. However, this subjectivity does not diminish the validity of the experience itself. The profound emotional and spiritual impact of NDEs on individuals is undeniable, regardless of how the experience might be explained from a scientific perspective.

The field of NDE research is a dynamic and evolving one, constantly refining its methodology and incorporating new insights from various disciplines. As our understanding of the brain, consciousness, and the nature of reality grows, so too will our understanding of NDEs. This ongoing dialogue between science, spirituality, and personal experience is crucial for building a more holistic and nuanced understanding of this fascinating and complex phenomenon.

The study of NDEs serves as a powerful reminder of the limitations of our current understanding of consciousness and the universe. It encourages us to question our assumptions, embrace the mystery of existence, and consider the possibility of realities beyond our immediate grasp. It also fosters an understanding that the human experience is far richer and more complex than our current scientific models can fully encompass. The continued exploration of NDEs, therefore, represents not just a scientific endeavor, but a profoundly philosophical and spiritual journey, inviting us to delve deeper into the fundamental questions of life, death, and the nature of consciousness itself. This exploration will lead to a profound shift in our understanding of ourselves and our place within the cosmos.

Eastern Spiritual Traditions

Eastern spiritual traditions offer profound and multifaceted perspectives on the nature of reality, consciousness, and the self, often diverging significantly from Western scientific and philosophical viewpoints. These traditions, encompassing diverse practices and philosophies, share a common thread: the exploration of inner experience as a path to understanding ultimate truth. Buddhism, Hinduism, and Taoism, three of the most influential Eastern traditions, provide particularly rich insights into the subjects raised by near-death experiences (NDEs), offering frameworks for interpreting the transformative aspects reported by many individuals.

Buddhism, originating in ancient India with Siddhartha Gautama (the Buddha), emphasizes the impermanence of all phenomena (anicca), the inherent suffering (dukkha) arising from attachment to impermanent things, and the path to liberation (nirvana) through the cessation of this attachment. This path, often described as the Eightfold Path, involves ethical conduct, mental discipline, and wisdom, aiming to cultivate a state of equanimity and insight. From a Buddhist perspective, NDEs could be interpreted as glimpses into the nature of impermanence, a direct experience of the fluidity and interconnectedness of all things. The visions of light and blissful realms might reflect the inherent potential for peace and liberation present within consciousness, independent of the physical body. The sense of detachment from the physical body resonates with Buddhist concepts of the non-self (anatman), emphasizing that there is no permanent, unchanging soul or ego. The experience of unity with all beings could be seen as an experiential validation of interconnectedness, a cornerstone of Buddhist cosmology.

Reincarnation, a central tenet in many Buddhist traditions, aligns with the potential for consciousness to continue beyond physical death. While not explicitly addressed in early Buddhist scriptures, the concept of rebirth became integrated into later Buddhist schools, suggesting that the experiences within an NDE could be interpreted as a transitional phase, a fleeting glimpse into the process of rebirth or even a karmic consequence. The nature of this rebirth, however, is not one of a fixed entity transmigrating, but rather a continuous process of arising and ceasing, shaped by karmic actions. The intensity of emotional experiences within NDEs could reflect the imprints of past actions and the karmic consequences that will shape future experiences. The seemingly verifiable details sometimes reported in NDEs could be viewed as a manifestation of subtle mental processes, carrying over into the new life, rather than a direct interaction with external phenomena.

Hinduism, a diverse tapestry of traditions and philosophies, offers another perspective on NDEs. The concept of Atman, the eternal, unchanging self, is central to many Hindu schools of thought. This concept contrasts sharply with the Buddhist notion of Anatman. The Atman is seen as the ultimate reality, the divine spark within each individual, that unites all beings. From a Hindu perspective, an NDE might represent a temporary separation of the Atman from the body, a journey back towards its true nature. The experiences of light, peace, and unity might reflect the inherent connection of the Atman to Brahman, the ultimate reality, a mystical union often described in Hindu scriptures and traditions.

Reincarnation is also crucial in Hindu thought, shaping the cycle of birth, death, and rebirth. Karma, the principle of cause and effect, plays a central role, influencing the type of rebirth an individual experiences. NDEs could be interpreted within this framework as a reflection of one's karmic balance, offering a preview of future consequences or even acting as a bridge between past lives and the present. Encounters with deceased loved ones might be understood as interactions within the subtle planes of existence, reflecting the continuity of consciousness beyond physical death.

Taoism, focusing on the harmony and balance of life, offers a unique approach to understanding NDEs. Taoism emphasizes the Tao, the underlying principle of the universe, an indescribable force that governs all things. From a Taoist perspective, an NDE might represent a temporary alignment with the Tao, a merging of individual consciousness with the universal flow. The experiences of peace and unity could reflect the inherent harmony present within the Tao, a state of complete acceptance and surrender. The concept of Wu Wei, effortless action, aligns with the passive nature of many NDEs, suggesting that the experience arises spontaneously, without intentional effort or control. The reported sense of timelessness within NDEs reflects the Taoist perspective on time as an illusion, a construction of the mind.

Compared to the Western emphasis on objective observation and linear causality, these Eastern traditions highlight the importance of subjective experience and cyclical processes. The emphasis on introspection and meditation in these traditions aligns with the profound introspective nature of NDEs. The experiences of unity, peace, and transcendent realms reported by many individuals might be seen as reflections of the deeper layers of consciousness, accessible through these practices. The transformative effects of NDEs resonate strongly with the emphasis on spiritual awakening and liberation in these traditions. The exploration of consciousness through both scientific and spiritual lenses highlights the potential for synergy between these different frameworks.

While these Eastern spiritual traditions offer valuable perspectives on NDEs, it's important to recognize their limitations. Many of these interpretations are based on faith and subjective experience, rather than empirical evidence. The lack of consistent, verifiable data makes it difficult to empirically validate these claims. Nevertheless, the insights offered by these traditions challenge conventional Western perspectives, prompting a re-evaluation of our understanding of consciousness, death, and the nature of reality. The juxtaposition of scientific investigation with these spiritually rich interpretations can contribute to a more nuanced and holistic approach to the study of NDEs, allowing for a broader understanding of the human experience and its implications for our understanding of the universe. The common thread across many of these diverse traditions lies in their emphasis on the potential for human consciousness to transcend the limitations of the physical body and perceive realities beyond our conventional sensory experiences. The ongoing dialogue between science and spirituality, in the context of NDEs, is vital in expanding our collective understanding of the nature of consciousness and our place within the cosmos.

Furthermore, it is crucial to acknowledge the vast diversity within each of these traditions. Interpretations of NDEs will vary significantly depending on the specific school of thought, the individual's personal beliefs, and their level of spiritual practice. While common themes emerge, the precise meaning ascribed to the experiences will remain deeply personal and culturally situated. The exploration of these interpretations, therefore, demands a sensitivity to the complexities and nuances inherent in each tradition, respecting their unique contributions to the larger human quest for understanding. This respect for diverse interpretations reflects a vital part of the ongoing scholarly engagement with the phenomenon of NDEs, fostering intellectual humility and open dialogue.

The study of NDEs across various cultural and spiritual contexts highlights the universality of certain core experiences, suggesting a potential underlying reality independent of specific belief systems. While the interpretations may differ significantly, the profound impact on individuals' lives remains a constant factor, regardless of their cultural background or spiritual beliefs. This commonality underscores the need for further interdisciplinary research, combining rigorous scientific methodology with a deep respect for the subjective experiences and diverse interpretations arising from different cultural and spiritual perspectives. The integration of scientific inquiry and spiritual understanding offers the potential for a more comprehensive and nuanced understanding of NDEs, avoiding reductionist explanations that fail to capture the full scope of these extraordinary experiences. The journey towards such an understanding necessitates a continued effort in fostering collaboration between scientists, spiritual leaders, and individuals who have undergone these transformative events. Only through a collective effort can we begin to fully grasp the profound implications of NDEs for our understanding of consciousness, the nature of reality, and the human condition. The open-ended nature of the inquiry continues to challenge and inspire, highlighting the inherent mystery and wonder at the heart of human existence.

Western Spiritual Traditions

Western spiritual traditions, while often framed within a distinct theological and philosophical framework compared to their Eastern counterparts, offer equally compelling perspectives on the nature of consciousness, reality, and the human experience, particularly regarding near-death experiences (NDEs). These traditions, deeply interwoven with the historical and cultural fabric of the West, provide unique lenses through which to interpret the transformative aspects of NDEs, enriching the ongoing dialogue between science and spirituality.

Christianity, arguably the most influential Western religious tradition, presents a multifaceted view on NDEs. The concept of the soul, an immortal entity distinct from the physical body, is central to Christian theology. Many Christians believe that upon physical death, the soul departs from the body and enters a state of either eternal bliss (Heaven) or eternal punishment (Hell), depending on one's actions and faith during earthly life. From this perspective, an NDE might be viewed as a temporary glimpse into one of these realms, a preview of the soul's ultimate destiny. Reports of encounters with deceased loved ones could be interpreted as interactions within a spiritual realm, reflecting the enduring nature of human relationships beyond physical death. The frequent descriptions of light and peace in NDEs could symbolize divine presence, a communion with the ultimate source of goodness and love.

However, the diversity within Christianity complicates any single interpretation of NDEs. Different denominations and theological perspectives hold varying views on the afterlife, the nature of the soul, and the interpretation of mystical experiences. Some emphasize the literal interpretation of scripture, while others embrace more symbolic or metaphorical understandings. Furthermore, the Christian tradition itself has a rich history of mystical experiences, encompassing various forms of prayer, contemplation, and ecstatic states, which offer potential parallels to the altered states of consciousness described in NDE accounts. The works of Christian mystics, such as St. Teresa of Avila and St. John of the Cross, provide invaluable insights into the subjective experience of union with the divine, a state that echoes the profound sense of unity and connectedness reported in many NDEs.

Sufism, a mystical branch of Islam, offers a unique perspective on NDEs, deeply rooted in its emphasis on direct experience and union with God. Sufis emphasize the importance of spiritual purification, self-discipline, and love as pathways to experiencing the divine reality. From a Sufi perspective, an NDE could be understood as a temporary unveiling of the divine presence, a glimpse into the ultimate reality that transcends ordinary perception. The reports of peace, love, and unity align with the Sufi emphasis on experiencing the oneness of existence, a state of interconnectedness with all beings and the divine. The experiences of timelessness and boundless space resonate with Sufi teachings on the transcendence of earthly limitations and the experience of divine immensity. Sufi poetry and literature often explore themes of death and the afterlife, providing rich metaphors and symbolic interpretations that can shed light on the transformative nature of NDEs. The journey of the soul, in Sufi tradition, is often portrayed as a pilgrimage towards divine union, mirroring the profound spiritual journey often described by individuals who have undergone NDEs.

Kabbalah, a mystical tradition within Judaism, offers another perspective, emphasizing the hidden dimensions of reality and the potential for human beings to attain a deeper understanding of God and the universe. Kabbalistic teachings describe a complex cosmology of divine emanations and interconnected realms, potentially offering a framework for understanding the experiences described in NDEs. The descriptions of light, unity, and encounters with deceased individuals might be interpreted as interactions within these hidden realms, revealing the interconnectedness of all things and the profound unity of existence. Kabbalistic practices, such as meditation and contemplation, aim to facilitate a direct experience of these hidden realities, thereby resonating with the introspective and transformative nature of NDEs. The emphasis on divine names and their mystical significance also suggests a potential correspondence between the symbolic language of NDE accounts and the symbolic language of Kabbalistic teachings. The intricate symbolism of Kabbalah allows for a rich and multi-layered interpretation of the reported experiences, going beyond a purely literal understanding of what transpired during the NDE.

Comparing these Western spiritual traditions with their Eastern counterparts reveals both parallels and contrasts.

While Eastern traditions often emphasize the impermanence of self and the interconnectedness of all things, Western traditions, particularly Christianity, often focus on the immortality of the soul and the existence of a distinct self. However, both sets of traditions acknowledge the transformative power of spiritual experiences and the potential for human consciousness to transcend the limitations of the physical body. The emphasis on mystical experiences, introspection, and spiritual practices is a common thread linking both Eastern and Western traditions, suggesting that the profound insights gained from NDEs may transcend cultural and religious boundaries.

The subjective nature of spiritual experiences necessitates acknowledging the inherent limitations of these interpretations. The lack of empirical evidence poses a challenge to scientifically validating the claims made by these traditions. However, the richness and depth of these spiritual perspectives offer valuable insights into the human experience and the potential for human consciousness to extend beyond the confines of the physical realm. The integration of scientific methodologies with the rich tapestry of Western spiritual traditions opens up avenues for more holistic and comprehensive explorations of consciousness, death, and the nature of reality, moving beyond reductionist explanations and embracing the full spectrum of human experience. The ongoing dialogue between science and spirituality, informed by both rigorous scientific inquiry and the profound wisdom of spiritual traditions, will continue to shape our understanding of NDEs and the mysteries of human existence. This interdisciplinary approach promises a deeper appreciation of the human spiritual journey and its profound implications for our understanding of the cosmos. The convergence of these diverse perspectives fosters a more inclusive and comprehensive approach to exploring these transformative experiences, emphasizing the need for humility, open dialogue, and respectful engagement with diverse viewpoints. The exploration of NDEs through this multifaceted lens highlights the profound questions that lie at the heart of the human condition, challenging us to continually refine our understanding of ourselves and our place within the universe.

Science and Spirituality A Dialogue

The exploration of near-death experiences (NDEs) has inadvertently illuminated a fascinating intersection—a point of potential convergence and productive tension—between the rigorous methodologies of science and the profound insights offered by spirituality. While seemingly disparate, these two domains share a common quest: to understand the fundamental nature of reality, consciousness, and the human experience. Science, with its emphasis on empirical observation and quantifiable data, seeks to unravel the mechanisms of the physical world, while spirituality, embracing subjective experience and inner exploration, delves into the realms of meaning, purpose, and the transcendent. The apparent incompatibility between these approaches is often overstated, as both fields grapple with fundamental questions that, although approached differently, ultimately point towards a deeper comprehension of existence.

One area of potential synergy lies in the study of consciousness itself. Neuroscience, through its exploration of brain function and neural activity, has made significant strides in understanding the physiological correlates of consciousness. However, the subjective nature of consciousness, the "what it's like" aspect of experience, remains a profound mystery, one that eludes purely reductionist explanations. Spiritual traditions, across cultures and throughout history, offer rich accounts of altered states of consciousness, mystical experiences, and profound shifts in perception, providing qualitative data that complements the quantitative findings of neuroscience. While scientific methods may struggle to directly measure the subtle nuances of spiritual experiences, the experiential narratives themselves provide valuable insights into the multifaceted nature of consciousness, suggesting that it may extend beyond the confines of the physical brain.

The phenomenon of NDEs provides a particularly compelling case study for this interdisciplinary dialogue. Scientific investigations into NDEs often focus on physiological factors, attempting to correlate reported experiences with brain activity, neurochemical changes, or other physical processes. These studies offer important insights into the potential neurological basis of these experiences, providing a framework for understanding how certain brain states might give rise to the subjective phenomena reported by NDErs. However, the recurring themes reported in NDEs—feelings of peace, unity, encounters with deceased loved ones, out-of-body experiences, and a sense of transcendence—suggest a dimension beyond purely physiological explanations.

Spiritual interpretations of NDEs often emphasize the soul's journey, the continuity of consciousness beyond physical death, or a glimpse into a realm beyond ordinary perception. These interpretations are not necessarily incompatible with scientific findings, but rather offer a complementary framework for understanding the deeper meaning and implications of these extraordinary experiences. For instance, the scientific study might focus on the brain's response to oxygen deprivation or the release of endorphins, while the spiritual perspective could explore the significance of these experiences in relation to the individual's spiritual path, the nature of the soul, or the interconnectedness of all beings.

The integration of scientific and spiritual perspectives requires a careful and nuanced approach, acknowledging the strengths and limitations of each methodology. Science excels at empirical observation, experimentation, and the formulation of testable hypotheses, but its reductionist approach may sometimes overlook the richness and complexity of subjective experience. Spirituality, on the other hand, provides valuable insights into subjective experience and the realm of meaning, but its reliance on personal testimony and interpretation can be subject to biases and individual variations. A truly productive dialogue between these two approaches requires a recognition of these inherent differences and a commitment to mutual respect and open-minded exploration.

One key aspect of this integration is the development of new methodologies that bridge the gap between scientific rigor and the subjective nature of spiritual experience. This might involve incorporating qualitative research methods, such as phenomenological analysis or hermeneutic interpretation, into scientific studies of NDEs and other spiritually significant experiences. It also requires a willingness to explore altered states of consciousness, not merely as aberrant neurological phenomena, but as potential pathways to deeper levels of understanding and awareness.

Furthermore, the integration of science and spirituality requires a shift in perspective, moving beyond a strict dichotomy of either/or towards a more holistic and integrated view. It is not a matter of choosing between scientific explanations and spiritual interpretations, but rather of recognizing that both fields contribute valuable insights to our understanding of human consciousness and reality. This integrated perspective emphasizes the complementary nature of scientific inquiry and spiritual exploration, highlighting the need for interdisciplinary collaboration and the development of new theoretical frameworks that encompass both the material and the immaterial aspects of existence.

The dialogue between science and spirituality is not without its challenges. The inherent differences in methodology, language, and assumptions can lead to misunderstandings and conflicts. The scientific community, with its emphasis on empirical evidence and falsifiable hypotheses, may be skeptical of claims that cannot be empirically verified. Similarly, spiritual traditions, with their emphasis on faith and personal experience, may resist attempts to impose scientific methods onto inherently subjective experiences. Overcoming these challenges requires a commitment to respectful dialogue, a willingness to engage with differing perspectives, and a recognition that the quest for understanding is a continuous process, marked by both progress and uncertainty.

In conclusion, the intersection of science and spirituality in the exploration of NDEs and other profound human experiences represents a vital frontier in our understanding of reality and consciousness. The potential for a productive dialogue between these two approaches is immense, promising a more comprehensive and nuanced understanding of the human condition. While challenges remain, the benefits of this integration are significant, potentially leading to the development of new methodologies, theoretical frameworks, and a deeper appreciation for the multifaceted nature of human existence. The ongoing exploration of this fascinating interplay promises to enrich our understanding of both the physical and spiritual dimensions of being, guiding us toward a more holistic and integrated view of ourselves and the cosmos in which we reside. This, ultimately, is a journey of discovery, demanding both intellectual rigor and spiritual humility, in the ceaseless search for truth and understanding.

CHAPTER 5

The Search for Meaning and Purpose

Existentialism and the Absurd

The previous exploration of near-death experiences and the potential convergence of scientific and spiritual perspectives naturally leads us to a consideration of existentialism, a philosophy that grapples directly with the fundamental questions of meaning and purpose in the face of a seemingly indifferent universe. Existentialism, in its various forms, doesn't offer easy answers or comforting resolutions. Instead, it confronts us with the stark reality of our existence, a reality often characterized by a profound sense of absurdity.

This absurdity, central to the existentialist worldview, stems from the inherent conflict between our innate human desire for meaning and purpose, and the apparent lack of inherent meaning or preordained purpose in the universe itself. We are born into existence without a pre-defined script, without a cosmic blueprint dictating our path or bestowing upon us a predetermined significance. The universe, from this perspective, doesn't care about our hopes, dreams, or aspirations; it simply unfolds according to its own impersonal laws, leaving us to grapple with the consequences of our own choices and actions within a seemingly meaningless framework.

Albert Camus, in his seminal work *The Myth of Sisyphus*, vividly captures this existential absurdity. He portrays Sisyphus, condemned to eternally roll a boulder uphill, only to watch it tumble back down each time, as a symbol of the human condition. The task is futile, repetitive, and utterly meaningless, yet Sisyphus continues, driven by a stubborn refusal to surrender to despair. Camus argues that it is precisely in the face of this meaningless struggle, this absurd confrontation with the universe's indifference, that we find the possibility of authentic existence. The absurdity isn't something to be overcome or escaped; it's the very condition of our being, the foundation upon which we build our lives and create our own meaning.

This creation of meaning, however, is not a passive or pre-ordained process. It requires conscious effort, a constant engagement with the choices and responsibilities that define our existence. Existentialism emphasizes the radical freedom inherent in the human condition. We are not merely products of our environment or our genetic makeup; we are free to choose, to create ourselves through our actions and commitments. This freedom, however, is a double-edged sword. While it allows us to shape our own destiny, it also places the burden of responsibility squarely on our shoulders. There are no external authorities or pre-defined paths to guide us; we are entirely accountable for the choices we make and the lives we lead.

Jean-Paul Sartre, another prominent figure in existentialist thought, further develops this theme of freedom and responsibility. In his view, "existence precedes essence," meaning that we are born into existence without a pre-defined nature or purpose. Our essence, our identity, is not something we are given; it's something we create through our choices and actions throughout our lives. This implies a profound sense of responsibility, as every choice we make contributes to the shaping of our own being and influences the lives of others. The weight of this responsibility can be overwhelming, leading to anguish and anxiety, but it is also the source of our authentic existence. To evade this responsibility, to deny our freedom, is to live inauthentically, to conform to societal expectations rather than to embrace the unique potential inherent in our own being.

The existentialist perspective doesn't shy away from the darker aspects of human existence. It acknowledges the possibility of despair, anguish, and even absurdity. However, it doesn't view these experiences as signs of failure or weakness. Instead, it recognizes them as integral components of the human condition, as inevitable consequences of our freedom and our confrontation with the meaningless universe. The challenge, then, is not to escape these experiences, but to confront them directly, to engage with them authentically, and to find a way to live meaningfully in the face of absurdity.

This confrontation with absurdity doesn't necessarily lead to nihilism, the belief that life is without meaning or purpose. While some interpretations of existentialism might seem nihilistic on the surface, the core message is not one of despair but one of empowerment. It's an invitation to create our own meaning, to forge our own paths, and to embrace the responsibility that comes with our radical freedom. It calls for a rejection of passive acceptance of pre-determined roles or societal expectations, urging us to actively shape our lives and create a sense of purpose within a universe that doesn't inherently provide one.

The process of creating meaning is deeply personal and often involves confronting our own mortality. The awareness of our finitude, the fact that our lives are limited and that death is inevitable, can be a powerful catalyst for authentic living. Knowing that our time is finite can heighten our appreciation for the present moment, motivating us to engage fully in life's experiences and to make the most of our limited time. This isn't about avoiding death or denying its reality; rather, it's about living a life that is true to ourselves and that makes a difference in the world.

The existentialist perspective, though challenging, offers a compelling alternative to more conventional views of meaning and purpose. It shifts the locus of meaning from external sources – religious doctrines, societal norms, or predetermined destinies – to the individual's own choices, actions, and commitments. It emphasizes the importance of self-awareness, personal responsibility, and the active creation of meaning in a world that offers no inherent guarantees.

One might argue that the existentialist emphasis on individual freedom and responsibility overlooks the importance of community and intersubjectivity. While existentialism prioritizes individual experience and the creation of personal meaning, it's crucial to acknowledge the profound influence of our relationships, social structures, and shared human experience on our sense of self and our capacity for meaning-making. The search for meaning isn't a solitary endeavor; it is often enriched and deepened through our connections with others and our participation in a wider community.

Furthermore, the existentialist focus on the inherent meaninglessness of the universe shouldn't be interpreted as a denial of the possibility of beauty, love, or joy. These experiences, while not guaranteed or inherently meaningful in a cosmic sense, are nonetheless profoundly significant in the human realm. The existentialist perspective doesn't negate these experiences; rather, it challenges us to appreciate their fragility and their inherent value within the context of a finite existence. It's in embracing both the light and the darkness, the joy and the sorrow, that we fully engage with the richness and complexity of the human experience.

The concept of absurdity, then, is not a bleak resignation to meaninglessness. Instead, it serves as a catalyst for authentic living, pushing us to confront the limitations of our existence and to create meaning from the seemingly meaningless. It encourages us to embrace our freedom, to take responsibility for our choices, and to live with a profound sense of awareness and commitment.

The existentialist framework provides a unique lens through which to examine near-death experiences. If the universe is indeed indifferent to our individual existence, as existentialism suggests, then the reported experiences of NDEs – the feelings of peace, unity, and transcendence – take on a different significance. They become not proof of an afterlife or a pre-ordained cosmic plan, but rather powerful demonstrations of the human capacity for profound subjective experience, even in the face of mortality. These experiences, therefore, can be understood as intensely personal expressions of meaning and purpose, created within the limitations of human consciousness rather than revealed by an external source.

The apparent contradiction between the scientific investigation of NDEs and the existentialist understanding of the absurd isn't necessarily insurmountable. Science seeks to understand the physical mechanisms underlying these experiences, while existentialism focuses on their subjective meaning and significance. These approaches, though different, are not mutually exclusive. The scientific exploration may shed light on the physiological processes involved, while the existentialist perspective offers a framework for interpreting the subjective meaning and implications of these profoundly personal experiences.

In conclusion, the existentialist perspective on meaning and purpose, with its emphasis on freedom, responsibility, and the confrontation with absurdity, provides a valuable framework for understanding the human condition and our search for meaning in a seemingly meaningless universe. It doesn't offer easy answers or comforting illusions, but instead challenges us to engage authentically with our own existence, to embrace our freedom, to take responsibility for our choices, and to create our own meaning in a world without inherent purpose. This ongoing process of creating meaning, while challenging, is precisely what gives our lives their significance and their unique value. The inherent absurdity, therefore, becomes not a source of despair but a catalyst for authentic living. The search for meaning, then, becomes not the pursuit of a pre-ordained truth but a continual creation of self and purpose in a world that gives us the radical freedom to choose.

Nihilism and its Alternatives

The exploration of existentialism, with its emphasis on individual freedom and the creation of meaning in a seemingly absurd universe, naturally leads us to consider nihilism. Nihilism, in its broadest sense, is the philosophical position that asserts the absence of inherent meaning, purpose, or value in life. It's a perspective that challenges the very foundations upon which many of our beliefs and values are built, prompting a profound reevaluation of our existence. However, nihilism isn't a monolithic doctrine; it manifests in various forms, each with its own nuances and implications.

One form is metaphysical nihilism, which denies the existence of objective meaning or purpose in the universe. From this viewpoint, the universe is simply a collection of physical processes unfolding according to natural laws, devoid of any inherent moral or ethical framework. There's no pre-ordained plan, no cosmic design, and no ultimate significance to human existence. This doesn't necessarily imply that individual experiences are meaningless; rather, it asserts that any meaning we ascribe to our lives is subjective, created by ourselves rather than inherent in the fabric of reality.

Moral nihilism, a closely related concept, challenges the existence of objective moral values. It argues that there are no universally valid moral principles or truths, and that concepts like good and evil are merely social constructs or subjective opinions. This perspective can be unsettling, as it challenges traditional moral frameworks and raises questions about the legitimacy of ethical systems. However, it doesn't necessarily lead to moral relativism or moral apathy. Some moral nihilists argue that, while there are no objective moral truths, we can still cultivate personal values and act in ways that we deem ethical, based on our own chosen principles.

Existential nihilism, although frequently associated with existentialism itself, represents a darker, more despairing interpretation. While existentialism emphasizes the freedom to create meaning, existential nihilism emphasizes the inherent absurdity and meaninglessness of existence, leading to a sense of despair and hopelessness. It accepts the lack of inherent meaning but offers little in the way of constructive alternatives, emphasizing the bleakness of a life devoid of inherent purpose. This position often leads to a sense of profound alienation and isolation.

Political nihilism expresses itself as a rejection of political systems and authority. This form of nihilism challenges the legitimacy of existing power structures, often advocating for their overthrow or dismantling. It can manifest as revolutionary fervor, aiming to create a new order free from the perceived injustices and limitations of the current systems. However, it can also lead to anarchic tendencies or outright violence if not guided by clear, constructive goals.

The criticisms of nihilism are numerous and varied. One major critique centers on its seemingly inescapable pessimism. Critics argue that the nihilistic worldview, while intellectually stimulating, can lead to moral paralysis, apathy, and a sense of purposelessness that undermines human flourishing. It's argued that a lack of inherent meaning doesn't necessarily preclude the possibility of creating meaning, and focusing solely on the absence of inherent meaning can be paralyzing and detrimental to mental wellbeing.

Furthermore, many argue that nihilism fails to adequately account for the richness and complexity of human experience. Emotions such as love, joy, sorrow, and compassion, all hold deep significance for individuals and societies, regardless of the absence of an inherent cosmic purpose. To dismiss these experiences as meaningless, or merely subjective constructions, is to disregard a crucial aspect of the human condition.

A powerful response to nihilism lies in the concept of subjective meaning creation. While the universe might lack inherent meaning, humans possess the capacity to create meaning for themselves through their values, beliefs, relationships, and actions. This perspective, aligning with existentialism, asserts that the search for meaning is not a quest for an external, pre-ordained truth, but rather a process of ongoing self-creation and engagement with the world.

This subjective meaning-making is often deeply personal and unique to each individual. What provides meaning for one person may not resonate with another. This process might involve pursuing passions, developing meaningful relationships, contributing to society, or engaging in creative endeavors. The crucial element is the active creation and investment in a personal value system that guides and shapes one's life choices.

Religious and spiritual perspectives offer alternative responses to nihilism by grounding meaning in a transcendent reality. Many religious systems propose the existence of a higher power, a divine purpose, or an afterlife that provides inherent meaning and significance to human existence. The specific nature of this meaning varies greatly across different faiths, but the common thread is the belief that human life is part of a larger cosmic plan, lending purpose and value to individual actions and experiences.

However, even within religious frameworks, questions of meaning can arise. The problem of evil, for instance, challenges the traditional theodicies that attempt to reconcile the existence of a benevolent God with the prevalence of suffering in the world. Similarly, the question of faith versus reason can lead to profound internal conflicts and doubts. Even strong religious beliefs don't necessarily eliminate the need for self-reflection, meaning creation, and finding personal significance within the chosen faith.

Beyond religion, various humanistic and secular approaches also offer ways of finding meaning. Humanism emphasizes human reason, ethics, and social justice, finding meaning in human relationships, creative endeavors, and the pursuit of knowledge. Secular humanism, in particular, rejects supernatural explanations for meaning, instead focusing on the inherent value of human life and the importance of creating a just and compassionate society.

Furthermore, the pursuit of knowledge and understanding, for its own sake, can serve as a powerful source of meaning. The ongoing quest to unravel the mysteries of the universe, to understand the natural world, and to expand human knowledge provides a framework for purpose and fulfillment. This pursuit can inspire intellectual curiosity, foster collaboration, and lead to advancements that benefit humanity.

Ultimately, the response to nihilism depends on the individual's unique worldview, experiences, and values. There is no single "correct" answer, and the search for meaning is an ongoing process, requiring self-reflection, critical examination, and a willingness to engage with the complexities of human existence. While nihilism presents a powerful challenge to traditional notions of meaning, it also opens up the possibility for a more profound and deeply personal understanding of our own lives and the significance we create within a universe that doesn't offer inherent guarantees.

The journey towards finding meaning, therefore, isn't a passive acceptance of pre-ordained truths but an active process of self-discovery, creating and living by our chosen values. The apparent meaninglessness of the universe can be seen not as a source of despair, but as an invitation to forge our own path, to create our own sense of purpose, and to embrace the responsibility that comes with the radical freedom to shape our own lives and leave our unique mark on the world. The challenge lies not in escaping the inherent uncertainties of existence, but in engaging with them authentically, finding beauty and purpose in the face of the unknown, and creating a life that is both meaningful and fulfilling. The absence of inherent meaning doesn't negate the possibility of subjective meaning; rather, it invites us to actively participate in its creation.

The Nature of Purpose and Intention

The preceding discussion of nihilism and the search for meaning naturally leads us to a deeper examination of purpose and intention. These concepts, seemingly straightforward, unravel into complex philosophical and scientific inquiries when scrutinized. Is purpose inherent in the universe, a pre-ordained design woven into the fabric of reality, or is it a human construct, a projection of our desire for order and significance onto a fundamentally indifferent cosmos? The answer, as with so many existential questions, is multifaceted and resists easy categorization.

From a scientific perspective, the concept of purpose often seems at odds with the mechanistic worldview dominant in many scientific disciplines. Physics, for example, describes the universe in terms of physical laws and causal relationships, suggesting that events unfold according to deterministic or probabilistic processes without inherent intention. A falling apple doesn't "intend" to fall; it obeys the law of gravity. Similarly, the evolution of life on Earth, as described by Darwinian theory, is a process driven by natural selection, not a purposeful striving towards some predetermined end. This perspective, often termed "mechanism," sees the universe as a vast, intricate clockwork, operating according to its own internal logic without any overarching goal or design.

However, the mechanistic view doesn't fully account for the emergence of consciousness and intentionality. Conscious beings, unlike inanimate objects, appear to act with purpose. We set goals, make plans, and strive to achieve them. Our actions are often guided by intentions, desires, and beliefs about the world, giving a sense of agency and purpose to our lives. The question then becomes: how does this intentionality arise from a seemingly purposeless universe? One might argue that intentionality is an emergent property of complex systems, arising from the intricate interactions of neurons in the brain, or even from the complex interplay of individuals within a society.

Philosophically, the question of purpose takes on even greater complexity. Teleological arguments, which posit that the universe has a purpose or goal, have been debated for centuries. The classic cosmological argument, for example, posits that the universe's order and complexity imply a designer or creator, imbuing the universe with inherent purpose. However, this argument has been challenged on numerous grounds, including the problem of evil and the difficulty of proving the existence of a divine creator.

The debate over inherent purpose also intersects with questions about free will and determinism. If the universe is deterministic, with every event causally predetermined, does this negate the possibility of genuine purpose and intention? If our actions are simply the inevitable outcome of prior causes, how can we claim to act with true purpose? Conversely, if free will exists, allowing for genuine choices and actions independent of prior causation, does this imply an inherent purpose within us, a capacity to shape our own destiny and imbue our lives with meaning?

Consider the concept of "emergent properties." Complex systems, like the human brain, exhibit properties that are not present in their individual components. Consciousness, for example, is an emergent property of the intricate network of neurons in the brain. Similarly, intentionality could be an emergent property of consciousness, arising from the complex interplay of cognitive processes. This doesn't necessarily resolve the question of inherent purpose, but it offers a possible explanation for how purpose might appear in a universe governed by physical laws.

The question of whether the universe itself has a purpose is a profound and ultimately unanswerable question. Scientific investigation can reveal the laws that govern the universe and the processes that have shaped its evolution, but it cannot provide definitive answers to questions about ultimate purpose or meaning. Many find meaning in their lives through their relationships, their work, their creative endeavors, or their contributions to society. These are subjective sources of meaning, but they are no less real or valuable for being subjective. The meaning of life, it seems, is not something to be discovered but something to be created.

This process of creating meaning often involves the setting of goals and intentions. We project ourselves into the future, envisioning what we want to achieve, and then we act to bring those visions into reality. This process of intention-setting is a crucial aspect of human agency and a powerful source of purpose. It allows us to shape our lives in accordance with our values and aspirations, giving direction and significance to our actions.

However, the creation of meaning isn't a linear, predictable process. Life often throws unexpected curveballs, challenges our assumptions, and forces us to adapt and recalibrate our intentions. The ability to adjust our goals and strategies in light of new information and experiences is a critical element of resilience and personal growth. Indeed, the very act of confronting setbacks and adapting to unforeseen circumstances can often be a powerful source of meaning and growth.

Furthermore, the nature of intention itself warrants deeper contemplation. Is it a conscious, deliberate act, or is it influenced by unconscious drives and biases? The study of cognitive biases reveals the extent to which our decisions and actions are shaped by factors outside our conscious awareness. This raises questions about the degree to which our intentions reflect our true selves and the extent to which we are truly the authors of our own lives.

Different philosophical perspectives offer diverse approaches to the issue of purpose. Existentialism emphasizes individual freedom and responsibility, suggesting that each person creates their own purpose through their choices and actions. While the universe may lack inherent meaning, individuals have the capacity to imbue their lives with significance. This perspective challenges us to actively engage in the process of meaning-making, to take ownership of our lives, and to forge our own paths.

In contrast to existentialism, some religious and spiritual perspectives offer a transcendental view of purpose. Many religious traditions posit the existence of a divine plan or purpose that transcends human understanding. Human life, in this context, is seen as part of a larger cosmic scheme, with each individual playing a specific role in the unfolding of this plan. The source of purpose, therefore, lies outside the individual, residing in a higher power or transcendent reality.

Ultimately, the question of purpose and intention is a profoundly personal one. There is no single, universally accepted answer, and the search for meaning is an ongoing process of self-discovery and reflection. Whether we find purpose in a pre-ordained cosmic design, in the creation of our own subjective meaning, or in a combination of both, the pursuit of purpose remains a fundamental aspect of the human experience, driving us to strive, to create, and to leave our mark on the world. The inherent ambiguity of the question, far from being a source of despair, can be seen as an invitation to explore the full spectrum of human possibility, to create a life rich in purpose and meaning, even within a universe that offers no inherent guarantees. The very act of searching for purpose can be a purpose in itself, a testament to the enduring human spirit's capacity to find meaning in the face of the unknown.

MeaningMaking and Human Experience

The preceding exploration of purpose and intentionality naturally leads us to consider how humans, as conscious beings, actively engage in the process of meaning-making. While the universe may or may not possess inherent purpose, the human experience is undeniably characterized by the persistent search for significance and the active creation of meaning within the context of our lives. This meaning-making process is not a passive reception of pre-ordained truth; rather, it's a dynamic, creative act deeply interwoven with our individual narratives, our relationships, and the cultural frameworks within which we exist.

One of the most fundamental aspects of human meaning-making is the construction of personal narratives. From our earliest memories, we begin to weave together our experiences into a coherent story, shaping our self-perception and understanding of our place in the world. This narrative isn't simply a chronological account of events; it's a selective interpretation, a carefully constructed tapestry woven from memories, emotions, and beliefs. We emphasize certain events, downplay others, and create connections between seemingly disparate experiences to form a cohesive sense of self and purpose. The narrative we construct, consciously or unconsciously, influences our decisions, our relationships, and our overall sense of well-being. A narrative dominated by feelings of failure and inadequacy will naturally lead to a different sense of purpose than a narrative focused on accomplishment and resilience.

The power of storytelling extends beyond personal narratives. Myths, legends, religious texts, and works of literature all contribute to our understanding of the world and our place within it. These stories provide frameworks for understanding our lives, offering models of heroism, suffering, redemption, and ultimate purpose. They offer comfort, inspiration, and a shared sense of meaning within a community. The narratives we encounter throughout our lives shape our values, our beliefs, and our expectations of the world. They provide moral compasses, helping us navigate complex ethical dilemmas and make sense of life's uncertainties. The impact of these shared narratives cannot be overstated; they form the bedrock of cultural identity, influencing everything from political systems to artistic expression.

Furthermore, our relationships are crucial in the creation of meaning. The connections we forge with others – family, friends, romantic partners, colleagues – provide a sense of belonging, support, and shared purpose. These relationships offer opportunities for mutual growth, collaboration, and the experience of love, empathy, and compassion. They provide context for our individual narratives, enriching and expanding our understanding of ourselves and the world.

The meaning we find in relationships often surpasses the meaning derived from individual accomplishments; the bonds we share with others provide a sense of stability, security, and enduring significance. The support and encouragement we receive from those we love can be crucial in navigating life's challenges and sustaining our sense of purpose in the face of adversity.

However, the cultural frameworks within which we live can both facilitate and hinder our ability to create meaningful lives. Societal expectations, cultural norms, and dominant ideologies can exert a powerful influence on our sense of self-worth and purpose. In some cultures, the pursuit of wealth, power, or status may be prioritized above other values. This can lead individuals to prioritize external validation over internal fulfillment, hindering their ability to discover authentic purpose. Conversely, other cultures may emphasize community, spiritual growth, or artistic expression as pathways to meaning. The specific cultural context within which we develop influences our values, our aspirations, and our capacity to create a life rich in purpose. Awareness of these influences is critical to developing a sense of meaning independent of societal pressures.

The importance of finding personal meaning, independent of external validation or societal expectations, cannot be overstated. External markers of success, such as wealth, fame, or professional achievement, can provide a temporary sense of fulfillment, but they are ultimately insufficient in providing lasting meaning. True meaning stems from a deeper engagement with our values, our passions, and our unique contributions to the world. This involves self-reflection, introspection, and a willingness to question societal norms and expectations. It requires the courage to pursue our authentic selves, even if it means diverging from the paths prescribed by society.

The search for meaning is a lifelong journey, not a destination. It requires ongoing reflection, adaptation, and a willingness to embrace uncertainty. As our lives unfold, our values, aspirations, and understanding of ourselves may evolve, necessitating a continuous re-evaluation of our sense of purpose. This process of self-discovery is not linear or predictable; it involves navigating setbacks, confronting challenges, and learning from our experiences. The ability to adapt to change, to learn from adversity, and to maintain a sense of hope in the face of uncertainty is critical in sustaining a meaningful life. Ultimately, the creation of meaning is a deeply personal and subjective endeavor, shaped by our individual experiences, relationships, and values. It is a testament to the resilience of the human spirit and our inherent capacity to find significance and purpose even in the face of existential uncertainty. The act of searching, of striving to create meaning, is itself a powerful affirmation of the human spirit and the relentless quest for understanding.

Living a Meaningful Life

Building upon our understanding of the dynamic and deeply personal nature of meaning-making, let's now delve into the practical aspects of cultivating a life rich in purpose and fulfillment. The search for meaning isn't a passive pursuit; it requires active engagement, conscious choices, and a willingness to embrace the inherent uncertainties of existence. While external factors undoubtedly influence our lives, the ultimate responsibility for creating meaning rests with each individual. This section explores several strategies for navigating this path, empowering you to actively shape your own journey towards a meaningful life.

One of the most potent tools in the pursuit of meaning is mindfulness. Mindfulness, often associated with meditation and contemplative practices, involves cultivating a present-moment awareness without judgment. It's about paying attention to the sensations, thoughts, and emotions arising in the present, observing them without getting swept away by them. This practice allows us to step back from the constant stream of thoughts and anxieties that often distract us from the richness of our lived experience. By cultivating mindfulness, we become more attuned to the subtle nuances of our internal world and the external environment, appreciating the beauty and wonder that often goes unnoticed in the rush of daily life. This increased awareness can lead to a deeper appreciation of simple pleasures, a greater sense of presence, and a more profound connection with ourselves and the world around us. The practice of mindfulness isn't about escaping life's challenges; instead, it equips us to face them with greater clarity, resilience, and a deeper understanding of our own inner landscape. Regular mindfulness practice, even in short bursts throughout the day, can significantly enhance our capacity for joy, compassion, and a more meaningful engagement with life.

Self-reflection is another crucial aspect of living a meaningful life. This involves taking the time to honestly examine our thoughts, feelings, beliefs, and values. It's a process of introspection, of looking inward to understand our motivations, our fears, and our aspirations. Self-reflection isn't just about identifying our strengths and weaknesses; it's about understanding how our past experiences have shaped our present and how our current choices will influence our future. This process can be facilitated through journaling, meditation, or simply dedicating time for quiet contemplation. Asking ourselves probing questions—What truly matters to me? What are my values? What am I passionate about?—can illuminate our deepest desires and guide us toward a life aligned with our authentic selves. The self-reflective process is ongoing and often reveals surprising insights. It is a continuous process of uncovering deeper layers of understanding about our selves and our relationship with the world. By engaging in self-reflection, we gain a clearer understanding of our purpose and become more empowered to create a life that aligns with our values.

Engaging with the world around us is another vital component of a meaningful life. This doesn't necessarily mean grand gestures or heroic actions. It can involve simple acts of kindness, volunteering our time, engaging in meaningful conversations, or immersing ourselves in activities that spark our curiosity and creativity. Connecting with nature, through hiking, gardening, or simply observing the natural world, can be incredibly grounding and restorative. Participating in our communities, contributing to causes we care about, and building strong relationships can imbue our lives with a sense of purpose and belonging. The act of contributing, even in small ways, fosters a sense of connection and shared purpose, strengthening our bonds with others and enriching our own lives. Engaging with the world, whether through acts of service or creative endeavors, allows us to transcend the limitations of our individual experiences and connect with something larger than ourselves.

Gratitude plays a pivotal role in cultivating a meaningful life. Taking time to appreciate the good things in our lives, both big and small, can shift our perspective and enhance our overall sense of well-being. Keeping a gratitude journal, expressing appreciation to others, or simply taking moments throughout the day to acknowledge the positive aspects of our experiences can have a profound impact on our emotional state. Gratitude helps us to focus on what we have, rather than what we lack, fostering a sense of contentment and reducing feelings of envy or dissatisfaction. This practice not only enhances our emotional well-being but also strengthens our relationships and fosters a more positive outlook on life. Cultivating gratitude is an active practice that requires conscious effort, but the rewards are immeasurable, leading to greater resilience and a deeper appreciation for the beauty and abundance in our lives.

Cultivating compassion is another essential step toward living a meaningful life. Compassion involves understanding and sharing the feelings of others, extending empathy and kindness even to those who have caused us pain. It's about recognizing our shared humanity and extending our circle of concern beyond ourselves. Practicing compassion can involve acts of kindness, volunteering our time to help others, or simply listening attentively to those who are suffering. Cultivating compassion not only benefits those we help but also enriches our own lives, fostering a sense of connection, purpose, and emotional well-being. The ability to empathize with others, to understand their perspectives, and to extend kindness even in the face of difficulty strengthens our ability to navigate complex relationships and fosters a deeper sense of belonging within our communities.

Finally, fostering a sense of connection with something larger than ourselves can contribute significantly to a meaningful life. This connection can take many forms, from religious or spiritual practices to engagement with nature or involvement in a community or cause. It can be a connection with something transcendent, something that gives our lives meaning and purpose beyond our individual experiences. This connection provides a sense of belonging, a sense of purpose, and a perspective that transcends the limitations of our individual existence. Whether this connection is through nature, spirituality, community involvement or a shared belief system, it provides the framework for finding a sense of belonging within something larger than ourselves, giving our lives a sense of significance. It provides a source of strength, resilience and guidance in navigating the challenges of life. This connection provides an anchor, a source of strength, and a sense of meaning that can sustain us through difficult times and enhance our appreciation for the wonder and mystery of existence.

Living a meaningful life is not a passive state to be achieved; it is an active, continuous process of self-discovery, engagement, and conscious choice. It requires embracing uncertainty, fostering self-compassion, and actively cultivating gratitude, mindfulness, and compassion. It's about aligning our lives with our deepest values, engaging with the world around us, and finding connection with something larger than ourselves. This journey unfolds uniquely for each individual, shaped by our personal experiences, relationships, and values. The path may be winding and unpredictable, but the pursuit itself is a powerful affirmation of the human spirit and its inherent capacity for meaning and purpose. The creation of meaning is not a destination; it is a lifelong journey of growth, transformation, and continuous self-discovery.

CHAPTER 6

Time and Space

The Nature of Time

Our exploration of meaning-making thus far has focused on the internal landscape—the conscious choices, mindful practices, and self-reflection that shape our individual experiences. However, the quest for meaning is inextricably linked to the external world, a world profoundly shaped by the passage of time and the vast expanse of space. To fully comprehend our place within the universe and to deepen our understanding of the meaning we create, we must now turn our attention to these fundamental aspects of reality. This section delves into the enigmatic nature of time, a concept both deeply familiar and profoundly mysterious.

The everyday experience of time is a linear progression, a unidirectional flow from past to future. We remember the past, experience the present, and anticipate the future. This seemingly simple perception, however, belies a complex and multifaceted reality. From the perspective of classical physics, time was considered absolute and universal, a constant backdrop against which events unfolded. Newtonian mechanics, for example, assumed a uniform and unchanging time that flowed identically for all observers, regardless of their location or motion. This view of time as a fixed, objective entity permeated our understanding of the cosmos for centuries.

Einstein's theory of relativity, however, revolutionized our understanding of time, demonstrating its intricate relationship with space and gravity. In special relativity, time is no longer absolute but relative, dependent on the observer's frame of reference. Two observers moving relative to each other will experience time differently; the faster an observer moves, the slower time passes for them relative to a stationary observer. This effect, known as time dilation, has been experimentally verified and has profound implications for our understanding of the universe. For instance, astronauts orbiting Earth in the International Space

Station experience time slightly slower than those on the ground, although the difference is minuscule in everyday terms.

General relativity further expands this concept, demonstrating that time is also affected by gravity. Time slows down in stronger gravitational fields. This means that time passes slightly slower at sea level than it does on a mountaintop, or even that time passes slower near a black hole compared to further away. While these differences are often imperceptible in our daily lives, they are significant at cosmological scales and are essential to our understanding of phenomena like gravitational lensing and the evolution of the universe.

The relativity of time challenges our intuitive understanding of its linearity. If time is relative, dependent on the observer's frame of reference, then the concept of a single, universal "now" becomes problematic. What constitutes "present" for one observer may be "past" or "future" for another. This raises fundamental questions about the nature of time itself: Is it a real entity, an independent dimension of reality, or simply a construct of our minds? Philosophers have debated this question for centuries, with some arguing that time is merely a subjective experience, a human interpretation of the flow of events, while others maintain that time possesses an objective reality, independent of our consciousness.

Further complicating our understanding of time is the concept of the "arrow of time," the seemingly irreversible flow of time from past to future. This unidirectional nature of time is intimately linked to the second law of thermodynamics, which states that the entropy of a closed system never decreases. Entropy is a measure of disorder or randomness. The arrow of time reflects the universe's tendency to move from states of lower entropy (order) to states of higher entropy (disorder). This inherent tendency toward increasing disorder explains why we remember the past but not the future, why broken eggs don't spontaneously reassemble, and why heat flows from hot objects to cold objects, and not the reverse.

However, the arrow of time presents a paradox in the context of fundamental physical laws. Many of the equations describing the universe are time-reversible, meaning that they work equally well whether time flows forward or backward. This raises the question of why the universe exhibits this irreversible arrow of time, even though the fundamental laws governing it are time-symmetric. This discrepancy remains one of the most profound unsolved mysteries in physics, challenging our understanding of the universe's fundamental nature.

The potential for time travel further complicates our perception of time's linearity and reality. While time travel remains firmly in the realm of science fiction for now, the laws of physics, at least as we currently understand them, do not explicitly forbid it. However, time travel introduces a multitude of paradoxes, such as the grandfather paradox, where traveling back in time and preventing one's own birth creates a logical contradiction. Resolving these paradoxes requires either revising our understanding of causality or accepting the existence of parallel universes or alternate timelines.

The subjective human experience of time adds another layer of complexity. Our perception of time is not constant; it can seem to fly by during periods of intense engagement or to drag on during moments of boredom or anxiety. Factors like age, emotional state, and even cultural background can influence our subjective experience of time's passage. Children often perceive time as stretching out indefinitely, while older adults may find time accelerating as they age. These subjective perceptions highlight the disconnect between our internal, experiential sense of time and the objective, physical reality of time as described by physics.

Furthermore, the concept of time intertwines intricately with our understanding of consciousness and the nature of reality itself. Some theories propose that time is an emergent property of consciousness, a product of our minds' attempts to make sense of the flow of events. Others argue that consciousness itself is intimately bound up with time, that the conscious experience is inherently temporal, unfolding through the passage of time. These perspectives emphasize the deep philosophical implications of time, linking its nature to fundamental questions about the nature of reality, free will, and the human experience.

In conclusion, the nature of time remains a profoundly challenging and fascinating topic, one that bridges the gap between physics, philosophy, and our subjective human experiences. From the relativity of time in physics to the arrow of time's irreversibility and the potential for time travel, the concept presents a series of paradoxes and unsolved mysteries. The subjective human experience further complicates our understanding, underscoring the multifaceted and enigmatic nature of this fundamental aspect of reality. Understanding time is not just a scientific pursuit; it is a journey into the heart of existence itself, a quest to grasp the very fabric of our reality and our place within it. The more we delve into the nature of time, the more we confront the limitations of our understanding and the infinite possibilities that lie beyond the boundaries of our current knowledge. It is in this continuous process of questioning, exploring, and refining our understanding that we approach a deeper understanding of our place in the universe and the meaning we create within its grand tapestry. The mystery of time serves as a reminder of the limits of human understanding and the boundless potential for discovery. The ongoing exploration of time's nature will continue to shape our comprehension of the universe and our role within it, leading us towards a richer, more nuanced understanding of our existence and the meaning we strive to find.

Space and the Cosmos

Our journey into the depths of meaning has thus far navigated the intricacies of time, a concept both intimately familiar and profoundly mysterious. Now, we shift our gaze outward, to the vast expanse of space and the cosmos, a realm of staggering scale and equally profound enigma. The human understanding of space, like that of time, has undergone a dramatic evolution, progressing from ancient mythological interpretations to the sophisticated models of modern astrophysics. Early cosmologies, often entwined with religious beliefs and philosophical speculation, envisioned a geocentric universe, with Earth at its center, a cosmic stage upon which celestial dramas played out. These models, while limited by their technological and observational capabilities, reflected humanity's innate drive to comprehend its place in the grand scheme of existence.

The shift from geocentrism to heliocentrism, championed by Copernicus, Galileo, and Kepler, marked a pivotal moment in our understanding of the cosmos. The realization that Earth was not the static center of the universe but a planet orbiting the sun profoundly altered our perception of space and our place within it. Suddenly, the universe expanded enormously, transforming from a relatively small, Earth-centered system to one with potentially limitless expanse. This revolution was not solely a scientific achievement but a philosophical one, challenging established worldviews and prompting a reevaluation of humanity's place in the cosmos.

Newton's laws of motion and universal gravitation further refined our understanding of space, providing a mathematical framework for describing the movements of celestial bodies. Space, in Newtonian physics, was considered absolute and unchanging, a passive stage upon which gravitational forces acted. This conception of space as a static, three-dimensional container persisted for centuries, providing a relatively simple and intuitive framework for understanding the universe. However, this framework would ultimately prove insufficient to accommodate the complexities revealed by later observations and theoretical advancements.

Einstein's theory of relativity once again revolutionized our understanding of space, just as it had our understanding of time. In special relativity, space and time are unified into a four-dimensional spacetime continuum, intrinsically linked and mutually influencing each other. The geometry of spacetime is not fixed but dynamic, warped and curved by the presence of mass and energy. This curved spacetime is the essence of Einstein's general relativity, which describes gravity not as a force but as a manifestation of the curvature of spacetime. Massive objects, like stars and planets, warp the fabric of spacetime, causing other objects to move along curved paths. This perspective fundamentally changed our conception of space, transforming it from a passive container into an active participant in the cosmic drama.

The implications of Einstein's theories are far-reaching, leading to predictions that have been experimentally confirmed and providing a foundation for modern cosmology. The expansion of the universe, one of the most remarkable discoveries of the 20th century, is a direct consequence of general relativity. Observations of distant galaxies reveal that the universe is not static but is expanding, with galaxies receding from each other at a rate proportional to their distance. This expansion suggests that the universe originated from an extremely hot, dense state – the Big Bang – and has been expanding and cooling ever since. This model, supported by a vast body of observational evidence, including the cosmic microwave background radiation, provides a powerful framework for understanding the evolution of the universe from its earliest moments to its current state.

However, the expansion of the universe raises further questions about the nature of space and its extent. If the universe is expanding, what is it expanding into? This seemingly simple question has no easy answer. The concept of "outside" the universe is meaningless within the context of current cosmological models. The expansion itself is not an expansion into pre-existing space, but rather an expansion of space itself. It's a stretching of the fabric of spacetime, a continuous creation of new space between galaxies. The very notion of "space" becomes elusive, blurring the boundaries between our intuitive understanding and the complexities of relativistic cosmology.

Adding to the mystery are the concepts of dark matter and dark energy. Observations of galactic rotation curves and gravitational lensing reveal that a significant portion of the universe's mass-energy content is invisible, neither emitting nor absorbing light. This mysterious substance, dubbed dark matter, accounts for approximately 85% of the matter in the universe. Its nature remains unknown, and its detection continues to be a major focus of cosmological research. Furthermore, observations of distant supernovae indicate that the expansion of the universe is accelerating. This acceleration is attributed to a mysterious force, called dark energy, which constitutes approximately 68% of the universe's total energy density. Dark energy is even more enigmatic than dark matter; its precise nature and origin are currently unknown.

The existence of dark matter and dark energy challenges our understanding of the fundamental constituents of the universe. They represent a significant portion of the universe's mass-energy content, yet their composition remains shrouded in mystery. These unknowns highlight the limitations of our current scientific knowledge and underscore the vastness and complexity of the cosmos. The search for an understanding of dark matter and dark energy is a major driving force in contemporary astrophysics, pushing the boundaries of our knowledge and technologies. The development of more sophisticated instruments and theoretical models is crucial to unraveling the mysteries of these enigmatic components of the universe.

The scale of the cosmos is truly mind-boggling. The observable universe, the portion of the universe we can currently see, is estimated to be 93 billion light-years in diameter. This immense scale dwarfs even the most ambitious human constructions and imagination. The sheer number of galaxies, stars, and planets within the observable universe is almost incomprehensible, and we only have access to a small fraction of the universe. The universe may well extend far beyond our observable reach. The cosmic distances involved necessitate the use of specialized astronomical techniques and theoretical models to study distant celestial objects.

Consider the implications of this vastness. Our sun, a seemingly colossal star, is merely one of billions of stars in our galaxy, the Milky Way. And the Milky Way, in turn, is just one of billions of galaxies in the observable universe. Each galaxy contains billions or even trillions of stars, many of which likely harbor planetary systems. This vastness invites contemplation on the nature of life in the universe, raising the possibility, or even probability, that we are not alone. The sheer scale of the cosmos encourages a perspective shift, placing human existence into a broader context, reminding us of our relative insignificance in the grand scheme of the universe while simultaneously emphasizing the profound potential for discovery.

In conclusion, the exploration of space and the cosmos mirrors our exploration of time—a journey into the unknown, a quest for understanding that pushes the boundaries of human knowledge. From the geocentric models of antiquity to the sophisticated relativistic cosmology of today, our understanding of space has undergone a dramatic transformation. The expansion of the universe, the mysterious nature of dark matter and dark energy, and the sheer scale of the cosmos all contribute to the profound mystery and wonder that permeate our investigations. Our understanding of space is continually evolving, driven by ongoing observations, technological advancements, and the development of new theoretical models. It is through this ongoing exploration that we can hope to further unravel the mysteries of the universe and our place within its vast and awe-inspiring expanse. The more we understand, the more questions arise, highlighting the boundless potential for discovery and the humbling realization of how much we do not yet know. This inherent mystery fuels the pursuit of knowledge, inviting us to continue our journey into the cosmic depths, forever searching for a deeper understanding of our place in the grand, unfolding narrative of the universe.

Spacetime and Relativity

Before Einstein, space and time were considered separate and absolute entities. Newton's physics, while revolutionary in its own right, depicted space as a fixed, three-dimensional backdrop against which the drama of the universe unfolded. Time, meanwhile, marched uniformly forward, an independent variable unaffected by the events occurring within this cosmic stage. This Newtonian framework served remarkably well for centuries, accurately predicting the motions of planets and celestial bodies within a certain range of scales and velocities. However, it would ultimately prove inadequate to describe the universe at its extremes.

Einstein's special theory of relativity, published in 1905, irrevocably shattered this classical worldview. It demonstrated that space and time are not independent but intimately intertwined, forming a unified four-dimensional continuum known as spacetime. This revolutionary idea stemmed from the seemingly simple yet profound observation that the speed of light in a vacuum is constant for all observers, regardless of their relative motion. This seemingly simple fact has profound consequences.

To maintain the constancy of the speed of light, Einstein postulated that space and time must be relative, meaning their measurements depend on the observer's frame of reference. This relativity manifests in several striking ways. For instance, the concept of simultaneity, which appears self-evident in everyday experience, becomes relative in special relativity. Two events that appear simultaneous to one observer may appear to occur at different times to another observer moving relative to the first. This seemingly paradoxical result arises because the measurement of time and distance is intertwined with the observer's motion, a direct consequence of the constancy of the speed of light.

Furthermore, special relativity predicts time dilation, meaning that time passes slower for objects moving at high speeds relative to a stationary observer. This effect, though subtle at everyday speeds, becomes significant at velocities approaching the speed of light. Imagine two identical clocks, one stationary and one moving at a significant fraction of the speed of light. The moving clock will appear to run slower than the stationary clock, as measured by the stationary observer. This is not a matter of the clock malfunctioning, but a fundamental consequence of the spacetime continuum. This effect has been experimentally verified numerous times, for example through precision measurements of atomic clocks on high-speed aircraft and satellites.

The implications of time dilation extend beyond mere clock discrepancies; they affect the fundamental processes of nature. For instance, particles with short lifespans, such as muons created in the upper atmosphere, should decay before reaching the Earth's surface. However, due to relativistic time dilation, their lifespans are extended from the perspective of a terrestrial observer, allowing them to reach the ground. This observation is a clear testament to the validity of special relativity.

Special relativity revolutionized our understanding of space and time at high velocities, but it didn't account for gravity. Einstein's general theory of relativity, published a decade later in 1915, extended the concept of spacetime to incorporate gravity. Instead of viewing gravity as a force acting between masses, as Newton had proposed, Einstein described gravity as a manifestation of the curvature of spacetime.

Imagine spacetime as a flexible fabric, stretched across a vast expanse. Massive objects, like stars and planets, warp this fabric, creating dips and curves. Other objects, such as smaller planets or satellites, then follow the curved paths created by these dips in spacetime. This is why planets orbit stars; they're not being pulled by a force, but rather following the curves in spacetime created by the star's mass. This revolutionary concept not only explained gravitational phenomena but provided a unified description of gravity and the geometry of spacetime.

General relativity makes several remarkable predictions, some of which have been experimentally verified with remarkable precision. One significant prediction is gravitational time dilation, which states that time passes slower in stronger gravitational fields. This means that a clock placed near a massive object will run slower than an identical clock placed further away. This effect is tiny in everyday situations but becomes measurable in strong gravitational fields, such as those near black holes or neutron stars. GPS satellites, for instance, must account for both special and general relativistic effects on their onboard atomic clocks to maintain accurate positioning. If these relativistic corrections weren't applied, GPS navigation would quickly become unreliable.

The curvature of spacetime also has significant implications for the structure and evolution of the universe. General relativity predicts that the universe is not static but is either expanding or contracting. The discovery of the expansion of the universe, based on observations of redshifted galaxies, provided a powerful confirmation of general relativity. This expansion is not an expansion into an existing space but rather an expansion of space itself, with the fabric of spacetime stretching and carrying galaxies along with it.

Moreover, general relativity provides the theoretical framework for understanding the earliest moments of the universe, the Big Bang. The Big Bang theory postulates that the universe originated from an extremely hot, dense state approximately 13.8 billion years ago and has been expanding and cooling ever since. General relativity describes the dynamics of this expansion and evolution, allowing us to trace the universe's history back to very early times, albeit with some limitations at the very beginning when quantum effects become dominant.

But the story doesn't end there. Observations of galactic rotation curves and gravitational lensing suggest that a substantial portion of the universe's mass-energy content is invisible, interacting gravitationally but not emitting or absorbing light. This mysterious substance, dubbed dark matter, is believed to account for about 85% of the matter in the universe. Its nature remains one of the most pressing puzzles in modern astrophysics. We know it exists because of its gravitational effects, but its composition remains elusive. Many theoretical candidates have been proposed, ranging from weakly interacting massive particles (WIMPs) to modified Newtonian dynamics (MOND), but conclusive evidence remains elusive.

Even more perplexing is dark energy, a mysterious force that is accelerating the expansion of the universe. Observations of distant supernovae indicate that the rate of expansion is not slowing down, as might be expected due to gravitational attraction, but is actually speeding up. This acceleration is attributed to dark energy, which constitutes about 68% of the universe's total energy density. Dark energy's nature is even more enigmatic than dark matter; its origin and properties are largely unknown, and its presence profoundly impacts our understanding of the ultimate fate of the universe.

These observations highlight the limitations of our current understanding of the universe. Despite the remarkable success of Einstein's theory of relativity in explaining many aspects of the cosmos, the nature of dark matter and dark energy remains a profound mystery. The quest to understand these enigmatic components is driving intense research in astrophysics and cosmology, pushing the boundaries of our experimental techniques and theoretical models. New telescopes, detectors, and theoretical frameworks are constantly being developed in an attempt to unravel these cosmic riddles.

The exploration of spacetime and relativity leads us to contemplate the very nature of space and time, concepts deeply woven into our perception of reality. The fact that these fundamental aspects of our experience are not absolute but relative and intertwined challenges our intuitive understanding. It reminds us that our perception of the universe is fundamentally shaped by our frame of reference, a crucial lesson from Einstein's revolutionary ideas. As we continue our journey of exploration, delving ever deeper into the mysteries of the cosmos, we are continually humbled by the vastness of the universe and the limitations of our current understanding. The more we learn, the more we realize how much more there is to discover. This inherent mystery is precisely what fuels our relentless pursuit of knowledge, driving us to continue our exploration of spacetime and the universe it encompasses.

Quantum Gravity and the Nature of Spacetime

Our journey through the landscape of spacetime has led us to the precipice of a profound mystery: the incompatibility between general relativity and quantum mechanics. General relativity, Einstein's masterpiece, elegantly describes gravity as the curvature of spacetime caused by mass and energy, providing a powerful framework for understanding the universe at large scales, from the orbits of planets to the expansion of the cosmos. Quantum mechanics, on the other hand, reigns supreme at the subatomic level, governing the bizarre and counterintuitive behavior of particles, with its probabilistic nature and wave-particle duality. However, these two pillars of modern physics, while incredibly successful in their respective domains, clash violently when applied together. This incompatibility represents one of the greatest challenges facing theoretical physics today.

The crux of the problem lies in the fundamentally different ways general relativity and quantum mechanics describe the universe. General relativity is a classical theory, dealing with continuous fields and deterministic predictions. It operates seamlessly at large scales, where the effects of quantum fluctuations are negligible. Quantum mechanics, conversely, is intrinsically probabilistic, describing the universe in terms of discrete quanta and inherent uncertainties. It governs the realm of the very small, where quantum effects are dominant.

The incompatibility becomes glaring when we attempt to describe phenomena where both gravity and quantum effects are significant, such as the Big Bang or the singularities at the centers of black holes. In these extreme environments, the curvature of spacetime becomes so immense that quantum fluctuations can no longer be ignored. General relativity, in its current form, breaks down, predicting infinite densities and undefined quantities. This signals a fundamental limitation of our understanding, highlighting the need for a more comprehensive theory that can unify gravity with the quantum world.

This quest for a unified theory has given rise to the field of quantum gravity, a challenging and exhilarating area of research. The goal is to develop a framework that seamlessly incorporates both general relativity and quantum mechanics, providing a consistent description of the universe at all scales, from the infinitely large to the infinitesimally small. This is no easy task, and several competing approaches have emerged, each with its own strengths and weaknesses.

One of the leading contenders in the quantum gravity arena is string theory. This ambitious theory proposes that fundamental particles are not point-like objects but rather tiny, vibrating strings of energy. The different vibrational modes of these strings correspond to the different particles we observe in nature. String theory offers a potential solution to the unification problem by elegantly incorporating gravity as a fundamental interaction arising from the dynamics of these strings.

In the string theory framework, spacetime itself emerges as a consequence of the interactions between these fundamental strings. The extra dimensions predicted by string theory, beyond the four dimensions we experience (three spatial dimensions and one time dimension), are thought to be compactified or curled up at incredibly small scales, rendering them invisible to our current observational capabilities. While string theory offers a mathematically elegant and potentially complete framework, it faces significant challenges. The theory is highly complex, and it lacks experimental verification. Many of its predictions lie beyond the reach of our current experimental technologies, making it difficult to test its validity.

Another prominent approach to quantum gravity is loop quantum gravity (LQG). Unlike string theory, which attempts to unify gravity by modifying the nature of fundamental particles, LQG takes a different route, focusing on quantizing the fabric of spacetime itself. In LQG, spacetime is not a smooth, continuous background but rather a discrete, granular structure composed of fundamental loops or "spin networks." These loops represent quanta of space and time, analogous to the quanta of energy and momentum in quantum mechanics. The dynamics of these loops determine the geometry and evolution of spacetime.

LQG offers a compelling picture of spacetime at the Planck scale, the realm where quantum gravitational effects are expected to dominate. At this extremely small scale (approximately 10^{-35} meters), spacetime is predicted to lose its continuous nature and instead exhibit a "quantum foam-like" structure, a highly fluctuating and unpredictable landscape. While LQG is conceptually attractive and possesses certain mathematical advantages, it also faces challenges in making testable predictions and in the complexity of its calculations.

Beyond string theory and LQG, other approaches to quantum gravity exist, including causal set theory, which describes spacetime as a partially ordered set of events, and asymptotic safety, which suggests that quantum gravity may be a well-defined theory without needing to be quantized in the same way as other fundamental interactions. Each approach grapples with the inherent difficulties of reconciling general relativity's description of spacetime as a continuous manifold with quantum mechanics' inherently discrete nature.

The quest for a theory of quantum gravity is not merely an academic exercise; it has profound implications for our understanding of the universe's earliest moments, the nature of black holes, and even the very fabric of reality. A successful quantum gravity theory would revolutionize our understanding of the cosmos, providing a unified framework that describes all fundamental forces and the evolution of the universe from the Big Bang to its ultimate fate. Such a theory might also shed light on the nature of dark matter and dark energy, currently some of the most perplexing enigmas in modern cosmology.

However, the road to a complete theory of quantum gravity is paved with challenges. The mathematical complexities are immense, and the experimental verification of quantum gravitational effects remains a considerable hurdle. The scales involved are far beyond our current observational capabilities, requiring the development of new theoretical tools and experimental techniques. Despite these difficulties, the quest for quantum gravity continues to drive significant research, fueling advancements in our understanding of the universe's most fundamental aspects.

BEYOND HUMAN UNDERSTANDING

The search for a unified theory encompasses much more than simply merging the mathematics of relativity and quantum mechanics. It delves into the very nature of space and time, concepts that have been fundamental to our understanding of the cosmos since antiquity. The possibility that space and time themselves are not continuous, but rather discrete entities, or even emergent phenomena arising from a deeper underlying structure, profoundly challenges our intuitive grasp of reality.

The implications of a successful quantum gravity theory extend beyond the realm of theoretical physics. A complete understanding of quantum gravity may provide insights into the origins of the universe, the nature of black holes, and the ultimate fate of the cosmos. It could also have practical implications, influencing future technologies in ways we can currently only speculate upon. As we continue to grapple with these profound questions, we are reminded of the vastness of the unknown and the relentless pursuit of knowledge that drives the human spirit. The quest for quantum gravity is a testament to our unwavering desire to understand the universe and our place within it, a quest that promises both profound discoveries and unforeseen challenges. The journey, however arduous, is one that holds the potential to fundamentally reshape our view of reality.

Time Space and Consciousness

Our exploration of spacetime's intricate architecture has brought us to a fascinating juncture: the interwoven relationship between the objective reality of time and space, and the subjective experience shaped by consciousness. While physics endeavors to define time and space as fundamental components of the universe, characterized by their measurable properties and governed by precise laws, consciousness adds another layer of complexity, transforming our perception and interaction with this reality.

Consider our perception of time. The ticking of a clock provides an objective measurement, a seemingly constant progression from past to future. Yet, our subjective experience of time is highly malleable. Moments of intense engagement can seem to fly by, while periods of boredom stretch endlessly. The psychological phenomenon of "time dilation" underscores this discrepancy, where stressful or exciting experiences compress our perceived duration, contrasting starkly with the consistent ticking of the clock. This subjective distortion of time isn't merely a psychological quirk; it points towards the profound influence of consciousness on our apprehension of the temporal dimension.

Similarly, our perception of space is deeply interwoven with our conscious experience. Consider optical illusions, where our brain interprets visual information in ways that distort the perceived spatial arrangement of objects. These perceptual shifts demonstrate the active role of consciousness in constructing our spatial reality, going beyond the mere reception of sensory data. Our brains don't simply passively record the physical world; they actively interpret and construct a model of reality based on sensory input, prior experiences, and expectations. This conscious construction of spatial perception highlights the non-trivial influence of the observer on what is observed, raising questions about the extent to which our observed reality mirrors an objective "truth."

The implications of various models of consciousness further complicate our understanding. Materialist views, which equate consciousness solely with brain activity, struggle to fully explain the subjective experience of time and space. How can a purely physical process give rise to the qualitative richness of conscious experience, including our sense of the flow of time and the spatial extent of our surroundings? Dualistic models, proposing a separation between mind and matter, offer an alternative, suggesting consciousness may interact with, but isn't entirely reducible to, physical processes. However, dualism raises its own challenges, particularly in establishing a mechanism for this interaction.

Integrated Information Theory (IIT), a prominent theory of consciousness, attempts to bridge this gap by proposing that consciousness arises from the complexity and integrated information within a system. This suggests that the subjective experience of time and space could be intrinsically linked to the level of integration and information processing within the conscious system. A higher degree of integration could lead to a more unified and coherent experience of time and space, potentially explaining the subjective distortions described earlier. Further research exploring the relationship between information processing, neural complexity, and the subjective experience of time and space is needed to fully elucidate this connection.

Furthermore, the concept of spacetime itself becomes ambiguous when considering its relationship with consciousness. General relativity treats spacetime as a continuous and deterministic entity, a backdrop for physical events. However, quantum mechanics introduces inherent indeterminacy and probabilistic behavior, suggesting a less deterministic and perhaps more fluid structure of spacetime. The search for a quantum theory of gravity further complicates the picture, suggesting the possibility of a granular or even emergent nature of spacetime at the Planck scale. If spacetime is emergent, as some theories suggest, then its properties might be intricately linked to the fundamental nature of consciousness itself. Could consciousness play a role in shaping the structure or properties of spacetime, or is our subjective experience of spacetime simply a consequence of its objective properties?

The advent of advanced technologies introduces new dimensions to this complex interplay. Virtual reality (VR) and augmented reality (AR) systems offer compelling examples of how technology can manipulate our perception of time and space, creating immersive experiences that challenge our sense of reality. In VR environments, users can experience altered temporal flows, compressed or expanded, and navigate simulated spaces that exist only within the digital realm. These technologies illustrate the plasticity of our consciousness, highlighting its ability to adapt to drastically altered sensory inputs and construct entirely novel spatial and temporal frameworks.

Moreover, technological advancements in communication, such as instant messaging and global interconnectedness, seem to accelerate the perceived pace of life. The constant stream of information, the ability to connect with people across continents instantaneously, compresses our perception of time and distance, potentially reshaping our understanding of both. This constant influx of stimuli can also lead to cognitive overload, impacting our ability to process information effectively and potentially further distorting our experience of both time and space.

As we integrate increasingly sophisticated technologies into our daily lives, their impact on our perception of time and space will only intensify. The possibilities range from profound insights into the nature of consciousness to potentially problematic alterations of our subjective experience. The ethical considerations of manipulating our perception of time and space through technological intervention deserve serious consideration. The development of powerful new technologies requires a responsible approach, ensuring these tools are employed in a manner that benefits society and respects the integrity of the human experience.

The interplay of time, space, and consciousness remains a profound and largely unexplored territory. By exploring the relationships between objective physical laws, subjective experience, and technological influence, we can begin to unravel this complex tapestry. The answers we discover will undoubtedly reshape our understanding of the universe and our place within it, potentially leading to a more profound and nuanced comprehension of reality itself. The quest for understanding this intricate relationship underscores the human capacity for exploration, challenging us to move beyond conventional boundaries and embrace the mysteries that still lie before us. The journey promises both challenges and discoveries, with the potential to dramatically reshape our worldview and our place within the grand cosmic narrative.

CHAPTER 7

The Anthropic Principle

The FineTuning of the Universe

Our journey into the intricate dance between consciousness, time, and space leads us naturally to contemplate the very fabric of the universe itself. The previous sections touched upon the subjective experience of these fundamental aspects of reality, but now we delve into a more objective, yet equally perplexing, aspect: the remarkable fine-tuning of the universe. The physical constants and laws governing our cosmos appear exquisitely tailored to allow for the emergence of life, a fact that has spurred intense debate and speculation among scientists and philosophers alike.

This fine-tuning manifests in numerous ways. Consider the strength of the electromagnetic force, which governs the interaction of charged particles. If this force were even slightly stronger or weaker, the structure of atoms would be drastically altered, rendering the formation of stable molecules—the building blocks of life—impossible. Similarly, the gravitational constant, which dictates the strength of gravitational attraction, is finely tuned to a precise value. A slightly stronger gravitational force would result in a universe dominated by black holes, while a weaker force would preclude the formation of stars and galaxies. The balance between these fundamental forces is so delicate that even minute variations would lead to a universe radically different from the one we inhabit, a universe profoundly inhospitable to life as we know it.

The expansion rate of the universe is another example of this exquisite fine-tuning. If the initial expansion rate had been slightly different, the universe would either have collapsed back on itself shortly after the Big Bang or expanded so rapidly that stars and galaxies would never have formed. The density of matter in the early universe is another crucial parameter. A slightly higher density would have resulted in a universe that collapsed quickly, whereas a slightly lower density would have prevented the formation of the large-scale structures we observe today. The precise balance between these factors, along with others, allowed the universe to evolve into a place capable of supporting the complex chemistry and structures needed for life.

These observations have led many scientists and philosophers to grapple with the implications of this remarkable fine-tuning. One prominent explanation is the multiverse hypothesis, which postulates the existence of an enormous, perhaps infinite, number of universes, each with its own unique set of physical constants and laws. In this scenario, our universe is just one among many, a seemingly rare instance where the conditions are right for life to emerge. The sheer improbability of our universe's specific properties is then explained by the vast number of possibilities available across the multiverse. This hypothesis, while intriguing, remains highly speculative due to the lack of direct observational evidence for other universes.

The multiverse idea is often framed within the context of inflationary cosmology, a theoretical framework that explains the rapid expansion of the universe in its earliest moments. Inflationary models suggest that the universe may have undergone multiple periods of rapid expansion, each potentially giving rise to a separate universe with different properties. This process could naturally lead to a vast landscape of universes, each with a unique combination of physical constants and laws, a kind of cosmic lottery that yields a vast diversity of possible realities. The challenge, however, lies in testing these ideas empirically. The universes predicted by inflationary models are, by definition, beyond our observational reach, leaving the multiverse hypothesis firmly in the realm of theoretical speculation.

Other theoretical frameworks attempt to explain the fine-tuning without invoking the multiverse. Some physicists propose that the fundamental constants are not truly constant but rather vary over vast cosmic scales or across different epochs in the universe's history. This idea, while challenging our conventional understanding of fundamental physics, offers a potential explanation for the observed fine-tuning without requiring the existence of other universes. However, the evidence for such variations in physical constants remains inconclusive, and further research is needed to assess the viability of this approach.

Furthermore, the anthropic principle, explored in previous chapters, offers another perspective. This principle, in its various forms, asserts that the observed properties of the universe are constrained by the requirement that they allow for the existence of observers. In other words, we only observe a universe capable of supporting life because if it were otherwise, we wouldn't be here to observe it. While this principle doesn't explain the underlying reasons for the fine-tuning, it provides a framework for understanding why we find ourselves in a universe with these particular characteristics. The anthropic principle highlights the inherent limitations of our perspective, reminding us that our observation is shaped by the very conditions that make it possible.

The debate surrounding the fine-tuning of the universe is far from settled. The multiverse hypothesis, while elegant in its explanatory power, remains unproven. Alternative explanations, such as variations in physical constants or the anthropic principle, offer different perspectives, but each faces its own set of challenges and limitations. The fine-tuning of the universe remains a profound mystery, a testament to the depth and complexity of the cosmos and the limits of our current understanding. The very question of fine-tuning challenges us to reconsider our assumptions about the nature of reality, prompting a deeper exploration of the interplay between fundamental physics, cosmology, and the very nature of existence.

The implications of this ongoing debate extend beyond the purely scientific realm. Philosophical and theological considerations arise, touching upon questions of design, purpose, and the place of humanity within the grand cosmic scheme. Some interpret the fine-tuning as evidence for a divine creator, arguing that the precise balance of physical constants is too improbable to have arisen by chance. Others remain skeptical, emphasizing the need for empirical evidence and the power of natural processes to generate complex systems. This debate highlights the intricate relationship between science and belief, underscoring the inherent limitations of our understanding and the ongoing quest to decipher the universe's deepest secrets.

The fine-tuning of the universe forces us to confront the limitations of our knowledge and the vastness of the unknown. As we continue to explore the cosmos, new discoveries and theoretical advancements will undoubtedly shed further light on this enduring mystery. The debate itself is a testament to the human spirit's enduring quest for knowledge, our relentless pursuit of understanding our place in the universe, a quest that pushes the boundaries of science, philosophy, and our understanding of existence itself. This journey, filled with both wonder and uncertainty, underscores the profound and ongoing interaction between our quest for knowledge and the universe's willingness, or perhaps unwillingness, to reveal its secrets. The quest continues. The search for answers remains at the very heart of our human endeavor.

The Weak and Strong Anthropic Principles

The exploration of the universe's fine-tuning naturally leads us to the anthropic principle, a concept that attempts to reconcile the seemingly improbable conditions necessary for life with our very existence. This principle, however, is not a single, monolithic idea but rather a spectrum of interpretations, with the weak and strong anthropic principles representing two prominent extremes.

The weak anthropic principle (WAP) is arguably the more straightforward of the two. It essentially states that what we observe about the universe must be compatible with the existence of observers. This isn't a statement about the universe's fundamental properties being inherently designed for life; rather, it's a statement of logical necessity. If the laws of physics were such that life could not emerge, then we wouldn't be here to observe them. It's a tautology, a self-evident truth, highlighting the limitations of our observational perspective. Our existence acts as a selection effect, filtering out universes in which we couldn't exist. We can only experience a universe that allows for our existence; other universes, even if they exist, are inaccessible to our observation.

Consider the analogy of a lottery winner. The odds of winning a major lottery are astronomically low. Yet, someone always wins. The fact that *you* won doesn't imply the lottery was rigged or that the odds were somehow manipulated in your favor. It simply means that someone had to win, and you happen to be that person. Similarly, the WAP suggests that while the conditions for life may seem incredibly improbable, given the vastness of the universe (or multiverse, as we'll explore further), it's not surprising that *some* region within that vast expanse would possess the necessary conditions. The existence of life, then, isn't necessarily improbable in a cosmic sense; it's simply a consequence of the vastness of possibilities and the fact that we are, by definition, situated within a life-permitting region.

The WAP's strength lies in its relative simplicity and avoidance of overtly speculative claims. It doesn't posit any specific mechanisms or explanations for the fine-tuning; it merely acknowledges the observational bias inherent in our position as observers. However, its weakness lies in its limited explanatory power. It doesn't address the underlying reasons for the fine-tuning, merely stating that it must be compatible with our existence. It doesn't explain *why* the universe appears so finely tuned, only that it must be so given our presence.

This is where the strong anthropic principle (SAP) enters the picture. The SAP asserts a much stronger claim: the universe must have the properties it does because it must allow for the existence of observers. This statement moves beyond mere observation bias; it suggests a deeper connection between the universe's fundamental properties and the emergence of life. This implies a teleological aspect, suggesting that the universe, in some sense, is designed or destined to produce observers. This can be interpreted in various ways, from a purely naturalistic perspective involving self-organizing systems to a theistic perspective involving a divine creator.

The implications of the SAP are far more profound and arguably more controversial than those of the WAP. The SAP suggests that the universe's constants and laws are not merely compatible with life; they are, in some fundamental sense, necessary for it. This leads to questions about the nature of consciousness, the role of observers in shaping reality, and the potential for a universe designed with life in mind.

One interpretation of the SAP involves the idea of a self-organizing universe. Complex systems, under certain conditions, tend to spontaneously generate order and complexity. It's argued that the universe's apparent fine-tuning may be a consequence of this inherent tendency towards complexity, with life emerging as a natural outcome of this process. From this perspective, the emergence of observers isn't a miraculous event but rather a predictable consequence of the universe's inherent properties.

Another, more controversial interpretation of the SAP involves the concept of a multiverse. If multiple universes exist, each with different physical constants and laws, it's not surprising that at least one universe would possess the conditions necessary for life. In this context, our universe's specific properties are not uniquely special; they are simply one outcome among many possibilities. The multiverse hypothesis provides a framework for understanding the SAP without resorting to overtly theological explanations.

The theistic interpretation of the SAP, while not strictly scientific, remains a compelling explanation for some. The apparent fine-tuning of the universe is seen as evidence of a divine creator, a being who intentionally designed the universe with life in mind. This interpretation, however, relies heavily on faith and is difficult to reconcile with purely scientific approaches. It also raises further questions about the nature of this creator and their motivations.

The debate between the WAP and SAP, and the interpretations within each, highlights the deep philosophical implications of the anthropic principle. It challenges our understanding of causality, purpose, and the relationship between observation and reality. It pushes the boundaries of scientific inquiry, forcing us to confront the limitations of our current understanding of the universe and its fundamental properties.

The anthropic principle, in its various forms, raises profound questions about our place in the cosmos. It challenges us to reassess our assumptions about the universe's origins and purpose, prompting a deeper exploration of the interplay between physical laws, cosmological evolution, and the emergence of conscious life. It underscores the inherent limitations of our observational perspective, highlighting how our very existence shapes our understanding of reality. Are we witnessing a universe finely tuned for life, or are we simply observing a universe that allows for our observation? The answer, it seems, remains elusive, a testament to the depth and complexity of the cosmic enigma.

The ongoing debate surrounding the anthropic principle reveals the intricate relationship between science, philosophy, and theology. The scientific community grapples with the empirical evidence for or against a multiverse, the possibility of varying physical constants, and the implications of self-organizing systems. Philosophers grapple with the implications of observation bias, causality, and the nature of reality. And theologians ponder the implications for faith, creation, and the purpose of existence. This multifaceted debate underscores the profound mystery surrounding the fine-tuning of the universe and our place within it. The quest to unravel these mysteries continues, pushing the boundaries of human knowledge and fostering a deeper understanding of our place in the vast cosmic tapestry.

The exploration of the anthropic principle, therefore, transcends the realm of pure scientific inquiry. It delves into the heart of existential questions, challenging us to confront the limitations of our understanding and the vastness of the unknown. The pursuit of answers continues, driving us to explore the deepest secrets of the universe and our own place within it, reminding us that the journey itself, filled with both wonder and uncertainty, is as significant as the destination. The anthropic principle serves as a reminder of the intricate connections between the vastness of the cosmos and the singularity of our individual existence, a testament to the ongoing dialogue between the universe and the conscious observer. The quest to reconcile these seemingly disparate elements remains a central theme in our ongoing exploration of reality.

The Significance of the Anthropic Principle

The anthropic principle, in its various formulations, profoundly impacts our understanding of the universe and our seemingly improbable existence within it. It compels us to confront the inherent limitations of our observational perspective, recognizing that our very act of observing shapes our interpretation of reality. The seemingly improbable fine-tuning of the universe's physical constants, perfectly calibrated for the emergence of life as we know it, demands explanation. The anthropic principle offers a framework for grappling with this mystery, though not necessarily providing definitive answers.

One of the most significant implications of the anthropic principle lies in its influence on our understanding of life itself. The weak anthropic principle (WAP) simply points out the self-evident truth that we can only observe a universe compatible with our existence. But the strong anthropic principle (SAP), however, proposes a much more profound connection between the universe's fundamental properties and the emergence of life. It suggests that the universe's constants and laws are not merely compatible with life; they are, in some fundamental sense, necessary for it. This implies a deeper, perhaps even teleological, relationship between the universe and consciousness.

This teleological aspect of the SAP opens a Pandora's Box of philosophical and spiritual interpretations. Does the universe's apparent design imply a divine creator, a cosmic architect who intentionally crafted the universe to support life? Or can the fine-tuning be explained through purely naturalistic processes, such as the multiverse hypothesis or the inherent self-organizing tendencies of complex systems? These questions are not easily answered, and the debate continues to engage scientists, philosophers, and theologians alike.

The multiverse hypothesis, while highly speculative, offers a potential explanation for the seemingly improbable fine-tuning without resorting to divine intervention. If multiple universes exist, each with its unique set of physical constants and laws, then the emergence of life in at least one of them becomes statistically more probable. In this vast cosmic landscape, our universe, with its seemingly perfect conditions, is just one realization among countless possibilities. Our existence, in this context, is not a unique event but a statistically likely occurrence within an inconceivably vast multiverse.

However, the multiverse hypothesis, while scientifically plausible, doesn't eliminate the mystery entirely. It merely shifts the problem from "why is our universe so finely tuned?" to "why is the multiverse structured in such a way that at least one universe possesses life-permitting conditions?" This shift doesn't necessarily resolve the issue of fine-tuning but rather expands the scope of the mystery, placing it within a broader cosmological context. The question of the multiverse's origins and its inherent properties remains an area of active research and speculation.

The anthropic principle also profoundly impacts our search for extraterrestrial life. If the universe is indeed finely tuned for life, as the SAP suggests, it raises the possibility that life could be widespread throughout the cosmos. The conditions for life, while seemingly improbable within a single universe, become much more probable within the context of a multiverse. This perspective fuels the ongoing search for extraterrestrial life, making the discovery of life beyond Earth a compelling scientific endeavor with far-reaching philosophical implications. The discovery of even microbial life on another planet would revolutionize our understanding of the prevalence of life in the universe and strengthen the case for the anthropic principle's validity.

The philosophical ramifications of the anthropic principle extend beyond the scientific realm. It challenges our anthropocentric view of the universe, forcing us to reconsider our place within the cosmic scheme of things. For centuries, humanity held a privileged position in the universe, considered the central focus of creation. The anthropic principle, however, reminds us of our relative insignificance on a cosmic scale. Our existence, while remarkable, is merely a consequence of the universe's inherent properties. This shift in perspective can be both humbling and liberating.

Moreover, the anthropic principle touches upon fundamental questions about consciousness and its role in the universe. Is consciousness a mere byproduct of complex physical systems, or does it play a more active role in shaping reality? Some interpretations of the SAP suggest that the universe's inherent properties are inextricably linked to the emergence of consciousness, implying a deep relationship between the observer and the observed. This perspective challenges the traditional scientific view of an objective reality, independent of the observer. The ongoing debate on the nature of consciousness and its role in the universe continues to fuel scientific and philosophical inquiry.

From a spiritual perspective, the anthropic principle opens up a wide range of interpretations. Some may view the fine-tuning of the universe as evidence of a divine creator, a being who intentionally designed the universe to support life. Others might interpret it as an expression of the universe's inherent creative potential, its capacity to generate complexity and consciousness from simpler beginnings. Regardless of one's spiritual beliefs, the anthropic principle prompts a deeper contemplation of our existence and our place within the grand cosmic scheme. It challenges us to question our assumptions about the nature of reality, the purpose of life, and our relationship with the universe.

In conclusion, the significance of the anthropic principle extends far beyond the realm of cosmology and physics. It touches upon fundamental questions about life, consciousness, the universe's origins, and our place within it. The principle's various interpretations—from the relatively straightforward WAP to the more speculative SAP—offer diverse perspectives on the fine-tuning of the universe, stimulating ongoing scientific, philosophical, and spiritual discussions. Whether the universe's fine-tuning points towards a divine creator, a multiverse of possibilities, or the inherent self-organizing tendencies of complex systems, the anthropic principle remains a profound and thought-provoking concept, prompting us to engage in a deeper exploration of reality and our place within it. The journey of understanding, like the universe itself, is vast and complex, but the quest for knowledge and understanding is a journey worth undertaking. The pursuit of answers leads to a deeper appreciation of the intricate tapestry of existence, connecting the vastness of the cosmos to the singularity of our conscious experience. The anthropic principle serves as a constant reminder of this profound interconnectedness, pushing the boundaries of our understanding and enriching our experience of being alive in a universe seemingly designed for life itself. This profound mystery, far from being discouraging, should be a catalyst for continuous inquiry and a testament to the boundless capacity of human curiosity.

Criticisms and Alternatives

The anthropic principle, while offering a compelling framework for understanding our existence within a seemingly finely-tuned universe, is not without its critics. Several significant objections challenge its explanatory power and raise questions about its methodological soundness. One central criticism revolves around the principle's inherent subjectivity. The weak anthropic principle (WAP), while seemingly innocuous—stating simply that we can only observe a universe compatible with our existence—can be viewed as a tautology, offering little in the way of genuine explanation. It simply restates the obvious fact that we wouldn't be here to observe a universe that doesn't support life. This tautological nature diminishes its explanatory power, leaving some to argue that it doesn't provide a true insight into the underlying physical mechanisms of the universe.

The strong anthropic principle (SAP), while more ambitious, faces even more stringent criticisms. Its assertion that the universe's fundamental constants and laws are *necessary* for the emergence of life is a bold claim that lacks direct empirical evidence. While the fine-tuning is undeniable, the leap to necessity is a significant one, requiring a justification that many find unconvincing. The SAP often treads into teleological territory, suggesting a purpose or design inherent in the universe, which is at odds with the materialistic worldview favored by many scientists. This inherent teleological implication draws criticism from those advocating for purely naturalistic explanations of the universe's properties. The implication of a preordained outcome, a universe designed for life, clashes with the scientific preference for mechanistic explanations based on natural laws.

Furthermore, criticisms are leveled at the inherent limitations of our observational perspective. Our current understanding of physics might be incomplete, and what appears to be fine-tuning from our current vantage point may simply be a result of our limited understanding. Future discoveries in physics might reveal underlying mechanisms that explain the observed constants and laws without needing to invoke the anthropic principle. The apparent fine-tuning might be an artifact of our current knowledge, a temporary illusion that will dissipate with further scientific progress. New theoretical frameworks, currently unknown, might reveal a deeper, more fundamental reality that renders the apparent fine-tuning less remarkable. The history of science is replete with instances where apparent anomalies were later explained by more comprehensive theories, challenging previously held beliefs.

The application of Bayesian reasoning also casts doubt on the anthropic principle's explanatory power. Bayesian methods consider prior probabilities—the likelihood of an event occurring *before* observing any evidence—when assessing the probability of an event. Applying Bayesian analysis to the fine-tuning problem suggests that even a relatively small prior probability of a life-permitting universe, combined with the observation of our universe's suitability for life, might still result in a low posterior probability for the anthropic principle being the correct explanation. In simpler terms, even if our universe is finely tuned, this fact alone doesn't necessarily support the anthropic principle, given the vast number of possible universes and the chance element involved.

The lack of a clear and testable definition of "life" also plagues the anthropic principle. Defining life, especially in a cosmological context, is a challenge. Are we to consider only carbon-based life? What about silicon-based life, or other forms of life we can't even imagine? The very parameters used to define "life-permitting conditions" could be biased, reflecting our anthropocentric perspective rather than a universal truth. Different definitions of life will invariably lead to different assessments of the universe's fine-tuning and thus the applicability of the anthropic principle. This ambiguity makes evaluating and testing the principle exceptionally difficult.

Alternative explanations for the observed fine-tuning often avoid the anthropic principle altogether. The multiverse hypothesis, for example, suggests that our universe is just one among many, each with its unique set of physical constants and laws. Within this vast ensemble of universes, a universe like ours, with conditions suitable for life, would inevitably arise, even if the probability is extremely low for any single universe. The multiverse, therefore, shifts the focus from explaining the fine-tuning of *our* universe to explaining the conditions that gave rise to the multiverse itself, a problem that may or may not be easier to solve. However, it's important to note the lack of empirical evidence for the multiverse, which limits its status as a truly scientific explanation at present.

Another alternative focuses on the inherent self-organizing properties of the universe. Complex systems, such as the universe itself, possess an inherent tendency to self-organize into complex structures. Through the process of natural selection, which acts not just on biological organisms but on physical structures and processes, systems evolve towards states of greater complexity and stability. This self-organization might, therefore, explain the apparent fine-tuning without needing to invoke an anthropic principle. The universe's seemingly precise properties might simply be a natural outcome of its self-organizational dynamics, a reflection of the underlying laws of physics that govern the emergence of complexity.

Furthermore, the landscape of possibilities within fundamental physics itself might be explored as an alternative. The parameters of the universe may not be finely tuned in the sense of an improbable outcome, but rather represent a region of parameter space allowing for the emergence of complexity. In this scenario, the observed parameters are not specifically selected but emerge from the broader mathematical constraints of the theoretical framework. The apparent fine-tuning arises not from deliberate selection, but from the inherent restrictions on possible configurations. Such an approach shifts the problem from one of improbability to one of the exploration of permitted states within a theoretical landscape.

Finally, it's important to consider the limitations of our current scientific understanding. Our models of the universe are inevitably approximations, simplifications of a reality that may be far more complex than we can currently comprehend. Future advancements in physics, cosmology, and other relevant fields may provide new insights that significantly alter our perspective on the fine-tuning problem. The current state of our knowledge may simply not be sufficient to make a definitive judgment on the validity or necessity of the anthropic principle.

In conclusion, while the anthropic principle offers a framework for considering our seemingly improbable existence, it remains a subject of considerable debate. Criticisms regarding its tautological nature, its potential biases, and its lack of testability highlight the limitations of relying solely on this principle to explain the observed fine-tuning of the universe. Alternative explanations, such as the multiverse hypothesis, self-organization theory, or alternative explorations within the physical landscape offer potentially more robust, even if not entirely definitive, answers. The ongoing quest to understand the universe and our place within it requires continuous critical examination of all available models and theories, acknowledging both their strengths and weaknesses, to arrive at a more complete and nuanced comprehension of reality. The journey of scientific discovery, much like the vastness of the cosmos itself, is a continuous process of refinement and revision.

The anthropic principle, while thought-provoking, remains one piece of a complex and evolving puzzle, not necessarily the key to solving the entire mystery.

The Anthropic Principle and the Future of Cosmology

The ongoing debate surrounding the anthropic principle extends far beyond its philosophical implications; it deeply impacts the future direction of cosmological research. The principle, in its various forms, acts as a potent lens through which we examine the universe's fundamental properties and our place within it. Its influence on future cosmological inquiries is undeniable, even amidst ongoing criticisms of its explanatory power.

One significant area where the anthropic principle shapes future research is the search for extraterrestrial life. The very notion that the universe's constants appear finely tuned for the emergence of life, as suggested by the strong anthropic principle (SAP), fuels the pursuit of detecting life beyond Earth. If the universe is indeed predisposed towards life, then the sheer scale of the cosmos suggests the likelihood of other life forms, even if the probability remains extremely low for any given planet or star system. The search for biosignatures, technosignatures, and habitable exoplanets is fundamentally driven by this anthropic consideration – a universe that allows for life likely harbors it in multiple places. Future missions focused on exoplanet characterization, advanced telescopes capable of detecting atmospheric biosignatures, and sophisticated data analysis techniques will be heavily influenced by the philosophical implications of the anthropic principle.

Furthermore, the principle's influence extends to the theoretical landscape of physics and cosmology. The fine-tuning problem, central to the anthropic debate, directly challenges physicists and cosmologists to develop more comprehensive theories capable of explaining the observed values of fundamental constants. The anthropic principle, even if not directly explanatory, acts as a guiding principle, focusing research efforts on theories capable of addressing the apparent improbability of our universe's life-permitting conditions. This might lead to the development of new theoretical frameworks, such as more refined models of the multiverse or alternative theories of quantum gravity, all aimed at providing a more fundamental explanation for the observed physical laws and constants. This influence can be seen in the burgeoning field of string theory, where the vast landscape of possible universes provides a natural framework for understanding the anthropic principle.

The anthropic principle also prompts a deeper investigation into the nature of physical laws themselves. The principle highlights the fact that our very existence depends on these laws, raising questions about their origin and the conditions for their emergence. Future research may focus on understanding the underlying principles that govern the selection, or emergence, of these physical laws, potentially revealing deeper connections between seemingly disparate aspects of the universe. The search for a "theory of everything" is inextricably linked to the anthropic principle's implications, as such a theory must explain not only the universe's current state but also the conditions that allowed for its existence and the possibility of life.

However, the anthropic principle's impact is not without its caveats. The criticisms levied against the principle, particularly concerning its potential for tautology and lack of falsifiability, must be considered. Future research should focus on refining the principle's formulation and developing testable predictions. The development of more precise definitions of "life," moving beyond anthropocentric biases, is crucial for making the principle more scientifically rigorous. This could involve exploring alternative biochemical pathways to life, or even considering non-biological forms of intelligence.

Furthermore, a critical aspect of future research must involve developing rigorous methods for comparing different cosmological models in light of the anthropic principle. The multiverse hypothesis, for instance, offers a potential explanation for the fine-tuning, but it lacks direct observational evidence. Future research should explore methods of distinguishing between different multiverse scenarios and testing their predictions. This might involve analyzing the cosmic microwave background radiation for signs of multiple universes interacting or exploring the potential for detecting gravitational waves from the formation of baby universes.

The anthropic principle also pushes us to reconsider our epistemological limitations. Our current understanding of the universe is undoubtedly incomplete, and our current models are necessarily simplified representations of a complex reality. Future discoveries in physics, cosmology, and related fields might reveal underlying mechanisms that explain the apparent fine-tuning without invoking the anthropic principle. The anthropic principle, therefore, should be seen as a working hypothesis, a guide for research rather than a definitive answer. It serves as a reminder of the limitations of our current knowledge and the potential for future discoveries to revolutionize our understanding of the universe.

The principle's role in shaping future research will likely also depend on advancements in computational power and data analysis techniques. Simulations of universe formation and evolution are becoming increasingly sophisticated, allowing researchers to explore a wider range of cosmological models and parameters. This will allow for more rigorous testing of theories that attempt to explain the observed fine-tuning, and potentially to evaluate the likelihood of universes supporting life under different physical laws. The development of more advanced algorithms for data analysis could also help uncover subtle patterns and correlations in observational data that might hint at a deeper understanding of the universe's underlying structure.

Moreover, future philosophical inquiries will play a crucial role in refining our understanding and application of the anthropic principle. The ongoing debate between proponents of a purely materialistic worldview and those who see hints of design in the universe's fine-tuning requires further philosophical analysis. A clearer understanding of the relationship between scientific inquiry and philosophical interpretations will help to navigate the complex interplay between scientific findings and metaphysical implications. Future philosophical work needs to address the challenges of defining life within the context of a potentially vast multiverse, refining our understanding of probability in a cosmological setting, and clarifying the meaning and limits of "explanation" itself.

In conclusion, the anthropic principle, while controversial and debated, stands as a significant catalyst for future cosmological research. It encourages the search for extraterrestrial life, motivates the development of new theoretical frameworks in physics and cosmology, and prompts a deeper investigation into the nature of physical laws. The principle's influence, however, is not absolute. Future work must focus on refining its formulation, developing testable predictions, and critically evaluating alternative explanations. The ongoing dialogue between scientists and philosophers, fueled by advancements in observation, computation, and theoretical understanding, will be crucial in navigating the intricate implications of this provocative principle and shaping our understanding of the universe and our place within it for years to come. The journey of understanding the universe is a relentless pursuit, and the anthropic principle, whether ultimately proven correct or incorrect, will continue to play a significant role in guiding that journey. The future of cosmology is inextricably linked to our grappling with the questions it raises, questions that touch upon the very essence of existence itself.

CHAPTER 8

The Search for Extraterrestrial Life

The Drake Equation and its Implications

The search for extraterrestrial intelligence (SETI) is a vast and ambitious undertaking, fueled by a fundamental human curiosity about our place in the cosmos. Central to this quest is the Drake Equation, a probabilistic argument formulated by Frank Drake in 1961. While not a precise formula capable of yielding a definitive answer, the equation serves as a powerful framework for organizing our thinking about the prevalence of intelligent life in the galaxy. The equation itself is relatively simple, yet the profound uncertainties associated with its parameters highlight the immense challenges inherent in estimating the number of communicating civilizations.

The Drake Equation is typically expressed as:

$N = R \times f_p \times n_e \times f_l \times f_i \times f_c \times L$

Where:

N = the number of civilizations in our galaxy with which communication might be possible
R = the average rate of star formation in our galaxy
fp = the fraction of those stars that have planetary systems
ne = the average number of planets that can potentially support life per star that has planets
fl = the fraction of planets that could support life that actually develop life at some point
fi = the fraction of planets with life that actually go on to develop intelligent life (civilizations)
fc = the fraction of civilizations that develop a technology that releases detectable signals into space
L = the length of time such civilizations release detectable signals into space

While the values for some parameters, such as R, are relatively well-constrained by astronomical observations, significant uncertainty clouds the remaining terms. The fraction of stars with planetary systems (fp) has been dramatically revised upwards in recent decades thanks to the Kepler mission and other exoplanet surveys. We now know that planetary systems are incredibly common, with many stars possessing multiple planets, some potentially within their habitable zones. However, the habitable zone itself is a concept that is subject to refinement and depends on a variety of factors, including the star's type, planetary atmosphere, and the presence of liquid water.

The next parameter, ne, representing the average number of potentially habitable planets per star with planets, is equally challenging to estimate. The definition of "habitable" itself is a subject of ongoing debate, and it's possible that life could exist outside what we currently consider the habitable zone. Furthermore, the conditions necessary for life are not fully understood. While liquid water is often cited as a critical requirement, extremophiles on Earth demonstrate that life can thrive in incredibly harsh conditions, expanding the potential range of habitable environments.

The transition from abiogenesis (the origin of life) to actual life (fl) is one of the most profound and uncertain steps in the Drake Equation. The conditions necessary for life to arise from non-living matter are largely unknown, and despite intense research, we have yet to definitively recreate this process in a laboratory setting. The possibility that the emergence of life is exceedingly rare or, conversely, remarkably common, fundamentally impacts the overall estimate of N. The rarity of life might be due to very specific conditions required for abiogenesis or to subsequent evolutionary bottlenecks.

Similarly, the probability of intelligent life evolving (fi) is highly speculative. While life on Earth has diversified remarkably, the evolution of intelligence is a complex and potentially rare event. The leap from simple unicellular organisms to complex, self-aware beings represents an immense evolutionary hurdle. Multiple factors could influence this transition, including the environment, genetic drift, and even chance events. The assumption that intelligence is an inevitable outcome of life is not supported by current scientific understanding. It is entirely possible that many planets might harbor life, yet never reach the level of technological intelligence we observe in humans.

The fraction of intelligent civilizations that develop detectable signals (fc) introduces further uncertainty. While humans have been broadcasting radio signals into space for over a century, our current technology is relatively primitive in comparison to what future civilizations might develop. Advanced civilizations might utilize communication methods we cannot yet detect, or they might choose not to broadcast signals into space for various reasons, such as self-preservation or a lack of interest in communicating with other civilizations.

Finally, the lifetime (L) of a communicating civilization is a parameter fraught with uncertainty. Technological civilizations could face self-destruction through warfare, environmental collapse, or resource depletion. Alternatively, they might achieve a level of technological advancement and societal maturity that allows for long-term survival. The lifespan of a civilization significantly affects the likelihood of detecting other intelligent life, especially considering the vast distances involved in interstellar communication.

The Drake Equation, despite its inherent uncertainties, compels us to confront fundamental questions about life, intelligence, and our place in the universe. The very act of attempting to quantify these unknowns forces us to consider the vastness of the cosmos and the potential for life beyond Earth. Even if the equation's output remains uncertain, the process of estimating its parameters highlights the critical gaps in our knowledge and motivates research in fields ranging from astrobiology and planetary science to evolutionary biology and social science.

The search for extraterrestrial life is not merely a scientific endeavor; it carries profound philosophical implications. The discovery of extraterrestrial life would revolutionize our understanding of ourselves and our place in the universe. It would challenge our anthropocentric biases and force a re-evaluation of our unique position in the cosmos. The potential for contact with an advanced civilization would present ethical challenges, requiring careful consideration of our actions and responsibilities. Such an event would require international cooperation and a global dialogue to address the societal, cultural, and even spiritual ramifications of such a discovery.

The implications extend beyond our understanding of life itself. The discovery of extraterrestrial intelligence would also impact our understanding of the universe's fundamental laws and constants. The existence of life elsewhere would lend support to the hypothesis that life is not a unique phenomenon confined to Earth, suggesting a greater prevalence of life-supporting conditions in the universe than previously thought. It might also challenge our current cosmological models and our understanding of the universe's evolution.

Conversely, the failure to detect any sign of extraterrestrial life after decades of searching could lead to alternative interpretations. It might suggest that the conditions necessary for life are exceptionally rare, or that the transition from life to intelligent life is an extremely improbable event. It could even suggest that intelligent life has a tendency towards self-destruction or that there exist significant barriers that prevent the long-term survival of advanced civilizations. This would have profound implications for our understanding of our own future and the potential risks associated with our technological advancements.

Regardless of the eventual outcome of the search, the Drake Equation and the broader SETI program serve as a powerful reminder of the vastness of the universe and the potential for life beyond Earth. It encourages us to explore our universe, to test the limits of our scientific understanding, and to ponder the deepest questions about our place in the cosmos. The search for extraterrestrial life is an ongoing journey of discovery, one that continuously challenges our assumptions and broadens our understanding of the universe and ourselves. It is a testament to human curiosity, our insatiable desire to understand our origins, and our potential for discovering something truly extraordinary. The pursuit continues, driven by the profound implications inherent in the answer, whatever it may be. The universe waits to reveal its secrets, and the Drake equation provides a roadmap, albeit an imperfect one, for navigating this extraordinary quest.

The Search for Biosignatures

The search for extraterrestrial life extends beyond the quest for intelligent civilizations actively broadcasting signals into space. A parallel, and arguably even more fundamental, pursuit focuses on the detection of biosignatures – indicators of past or present life, however simple or complex. Unlike the search for technosignatures, which relies on detecting technologically advanced signals, the search for biosignatures delves into the chemical and physical evidence of life itself, regardless of its technological capabilities. This approach offers a broader scope, potentially revealing the presence of life even from long-extinct civilizations or microbial organisms.

The detection of biosignatures presents a unique set of challenges. Unlike the relatively straightforward (though still immensely difficult) task of detecting radio waves or laser signals, identifying biosignatures requires a deep understanding of both the processes that create them and the processes that might mimic them. False positives, arising from geological or chemical processes that mimic the characteristics of life, are a major concern, requiring meticulous analysis and rigorous verification.

One of the primary targets in the search for biosignatures is Mars. Decades of robotic exploration have revealed evidence of past liquid water on the Martian surface, a key ingredient for life as we know it. Missions like the Mars rovers Curiosity and Perseverance are actively searching for organic molecules—the building blocks of life—in Martian soil and rocks. The detection of specific organic molecules, particularly those with unusual isotopic ratios (indicating biological processes), could serve as compelling biosignatures. However, the harsh Martian environment, with its intense radiation and lack of a global magnetic field, could have degraded or destroyed any potential biosignatures over billions of years, posing a significant hurdle to their discovery.

Beyond Mars, other celestial bodies within our solar system are also being scrutinized for potential biosignatures. Europa, one of Jupiter's moons, is covered in a thick layer of ice, beneath which a vast ocean of liquid water is suspected to exist. The potential for hydrothermal vents on the ocean floor, similar to those found on Earth that support thriving ecosystems, makes Europa a prime target for future exploration. Missions are being planned to investigate the composition of Europa's subsurface ocean, searching for chemical imbalances that might indicate the presence of life. Similarly, Enceladus, a moon of Saturn, exhibits geysers erupting from its south polar region, spewing plumes of water vapor and ice particles into space. Analysis of these plumes has revealed the presence of organic molecules, further fueling speculation about the possibility of a subsurface ocean capable of supporting life.

The search for biosignatures extends beyond our solar system to exoplanets orbiting distant stars. This presents an even greater challenge, requiring extremely sensitive instruments and sophisticated detection techniques. One promising method involves analyzing the atmospheric composition of exoplanets using spectroscopy. By studying the light passing through a planet's atmosphere, astronomers can identify the presence of specific gases, some of which might be indicative of life. For example, the detection of oxygen, methane, and carbon dioxide in specific ratios could suggest the presence of photosynthetic life, as these gases are often produced and consumed in a balanced way by biological processes. However, abiotic processes can also produce these gases, making definitive identification extremely challenging.

The detection of biosignatures is not simply a matter of finding a single "smoking gun" but rather of accumulating multiple lines of evidence. The more independent lines of evidence that point towards the presence of life, the stronger the case becomes. This multi-faceted approach involves combining data from different sources, including remote sensing observations, in-situ measurements (from landers and rovers), and laboratory analyses of samples returned from other celestial bodies.

The interpretation of potential biosignatures also requires careful consideration of the geological and chemical context. The presence of certain minerals or isotopic ratios might be indicative of past or present life, but they could also be explained by purely abiotic processes. Researchers must rigorously rule out alternative explanations before concluding that a biosignature is genuinely indicative of life. Sophisticated computer models and simulations are used to model the formation and evolution of planetary atmospheres and surfaces, providing a framework for interpreting observational data and evaluating the plausibility of different hypotheses.

The challenges associated with detecting biosignatures underscore the need for innovative technologies and approaches. Future missions will likely involve advanced spectroscopic instruments capable of detecting a wider range of biosignatures, more sensitive detectors for organic molecules, and sophisticated robotic explorers capable of performing detailed in-situ analyses. The development of new analytical techniques and improved understanding of the processes that produce biosignatures are critical to advancing the search.

The implications of discovering biosignatures would be profound, reshaping our understanding of life's prevalence in the universe and its potential diversity. Finding even simple microbial life on another planet would revolutionize our understanding of biology and evolution, providing crucial insights into the origin and evolution of life itself. It would also impact our search for extraterrestrial intelligence, suggesting that the emergence of life is not a unique event confined to Earth. The discovery of complex life, or even evidence of extinct civilizations, would carry even more profound implications, forcing us to confront fundamental questions about our place in the cosmos and the potential for contact with other intelligent beings.

Conversely, the failure to detect biosignatures after decades of intensive research could lead to alternative interpretations. It might suggest that life is incredibly rare, requiring an exceptionally narrow set of conditions to arise and evolve. This could have profound implications for our understanding of our own planet's unique position in the universe, highlighting the fragility of life and the importance of protecting Earth's biodiversity. However, it's crucial to remember that the absence of evidence is not evidence of absence. Our current technologies may simply not be sensitive enough to detect subtle biosignatures or life forms vastly different from what we know.

The search for biosignatures is a challenging but incredibly rewarding endeavor, pushing the boundaries of scientific understanding and prompting us to confront fundamental questions about life, the universe, and everything. It is a journey of discovery that continues to unravel the secrets of the cosmos, potentially revealing answers to some of humanity's most profound questions. Whether we ultimately find evidence of life beyond Earth or not, the quest itself is a testament to human curiosity and our unwavering pursuit of knowledge. The search continues, driven by the immense potential implications and the sheer wonder of exploring the unknown.

The Fermi Paradox and its Resolutions

The search for biosignatures, as compelling as it is, leaves us grappling with a profound conundrum: the Fermi Paradox. This paradox highlights the stark contrast between the seemingly high probability of extraterrestrial life, given the vastness of the universe and the prevalence of potentially habitable planets, and the conspicuous absence of any detectable evidence of such life, particularly intelligent life. Where are they? This seemingly simple question has spurred decades of debate and speculation amongst scientists, philosophers, and science fiction writers alike.

The sheer scale of the universe argues strongly in favor of extraterrestrial life. Billions of galaxies, each containing billions of stars, many of which are likely orbited by planets, suggest an almost incomprehensible number of potential habitats. Even if the conditions necessary for life are incredibly rare, the sheer scale of the cosmos suggests that life should have arisen elsewhere, possibly numerous times. Further bolstering this argument are recent discoveries revealing the abundance of exoplanets, many of which reside within the habitable zones of their stars—the regions where liquid water could exist on the planet's surface.

Yet, despite decades of searching using increasingly sophisticated technologies, we have found no conclusive evidence of extraterrestrial life. We haven't received any interstellar signals, detected any alien artifacts, or observed any unambiguous signs of life beyond Earth. This absence of evidence fuels the Fermi Paradox, creating a tension between theoretical probability and observational reality.

One prominent attempt to resolve this paradox is the "Great Filter" hypothesis. This hypothesis posits that there is some critical hurdle—a "filter"—that prevents life from evolving beyond a certain stage. The exact nature of this filter remains highly speculative, but several possibilities have been proposed.

One possibility is that the filter lies in the very origins of life. The transition from non-living matter to self-replicating molecules may be an extraordinarily rare event, requiring a highly specific set of conditions that are unlikely to be replicated elsewhere. If this is the case, the emergence of life itself is the Great Filter, explaining why we haven't observed life beyond Earth. The conditions that allowed life to arise on Earth might have been exceptionally unique – a confluence of factors, from the specific composition of our early atmosphere to the impact of a Mars-sized object that likely created the moon and stabilized Earth's axial tilt. These factors might be so improbable as to make it a cosmic lottery that only Earth managed to win.

Another possibility is that the filter lies in the transition from simple life to complex, multicellular organisms. This transition required a series of significant evolutionary leaps, each involving a low probability event. Perhaps this leap is exceptionally difficult to achieve, acting as a bottleneck that prevents the evolution of complex life elsewhere in the universe.

A third possibility, and perhaps the most unsettling, is that the filter lies in the development of technologically advanced civilizations. Perhaps there's an inherent tendency for intelligent civilizations to destroy themselves before reaching a point where they could be detected by other civilizations. This could be through self-inflicted environmental damage, nuclear war, or some other form of catastrophic technological failure. This hypothesis suggests that the absence of detectable civilizations is not due to the rarity of life itself, but rather the rarity of civilizations surviving their own technological advancements. The rise and fall of civilizations might be a common occurrence, leaving only faint traces, if any, detectable across the vast distances of space.

The Great Filter hypothesis, while not offering definitive answers, provides a framework for considering the various stages in the development of life and civilization where a significant barrier might exist. It highlights the possibility that the rarity of life might not lie in the origins of life itself, but in the subsequent evolutionary or technological transitions.

Other resolutions to the Fermi Paradox have been proposed. Some suggest that interstellar travel might be far more difficult or expensive than we currently imagine, limiting the ability of advanced civilizations to explore or colonize other star systems. The vast distances involved and the energy requirements for interstellar travel could pose insurmountable challenges. Technological limitations might be preventing us from detecting signals from other civilizations, or our methods of detection might be too simplistic to find the unique signatures of an alien civilization.

The possibility of civilizations choosing to remain hidden, or to operate in ways that are undetectable to us, is another intriguing possibility. Advanced civilizations may have developed technologies that allow them to remain entirely invisible to our current methods of detection. This notion, while not scientifically testable, challenges our assumptions about the behavior of advanced extraterrestrial intelligence.

Further complicating the matter is the vast timescale involved. The universe is incredibly old, and even if civilizations have arisen and fallen numerous times, the probabilities of their existing concurrently and being close enough for us to detect might be extremely low. Our own civilization is still relatively young in cosmic terms, and it's possible that other civilizations have risen, flourished, and disappeared long before we even appeared on the scene. The sheer scale of space and time magnifies the difficulty of detection.

The Fermi Paradox continues to stimulate scientific inquiry and philosophical debate. While no single resolution has yet gained universal acceptance, the paradox forces us to confront fundamental questions about life, intelligence, and our place within the cosmos. It compels us to refine our methods of searching, to expand our understanding of the universe and the potential for life within it, and to carefully consider the implications of both finding and not finding extraterrestrial life. The paradox serves as a powerful reminder of the vast unknowns that lie ahead in the exploration of the cosmos, even as it spurs the ongoing quest to unveil some of its most profound mysteries. The search continues, fuelled by a blend of scientific curiosity and philosophical contemplation, underscoring the enduring human desire to understand our place in the grand scheme of things.

The Implications of Contact

The prospect of contacting an extraterrestrial civilization, after decades of searching, holds immense implications, ranging from the profoundly beneficial to the potentially catastrophic. While the discovery itself would represent a monumental leap in human understanding, the nature of that contact and its subsequent impact remain largely unknown, shrouded in speculation and uncertainty. The potential benefits are breathtaking, promising unprecedented advancements in science, technology, and philosophy. Imagine gaining access to knowledge and technologies far surpassing our own – solutions to pressing problems like climate change, disease, and even the limitations of human lifespan might be within reach. New forms of energy, propulsion systems, and materials could revolutionize our civilization, opening up possibilities previously confined to science fiction. A deeper understanding of the universe, gleaned from a perspective far removed from our own, could radically reshape our cosmological models and fundamental understanding of reality. The very act of communication, bridging the immense gulf between two vastly different species, would represent a profound philosophical achievement, reshaping our self-perception and our place within the cosmos. It would force humanity to confront our biases and assumptions, expanding our understanding of intelligence, culture, and societal structures. The potential for cultural exchange is equally compelling. Exposure to a radically different worldview could enrich our own, challenging long-held beliefs and expanding our creative horizons. Artistic, philosophical, and scientific collaborations could lead to innovations beyond our wildest imaginings. The diversity of thought and experience would undoubtedly enrich the human experience, enriching our collective consciousness.

However, alongside these tantalizing possibilities lie significant risks. The most immediate concern revolves around the potential for technological disparity. If we encounter a civilization far more advanced than ourselves, the power imbalance could be insurmountable. Their motives, whether benevolent or malevolent, could hold devastating consequences for humanity. The potential for exploitation, subjugation, or even annihilation cannot be dismissed. We might unwittingly expose ourselves to technologies or pathogens we are ill-equipped to handle, leading to unforeseen and potentially catastrophic consequences. The history of human interaction, marked by both cooperation and conflict, suggests that the encounter with another intelligent species may not be inherently peaceful. The competition for resources, territory, or even dominance could escalate into conflict, with potentially devastating consequences. This risk is amplified by the uncertainty surrounding the nature of extraterrestrial intelligence. We cannot assume their intentions or behavior will align with our own values or ethical framework. They may operate under vastly different principles, making peaceful coexistence challenging, if not impossible.

Beyond the immediate threat of technological or military conflict, the cultural and social disruption caused by contact could be profound. Our entire worldview, our sense of place in the universe, and our self-perception could be radically altered. The possibility of encountering life fundamentally different from ourselves—life based on different chemistries or possessing forms of intelligence we cannot comprehend—could challenge our most basic assumptions about life itself. This challenge to our established beliefs could lead to social unrest, religious upheaval, and widespread psychological disruption. The human psyche might struggle to adapt to the realization that we are not alone, and that our place within the cosmos is far less central than we have always assumed. The ensuing period of societal readjustment might be tumultuous, characterized by widespread anxiety, uncertainty, and societal upheaval. The very fabric of human societies could unravel under the weight of such a paradigm shift.

The ethical considerations surrounding contact are equally complex. Should we actively seek contact, or should we remain silent, observing from a distance? What protocols should govern our interactions with another species, ensuring mutual respect and avoiding exploitation? How do we ensure that the benefits of contact are shared equitably among all members of humanity, avoiding a situation where the rewards are concentrated in the hands of a few? These are not merely hypothetical questions. They are dilemmas that demand careful consideration and a robust framework for decision-making. The consequences of our actions could reverberate for generations to come. One of the most daunting ethical challenges relates to the potential for cultural contamination. Our contact could irrevocably alter another civilization's development, perhaps even leading to its decline or destruction. Conversely, exposure to another civilization's culture could have unforeseen and irreversible effects on our own culture. Striking a balance between the benefits of exchange and the risks of contamination is a delicate task.

Another crucial ethical consideration involves the potential for miscommunication or misunderstanding. The difficulties in bridging the communication gap between two vastly different species cannot be overstated. A simple misunderstanding could have disastrous consequences. Even our attempts at reaching out – through radio signals or probes – could be misinterpreted, leading to unintended hostility. The very act of transmitting signals into space raises questions about responsibility and the potential impact on other civilizations. We are essentially broadcasting our existence to the universe, without fully understanding the potential repercussions. We must weigh the potential benefits of contact against the risks of attracting unwanted attention.

The implications of contact extend beyond the immediate consequences. The long-term effects on human society, culture, and civilization remain largely uncharted territory.

The fundamental questions of our place in the universe, the nature of intelligence, and the meaning of existence would be subjected to intense scrutiny and re-evaluation. Our self-perception as a species might undergo a dramatic transformation, leading to profound changes in our values, beliefs, and societal structures. Furthermore, our technological and scientific progress could be accelerated exponentially, leading to an unprecedented era of innovation and development. However, this potential for progress is intertwined with the risk of catastrophic failure. The misuse of advanced technologies, the escalation of conflicts, or the inability to manage the social and psychological impacts of contact could lead to a dystopian future.

Ultimately, the search for extraterrestrial life is not just a scientific endeavor; it is a philosophical and ethical quest. The potential implications of contact are so profound, so far-reaching, and so uncertain that we must approach the matter with a combination of caution, curiosity, and a deep sense of ethical responsibility. The decisions we make today will determine the fate of humanity for generations to come. The answers lie not only in the realm of science and technology but also in the realm of philosophy, ethics, and our collective ability to navigate the complexities of a universe far larger and more enigmatic than we could have ever imagined. The future of humanity, intertwined with the potential for contact with extraterrestrial life, hangs delicately in the balance, awaiting the revelation of a discovery that could forever alter the course of human history. The implications, both wondrous and terrifying, demand our careful consideration, as we stand at the threshold of a new era in our understanding of the cosmos and our place within it.

The Future of SETI and the Search for Life

The challenges inherent in detecting extraterrestrial life are immense, demanding a multi-pronged approach that transcends the limitations of current methodologies. The future of SETI hinges on a convergence of technological advancements, methodological innovations, and a deeper understanding of the fundamental principles governing the emergence and evolution of life itself. Current radio astronomy techniques, while undeniably crucial, are but one piece of a much larger puzzle. The vastness of space and the limitations of our current technologies mean that we may be overlooking subtle signals, or employing methods that are simply ineffective in detecting life forms drastically different from ourselves.

One promising avenue for advancement lies in the development of more sensitive and sophisticated detection instruments. The next generation of radio telescopes, with their vastly increased collecting area and improved sensitivity, will be capable of detecting fainter and more distant signals than ever before. Projects like the Square Kilometre Array (SKA), a global network of radio telescopes planned to be the largest ever constructed, represent a quantum leap in our ability to scan the skies for faint radio emissions. Beyond radio waves, the search should expand to other electromagnetic spectrums. Optical SETI, for example, looks for laser pulses that might be used by advanced civilizations for interstellar communication. This technology, still in its infancy, holds the potential to reveal signals that might otherwise be missed.

Furthermore, the development of advanced signal processing algorithms is crucial. The sheer volume of data generated by modern telescopes requires sophisticated computational techniques to filter out noise and identify potentially meaningful signals. Machine learning and artificial intelligence are increasingly being employed in this process, providing a level of analysis that would be impossible for human observers. These algorithms can be trained to identify patterns and anomalies in data that might escape human notice, significantly increasing the probability of detecting weak or unusual signals. The development of novel algorithms capable of detecting non-traditional signals is paramount. Life may not necessarily communicate using signals easily interpreted by our current instruments.

Beyond technological improvements, a fundamental shift in our approach is needed. We must broaden our search beyond the conventional focus on radio waves and consider other potential biosignatures. These could include the detection of atmospheric gases indicative of biological activity on exoplanets (like oxygen, methane, or nitrous oxide), or even the observation of large-scale structures or engineering feats created by an extraterrestrial civilization (known as "technosignatures"). This necessitates a multi-wavelength approach that encompasses the entire electromagnetic spectrum, as well as other potential avenues of detection such as gravitational waves or neutrino emissions. The hunt for technosignatures requires a different strategy altogether, involving searches for anomalies in astronomical data, such as Dyson spheres or unusual energy signatures, that may point to the presence of a technologically advanced civilization.

Another critical area for improvement involves the targeting of the search. Instead of conducting indiscriminate searches of the entire sky, more focused efforts should be directed at regions of space with a higher probability of harboring habitable planets. This requires a comprehensive understanding of exoplanet formation and characteristics, as well as the factors that contribute to the habitability of a planet. Advances in astrobiology and planetary science are providing insights into the conditions necessary for life to emerge and thrive, enabling us to narrow down the most promising targets for future SETI searches. The study of extremophiles on Earth – organisms that thrive in extreme environments – provides valuable clues about the potential diversity of life beyond our planet and expands the range of environments we should consider in our search.

The future of SETI also rests on increased interdisciplinary collaboration. The search for extraterrestrial life requires a convergence of expertise from a wide range of fields, including astronomy, astrobiology, planetary science, computer science, artificial intelligence, and even the social sciences and humanities. A successful search requires the combined efforts of scientists, engineers, mathematicians, and ethicists working together to develop new techniques, analyze data, and address the ethical and societal implications of a potential discovery. This interdisciplinary approach can be fostered by creating dedicated research centers and collaborative projects that bring together scientists from different disciplines. The sharing of data and resources between different research groups is also vital to maximize the effectiveness of the search.

The ethical implications of contact with extraterrestrial intelligence cannot be understated. A rigorous framework for decision-making, developed through collaboration between scientists, ethicists, and policymakers, is necessary to guide our actions in the event of a discovery. This framework must address issues such as the potential risks of contact, the equitable distribution of benefits and responsibilities, and the protection of both human and extraterrestrial cultures. The potential for unintended consequences, whether through the transmission of harmful terrestrial pathogens or the disruption of a thriving extraterrestrial civilization, must be considered. Open and transparent discussions are essential to ensure that our actions are guided by ethical considerations and that the pursuit of knowledge is tempered with responsibility.

Furthermore, the public understanding of SETI and the search for extraterrestrial life is crucial for the success of these efforts. Increased public engagement and education can foster support for research, funding, and policy decisions related to the search. Promoting scientific literacy and critical thinking can help to counteract misinformation and promote a reasoned approach to the potential implications of contact. By fostering a global understanding of the potential benefits and risks associated with the search for extraterrestrial intelligence, we can create a more informed and responsible approach to this monumental undertaking.

The discovery of extraterrestrial life would have profound implications for humanity, reshaping our understanding of ourselves and our place in the cosmos. It would be a watershed moment in human history, comparable in significance to the Copernican Revolution or the discovery of the double helix. The social, political, and philosophical ramifications would be far-reaching, requiring a period of societal adjustment and adaptation. The future of SETI is not just about the detection of life beyond Earth; it is about our journey toward a deeper understanding of ourselves and the universe. It's a testament to humanity's enduring quest for knowledge and our innate curiosity about the cosmos. The challenges are considerable, but the potential rewards are immeasurable. The relentless pursuit of extraterrestrial life represents not just a scientific endeavor, but a testament to our resilience and our unwavering hope for discovery. The future of SETI and the search for life beyond Earth is a future brimming with both uncertainty and extraordinary potential – a future that demands our careful consideration and unwavering commitment.

CHAPTER 9

The Big Bang and the Origin of the Universe

Evidence for the Big Bang

The Big Bang theory, while elegantly explaining the origin and evolution of the universe, remains a theory, albeit one strongly supported by a wealth of observational evidence. This evidence isn't merely circumstantial; it's a convergence of independent lines of inquiry, each reinforcing the others, painting a compelling picture of a universe born from a hot, dense state and expanding ever since. Let's delve into the key pillars of this evidence.

One of the most compelling pieces of evidence is the Cosmic Microwave Background Radiation (CMB). Discovered accidentally in 1964 by Arno Penzias and Robert Wilson, the CMB is a faint, uniform afterglow of the Big Bang, a relic radiation permeating the entire universe. This radiation, detectable in the microwave region of the electromagnetic spectrum, is remarkably uniform, with a temperature of approximately 2.7 Kelvin—a mere 2.7 degrees above absolute zero. This uniformity strongly suggests that the early universe was incredibly homogeneous, a condition predicted by the Big Bang theory. Slight temperature variations within the CMB, discovered by the COBE and WMAP satellites, provide crucial insights into the initial density fluctuations that seeded the formation of galaxies and large-scale structures in the universe. These minute temperature anisotropies, only a few parts per hundred thousand, are considered the "seeds" of cosmic structure, acting as gravitational wells that attracted matter, leading to the clustering of galaxies we observe today. The detailed analysis of the CMB's power spectrum—a measure of the amplitude of these fluctuations at different angular scales—provides critical constraints on cosmological parameters, such as the density of dark matter and dark energy, further strengthening the Big Bang model. The precision with which the CMB's characteristics align with theoretical predictions represents a remarkable triumph of observational cosmology.

Another crucial piece of evidence is the redshift of distant galaxies. Edwin Hubble's groundbreaking observations in the 1920s revealed that galaxies are receding from us, with their velocity proportional to their distance. This observation, known as Hubble's Law, implies that the universe is expanding. The redshift of light from distant galaxies is a direct consequence of this expansion. As the universe expands, the wavelength of light stretches, shifting it towards the red end of the spectrum. The farther away a galaxy is, the greater its redshift, and the faster it is receding from us. This expansion, extrapolated backward in time, points towards an initial singularity—a state of infinite density and temperature—which is the essence of the Big Bang. The precise measurement of galaxy redshifts, achieved through advanced spectroscopic techniques, provides critical data for determining the expansion rate of the universe, known as the Hubble constant. While there are ongoing debates regarding the precise value of the Hubble constant, its very existence and its correlation with distance firmly support the expanding universe paradigm. The Hubble constant, along with other cosmological parameters, acts as a "tuning knob" in our understanding of the universe's expansion history, influencing our models of dark energy and the ultimate fate of the cosmos.

Furthermore, the abundance of light elements in the universe provides strong support for the Big Bang. In the very early universe, within the first few minutes after the Big Bang, conditions were hot and dense enough for nuclear reactions to occur, creating light elements like hydrogen, helium, and lithium. The Big Bang theory predicts the relative abundances of these elements based on fundamental physical constants and the initial conditions of the universe. Remarkably, these predictions are remarkably consistent with the observed abundances in the universe, as determined through astronomical observations and spectroscopy of stars and interstellar gas. The precise agreement between the predicted and observed abundances of light elements—particularly the ratio of hydrogen to helium—is a compelling piece of evidence that strongly supports the Big Bang model, and refutes competing models that do not account for this primordial nucleosynthesis. This successful prediction underscores the power of the Big Bang theory in explaining the fundamental composition of the universe.

However, our current understanding of the Big Bang is not without its limitations. The very early universe, within the first fraction of a second after the Big Bang, remains a realm shrouded in mystery. Our current physical theories, including Einstein's theory of general relativity, break down at extremely high energies and densities, making it challenging to describe the conditions of the early universe with complete accuracy. The period of inflation, a hypothesized period of extremely rapid expansion in the very early universe, addresses some of these challenges by smoothing out initial density fluctuations and explaining the large-scale homogeneity of the universe. However, the precise mechanism driving inflation remains an active area of research, with various theoretical models being proposed and tested.

Beyond inflation, another significant challenge lies in understanding the nature of dark matter and dark energy. These mysterious substances, which make up the vast majority of the universe's mass-energy content, remain largely unknown. Their existence is inferred from their gravitational effects on visible matter, but their fundamental nature is still a profound open question in cosmology and physics. Much research is currently focused on understanding the properties of dark matter and dark energy through observational studies and theoretical modeling. The detection and characterization of dark matter particles would be a revolutionary discovery, potentially altering our understanding of fundamental physics and the evolution of the universe.

Furthermore, ongoing research is aimed at refining our models of the Big Bang. The ongoing development of more sensitive telescopes and detectors, coupled with advanced data analysis techniques, promises to deliver increasingly precise measurements of cosmological parameters and to test the predictions of the Big Bang theory with ever-greater accuracy. This includes refined measurements of the CMB, improved galaxy redshift surveys, and improved constraints on the abundance of light elements. These advancements provide opportunities to test the limits of our current understanding of the Big Bang and to uncover new insights into the earliest moments of the universe. Projects like the James Webb Space Telescope are poised to make significant contributions in this domain, probing the universe's earliest galaxies and providing further observational constraints for our theoretical models. The future of Big Bang research is bright, promising continued refinement of our understanding and possibly revolutionary discoveries.

In conclusion, while the Big Bang theory is not a complete explanation of everything, it represents our best current understanding of the origin and evolution of the universe. The convergence of evidence—the CMB, the redshift of galaxies, and the abundance of light elements—provides a robust foundation for the theory. However, significant questions remain, highlighting the need for continued research and theoretical development. The ongoing quest to understand the very early universe, the nature of dark matter and dark energy, and the details of the Big Bang itself represents a central challenge and a powerful driving force in modern cosmology and physics. The continuing refinement of existing data and the ongoing quest to observe phenomena currently beyond our reach promise further advancements in our knowledge of the universe's origins. The mystery of the Big Bang, far from being solved, continues to inspire and motivate the next generation of cosmologists and physicists.

Inflationary Cosmology

The Big Bang theory, while remarkably successful in explaining the universe's large-scale structure and evolution, encounters certain limitations when we delve into its earliest moments. The initial conditions of the Big Bang, particularly the remarkable homogeneity and flatness of the observable universe, pose significant challenges. This is where the theory of inflationary cosmology enters the picture, offering a compelling solution to these puzzles.

Inflationary cosmology postulates a period of extraordinarily rapid expansion in the very early universe, occurring within a minuscule fraction of a second after the Big Bang. This exponential expansion, driven by a hypothetical field known as the inflaton field, dramatically alters the dynamics of the early universe, addressing several key observational conundrums. The inflaton field, possessing a potential energy density far exceeding that of matter or radiation, is thought to have dominated the universe's energy content during this period. As this field decayed, its potential energy was converted into the matter and radiation that constitute the universe we observe today.

One of the most significant problems that inflation elegantly addresses is the horizon problem. The observable universe exhibits remarkable uniformity in its temperature and properties, even at regions that were causally disconnected in the early universe. In a standard Big Bang scenario, these regions would have been too far apart to have interacted and equilibrated thermally. Inflation, however, provides a solution by exponentially expanding these regions, bringing them into causal contact in the very early universe. Before inflation, these regions were close enough to interact and achieve thermal equilibrium; the subsequent rapid expansion then separated them, preserving this homogeneity. This elegantly explains the observed uniformity of the Cosmic Microwave Background (CMB) across vast stretches of the cosmos.

Another critical issue resolved by inflation is the flatness problem. The universe's geometry is remarkably close to being flat, as evidenced by observations of the CMB. However, in a standard Big Bang model, a perfectly flat universe is an unstable state—the slightest deviation from flatness would lead to a rapidly expanding or contracting universe. Inflation, by its very nature, drives the universe towards flatness. The exponential expansion stretches the universe's curvature so much that, regardless of its initial curvature, it appears almost perfectly flat by the time inflation ends. This is akin to inflating a balloon with a slightly curved surface—as it inflates, the curvature becomes less noticeable.

Furthermore, inflation provides a natural mechanism for generating the initial density fluctuations that seeded the formation of galaxies and large-scale structures. Quantum fluctuations in the inflaton field during the inflationary epoch are stretched and amplified by the exponential expansion, resulting in tiny density perturbations. These perturbations subsequently acted as seeds for gravitational collapse, leading to the formation of the cosmic web we observe today. The amplitude and distribution of these initial density fluctuations are remarkably consistent with the predictions of inflationary models, and this match is a key piece of evidence supporting the theory. Detailed analysis of the CMB anisotropy power spectrum strongly supports the prediction of these fluctuations originating from inflation.

While inflation offers compelling solutions to these problems, it is not without its challenges and open questions. The nature of the inflaton field itself remains a mystery. Various theoretical models have been proposed, incorporating different types of scalar fields, but the precise nature of the inflaton remains an area of active research. Moreover, the observational evidence for inflation is largely indirect. While the predictions of inflation are consistent with many observations, a direct detection of the inflaton field or other unique signatures of inflation would significantly strengthen the theory.

One such potential signature of inflation is the detection of primordial gravitational waves. These gravitational waves, generated during the inflationary epoch, would leave a distinct imprint on the CMB polarization. Several experiments are actively searching for this imprint, and their findings could provide crucial evidence for or against inflationary cosmology. However, so far, this direct evidence remains elusive.

Beyond the inflaton field's nature, there exist alternative models attempting to explain the early universe's evolution. These models, while often less elegant or comprehensive than inflation, attempt to address the horizon and flatness problems without invoking a period of rapid expansion. One such model involves modifying the laws of gravity at very high energies, suggesting a different framework of how the universe evolves in its earliest stages. Other models involve investigating alternate initial conditions or proposing that the universe didn't begin with a singularity but from a pre-existing state. These alternatives, however, typically involve fine-tuning of parameters or require abandoning well-established physical principles.

The ongoing quest to understand the early universe is a vibrant and evolving field. New observational data from experiments such as the Planck satellite and the James Webb Space Telescope are continuously refining our understanding of the CMB and the large-scale structure of the universe, providing crucial constraints for cosmological models, including inflationary models and their alternatives. Theoretical advancements in string theory and quantum gravity might one day offer a deeper understanding of the underlying physics driving inflation, while continued refinement of experimental techniques may eventually lead to the direct detection of gravitational waves or other distinctive signatures of inflation.

The elegance and explanatory power of inflationary cosmology have made it the leading paradigm in our understanding of the early universe. Its ability to address the horizon and flatness problems, and to provide a mechanism for generating the initial density perturbations, makes it a compelling theory. However, several challenges remain, requiring further theoretical and observational research. The ongoing debate between proponents of inflation and alternative models reflects the dynamism and uncertainty inherent in cosmological research. Ultimately, further research, driven by both theoretical advancements and increasingly precise observational data, will be crucial in determining the ultimate fate of inflationary cosmology and our deeper understanding of the universe's origins. The quest to unravel the mysteries of the very early universe continues, pushing the boundaries of our knowledge and inspiring future generations of cosmologists and physicists. The pursuit of truth, whether it affirms or refutes inflationary cosmology, remains the fundamental driver of our scientific endeavor. This ongoing process of testing, refining, and revising our models constitutes the essence of the scientific method itself, constantly striving for a more accurate and complete understanding of the cosmos. The journey to understand the universe's origins is an ongoing narrative, constantly being written and rewritten as new evidence emerges and new theories are proposed and tested. The final chapter remains unwritten, awaiting the next generation of researchers to continue this grand exploration.

The Planck Epoch and Beyond

We have traced the universe's evolution from the aftermath of inflation, a period of exponential expansion that smoothed out the cosmic landscape and sowed the seeds for galaxies and large-scale structures. However, the story doesn't begin there. Inflation itself had a beginning, and before that lies a realm shrouded in mystery—the Planck epoch. This era, occurring within the first 10^{-43} seconds after the Big Bang (the Planck time), represents a frontier where our current understanding of physics breaks down. The conditions during the Planck epoch were so extreme—temperatures exceeding 10^{32} Kelvin and densities exceeding 10^{93} g/cm^3—that the known laws of physics, including general relativity and quantum mechanics, are insufficient to describe the dynamics.

The problem lies in the incompatibility of general relativity and quantum mechanics. General relativity, our most successful theory of gravity, excels in describing the universe's large-scale structure and evolution, but it fails at describing phenomena at extremely small scales, close to the Planck length (approximately 10^{-35} meters). Conversely, quantum mechanics provides an accurate description of the universe's microscopic behavior but struggles to reconcile with gravity. At the Planck epoch, both gravity and quantum effects were equally dominant, requiring a unified theory of quantum gravity to provide a coherent description. This is precisely the challenge physicists face—the creation of a theory that seamlessly unites these two pillars of modern physics.

Several promising candidates for a theory of quantum gravity are currently under investigation. String theory, for instance, proposes that the fundamental constituents of matter are not point-like particles but rather tiny, vibrating strings. This radical shift in perspective suggests a fundamentally different approach to gravity, where it is not described as a force mediated by particles but emerges as a geometric property of spacetime itself, influenced by the vibrational modes of these strings. Loop quantum gravity, another leading contender, approaches the problem from a different angle. It quantizes spacetime directly, proposing that spacetime itself is granular at the Planck scale, rather than being a smooth, continuous entity as portrayed in general relativity. These granular structures, analogous to pixels in a digital image, weave the fabric of spacetime at its most fundamental level.

These theories are currently highly mathematical and abstract, lacking direct experimental verification. The extremely high energies and densities involved are beyond the reach of any foreseeable experiment. However, the indirect implications of these theories are potentially testable. For example, certain predictions about the early universe's evolution derived from string theory or loop quantum gravity might leave detectable signatures in the cosmic microwave background (CMB) radiation or in the distribution of large-scale structures.

Furthermore, the search for a unified theory of quantum gravity isn't just an exercise in theoretical physics; it carries profound implications for our understanding of the universe's origins. Our current models of the Big Bang suggest a singularity at the beginning of time – a point of infinite density and curvature. This singularity is a mathematical artifact of general relativity, signaling the breakdown of the theory itself. A successful theory of quantum gravity is expected to resolve this singularity, possibly by suggesting a more profound and elegant scenario for the universe's inception.

One possibility is that the universe didn't emerge from a singularity but from a pre-existing state, perhaps a quantum fluctuation within a larger multiverse. This concept, while speculative, aligns with some interpretations of string theory and other quantum gravity approaches. Another intriguing possibility, arising from loop quantum gravity, suggests that spacetime itself was non-singular at the beginning, implying the existence of a "bounce" – a transition from a contracting phase to an expanding one. This concept offers an alternative to the Big Bang singularity, suggesting a cyclic universe that undergoes cycles of contraction and expansion.

While the Planck epoch remains deeply mysterious, ongoing research is slowly unveiling some of its secrets. The quest for a quantum theory of gravity represents one of the biggest challenges in modern physics, but its solution holds the key to understanding not just the earliest moments of the universe but also the very nature of spacetime, gravity, and ultimately, reality itself. The exploration of the Planck epoch is a journey into the heart of creation, a pursuit as fundamental and profound as human inquiry itself. The pursuit of such knowledge continues to drive scientific advancement, pushing the boundaries of our conceptual understanding and technological capabilities.

The implications extend beyond cosmology. A complete understanding of quantum gravity might revolutionize our understanding of black holes, providing insights into their inner workings and their ultimate fate. It might also shed light on the nature of dark matter and dark energy, two enigmatic components of the universe that currently defy explanation within the framework of our current understanding. Ultimately, the search for a unified theory of everything is a testament to our inherent human curiosity, our drive to explore the unknown, and our insatiable desire to unravel the secrets of the cosmos.

The development of more powerful telescopes and detectors, coupled with ongoing theoretical advancements, promises exciting breakthroughs in the coming decades. Future observations of the CMB, gravitational waves, and other cosmological phenomena might offer crucial clues about the Planck epoch, providing constraints on various models of quantum gravity. The analysis of these data requires not only sophisticated mathematical techniques but also an interdisciplinary approach that integrates diverse fields of physics, astronomy, and mathematics.

Furthermore, the exploration of the Planck epoch has prompted a profound re-evaluation of the fundamental concepts of physics. Questions about the nature of time, the origin of spacetime, and the ultimate fate of the universe are being revisited in the light of new theoretical developments. The very foundations of physics are being challenged, leading to a dynamic and exciting evolution in our understanding of the cosmos. It's a testament to the power of human ingenuity that we even dare to ponder these fundamental questions, and the scientific quest continues, driven by the insatiable curiosity inherent in the human spirit.

The journey into the Planck epoch is not simply a scientific endeavor; it is a philosophical journey. It forces us to confront the very limits of our knowledge and to grapple with questions that lie at the intersection of science and metaphysics. What existed before the Big Bang? Is our universe unique, or is it one among many in a multiverse? These are profound questions that may never have definitive answers, but the exploration itself enriches our understanding of our place in the universe. This humbling experience helps us to better appreciate the vastness of the cosmos and the beauty of the intricate laws that govern it.

In conclusion, while the Planck epoch remains beyond our current grasp, the ongoing quest to understand its mysteries represents one of the most intellectually stimulating and challenging endeavors in science. The development of a unified theory of quantum gravity is not merely a scientific goal; it represents a leap towards a deeper, more complete understanding of reality itself. The challenges are immense, but the potential rewards—a profound shift in our comprehension of the universe's origins, the nature of spacetime, and the fundamental laws of physics—are equally breathtaking. The journey continues, and the future holds the promise of exciting discoveries that will shape our understanding of the universe for generations to come. The quest to understand the Planck epoch and its implications is a testament to the enduring human spirit of exploration and the relentless pursuit of knowledge. It is a journey that reminds us of the immense beauty and mystery of the cosmos, and our own privileged position in being able to contemplate its origins and ultimate fate.

Dark Matter and Dark Energy

Having ventured into the enigmatic realm of the Planck epoch and the quest for a unified theory of quantum gravity, we now shift our focus to another profound mystery that permeates the cosmos: the nature of dark matter and dark energy. These elusive components constitute the vast majority of the universe's mass-energy content, yet their precise nature remains one of the most significant unsolved puzzles in modern cosmology. Their existence is inferred indirectly through their gravitational effects on visible matter and the expansion of the universe, but their fundamental properties remain largely unknown.

The evidence for dark matter first emerged from observations of galactic rotation curves. Stars orbiting the centers of galaxies move at speeds far exceeding what would be expected based on the visible matter alone. The gravitational force required to maintain these high orbital velocities implies the existence of a significant amount of unseen matter, dubbed "dark matter," which exerts a gravitational pull but does not interact with light or other forms of electromagnetic radiation. This lack of electromagnetic interaction is what renders dark matter invisible to our telescopes.

Further evidence for dark matter comes from gravitational lensing, a phenomenon predicted by Einstein's general relativity. Massive objects, including dark matter halos surrounding galaxies, bend the path of light passing nearby, acting like a cosmic lens. By observing the distortion of light from distant galaxies, astronomers can map the distribution of dark matter, revealing its presence in regions far beyond the extent of visible matter. These observations confirm that dark matter is not just a localized phenomenon within galaxies but a ubiquitous component of the universe, pervading the cosmic web that connects galaxies and galaxy clusters.

Beyond galactic scales, the large-scale structure of the universe also provides strong support for the existence of dark matter. Computer simulations of galaxy formation, incorporating dark matter, accurately reproduce the observed distribution of galaxies, galaxy clusters, and filaments. Without dark matter, the gravitational forces from visible matter alone are insufficient to explain the observed clustering of galaxies, and the cosmic web structure would look vastly different. These simulations demonstrate the crucial role dark matter plays in the formation and evolution of large-scale cosmic structures.

While the existence of dark matter is well-established through various observational lines of evidence, its precise composition remains a matter of intense investigation. Numerous candidates have been proposed, ranging from weakly interacting massive particles (WIMPs) to axions and sterile neutrinos. WIMPs, hypothetical particles predicted by some extensions of the Standard Model of particle physics, are among the leading contenders. Their weak interaction with ordinary matter makes them difficult to detect directly, but experiments like the Large Hadron Collider (LHC) and other dedicated dark matter detectors are actively searching for evidence of their existence. The absence of a definitive detection, however, highlights the challenges in directly probing dark matter's nature.

The exploration of dark matter goes beyond particle physics. Alternative explanations for the observed phenomena, such as modifications to the laws of gravity on galactic scales, have also been proposed. However, these modified gravity models face difficulties in explaining the full range of observational data, particularly the consistency between the small-scale and large-scale evidence for dark matter. The most compelling evidence still strongly favors the existence of a non-baryonic dark matter component.

In contrast to dark matter, which affects the structure formation of the universe, dark energy influences its expansion. The discovery of dark energy was a revolutionary moment in cosmology. Observations of distant supernovae in the late 1990s revealed that the expansion of the universe is not only accelerating but is doing so at an ever-increasing rate. This acceleration is attributed to a mysterious repulsive force, termed "dark energy," which counteracts the attractive force of gravity.

The nature of dark energy is even more elusive than that of dark matter. The simplest explanation, within the framework of general relativity, is that dark energy is a cosmological constant, a constant energy density that pervades all of space. This constant energy density exerts a repulsive gravitational force, causing the accelerated expansion. However, the value of the cosmological constant required to explain the observed acceleration is incredibly small, many orders of magnitude smaller than predicted by theoretical models. This discrepancy constitutes the "cosmological constant problem," one of the most significant challenges in modern physics.

Beyond the cosmological constant, alternative models for dark energy, such as quintessence, have been proposed. Quintessence posits a dynamic dark energy field, whose energy density can vary over time, rather than being constant. These models offer a more complex but potentially more satisfying explanation for the observed acceleration, although they require specific properties for the quintessence field that are not yet constrained by observations.

The implications of dark matter and dark energy for the ultimate fate of the universe are profound. The continued dominance of dark energy suggests that the universe's expansion will continue accelerating indefinitely. This scenario, commonly referred to as "the Big Freeze," implies that galaxies will eventually become so distant from one another that they will be effectively isolated, and the universe will become increasingly cold and empty. However, the uncertainties in our understanding of dark energy leave open the possibility of different scenarios, such as a Big Rip, where the accelerated expansion becomes so extreme that it tears apart even atoms and subatomic particles.

The ongoing research into dark matter and dark energy is multi-faceted. It involves a combination of theoretical investigations, aiming to understand their fundamental nature within the framework of particle physics and cosmology, and observational studies, striving to improve our measurements of their properties and distribution. New telescopes and detectors are being developed to provide more precise measurements of cosmological parameters and to probe the nature of dark matter and dark energy with greater sensitivity. These efforts aim to resolve the mysteries surrounding these elusive components of the universe and to shed light on the ultimate fate of the cosmos. The journey continues, promising both intriguing discoveries and a deeper understanding of the universe's composition and future evolution. The pursuit of such knowledge, as we have seen throughout this exploration of the Big Bang and its aftermath, represents not merely a scientific endeavor but a fundamentally human quest to comprehend our place in the vast and wondrous cosmos.

The Big Bang and the Future of Cosmology

The Big Bang theory, while remarkably successful in explaining the universe's evolution from its earliest moments, still leaves many profound questions unanswered. Its triumph lies in its ability to accurately predict the cosmic microwave background radiation, the leftover heat from the Big Bang, and the abundance of light elements like hydrogen and helium observed in the universe. However, the theory itself does not explain the initial conditions that gave rise to the Big Bang, nor does it fully account for the nature of dark matter and dark energy, which constitute the vast majority of the universe's mass-energy content. These unanswered questions drive ongoing research in cosmology, pushing the boundaries of our understanding and prompting new theoretical frameworks.

One of the most significant challenges is the singularity problem. The Big Bang theory suggests that the universe originated from an infinitely dense and hot singularity, a point where the known laws of physics break down. This singularity represents a boundary beyond which our current understanding cannot extrapolate. To overcome this limitation, physicists are actively exploring theories of quantum gravity, which aim to unify general relativity, the theory governing gravity on large scales, with quantum mechanics, the theory governing the behavior of matter at the subatomic level. A successful theory of quantum gravity could potentially provide a more complete description of the universe's origins, resolving the singularity problem and shedding light on the conditions that preceded the Big Bang.

String theory, loop quantum gravity, and causal set theory are among the leading contenders in the quest for a quantum gravity theory. These theories propose radical departures from our classical understanding of spacetime, suggesting that space and time may be emergent properties of a more fundamental underlying structure. For example, string theory proposes that fundamental particles are not point-like objects but rather tiny vibrating strings, and the different vibrational modes of these strings correspond to different particles. Loop quantum gravity, on the other hand, suggests that spacetime itself is quantized, meaning that it is composed of discrete units, akin to pixels in a digital image. These radical ideas, while still speculative, offer the possibility of resolving the singularity problem and providing a more complete picture of the very early universe.

Beyond the singularity problem, the nature of dark matter and dark energy remains a major focus of cosmological research. While their existence is strongly supported by observational evidence, their fundamental properties are still unknown. The search for dark matter particles is a prominent area of investigation, with numerous experiments employing diverse detection techniques. These experiments aim to directly detect dark matter particles through their interactions with ordinary matter, either in underground detectors shielded from cosmic rays or in particle colliders like the Large Hadron Collider. While no definitive detection has been achieved so far, ongoing research offers the potential for groundbreaking discoveries in the coming years.

The cosmological constant, a constant energy density that pervades all of space, is the simplest explanation for dark energy within the framework of general relativity. However, the value of the cosmological constant required to explain the observed accelerated expansion of the universe is vastly smaller than what is predicted by theoretical models, posing the cosmological constant problem. Alternative models for dark energy, such as quintessence, a dynamic energy field whose energy density can change over time, offer potential solutions, but they often introduce new parameters and assumptions that need to be constrained by observations. The quest to understand dark energy is intricately linked to the fundamental laws of physics and our understanding of the universe's ultimate fate.

The future of cosmology is deeply intertwined with advancements in observational astronomy and astrophysics. The development of new telescopes and detectors, operating across a wide range of wavelengths, including radio waves, infrared, visible light, ultraviolet, X-rays, and gamma rays, promises to significantly enhance our ability to probe the universe's farthest reaches. Space-based observatories, like the James Webb Space Telescope, offer unprecedented sensitivity and resolution, allowing us to observe the earliest galaxies and explore the distribution of dark matter and dark energy with greater precision. Ground-based telescopes, equipped with advanced adaptive optics, provide complementary observations, allowing astronomers to study cosmic phenomena in exquisite detail.

The analysis of data from these telescopes necessitates advanced computational techniques. Simulations of the universe's evolution, incorporating increasingly realistic models of dark matter, dark energy, and galaxy formation, play a crucial role in interpreting observational data and testing theoretical predictions. These simulations, often running on supercomputers, can reproduce the large-scale structure of the universe and provide insights into the processes that shaped the cosmic web. The interplay between theory, simulation, and observation is essential for advancing our understanding of the universe's origins and evolution.

Furthermore, multi-messenger astronomy, which combines data from different types of astronomical messengers, such as gravitational waves, neutrinos, and electromagnetic radiation, offers a powerful new approach to studying cosmic phenomena. The detection of gravitational waves from merging black holes and neutron stars has already revolutionized our understanding of these extreme objects, providing independent confirmation of Einstein's theory of general relativity and offering a new window into the universe's most energetic events. The combined analysis of data from multiple messengers promises to reveal even more about the universe's history and composition.

The ongoing quest to understand the Big Bang and the universe's evolution is a testament to humanity's insatiable curiosity and our inherent drive to explore the unknown. The challenges are immense, but the potential rewards – a deeper understanding of our place in the cosmos and the fundamental laws that govern the universe – are equally profound. The future of cosmology is likely to be filled with surprising discoveries, shifting paradigms, and an ever-evolving understanding of the universe's intricate tapestry. The journey of cosmic exploration continues, propelled by the relentless pursuit of knowledge and the awe-inspiring mysteries that still await us in the vast expanse of space and time. The story of the universe is far from complete, and each new discovery brings us closer to unraveling its grand narrative. The integration of cutting-edge technology, theoretical breakthroughs, and persistent scientific inquiry will undoubtedly illuminate many of the remaining dark corners of the cosmos in the years to come, unveiling a more complete and nuanced understanding of the Big Bang and its profound implications for the past, present, and future of the universe.

CHAPTER 10

Quantum Mechanics and its Interpretations

The Quantum World

Our journey from the vast expanse of the cosmos to the infinitesimally small realm of the quantum world might seem a jarring shift, yet the two are inextricably linked. The Big Bang, as we've explored, describes the universe's evolution from an incredibly hot, dense state. But what were the fundamental building blocks of this primordial soup? What governed their behavior in those earliest moments? To answer these questions, we must delve into the bizarre and beautiful world of quantum mechanics.

Quantum mechanics, unlike the classical physics that governs the macroscopic world we experience daily, unveils a reality that defies intuition. In the classical world, objects possess definite properties—a ball has a specific location and velocity, a planet follows a predictable orbit. But at the subatomic level, things are dramatically different. The fundamental components of matter—electrons, protons, neutrons, and others—exhibit a duality, behaving as both particles and waves. This is the cornerstone of quantum mechanics: *wave-particle duality*.

Imagine a pebble dropped into a still pond. Ripples, waves, spread outwards. This wave-like behavior isn't limited to water; it's a fundamental property of quantum particles. Electrons, for example, can be described by a wave function, a mathematical function that encapsulates the probability of finding the electron at a particular location. This probability distribution, rather than a precise position, is the quantum description of the electron's whereabouts. However, when we attempt to measure the electron's location, it suddenly behaves like a particle, appearing at a single point. This is the strange nature of quantum reality: a blend of wave-like probability and particle-like detection.

This inherent uncertainty is formalized by the Heisenberg uncertainty principle. It states that we cannot simultaneously know both the position and momentum of a particle with perfect accuracy. The more precisely we know its position, the less precisely we know its momentum, and vice versa. This isn't a limitation of our measuring instruments; it's a fundamental aspect of quantum reality, a manifestation of the wave-like nature of particles. This uncertainty isn't just a matter of imprecise measurements; it represents a genuine indeterminacy at the heart of the quantum world. The universe, at its most fundamental level, appears to be inherently probabilistic.

Another key concept is *superposition*. In the classical world, a light switch is either on or off. But in the quantum world, a quantum system can exist in multiple states simultaneously. Think of Schrödinger's famous thought experiment: a cat inside a box with a radioactive atom. Until the box is opened, the atom exists in a superposition of both decayed and undecayed states. Consequently, the cat is simultaneously alive and dead—a superposition of states. Only upon observation does the system "collapse" into a single definite state. The act of measurement, it seems, plays a crucial role in determining reality.

The concept of *entanglement* takes the strangeness of the quantum world even further. Two or more quantum particles can become entangled, meaning their fates are inextricably linked, regardless of the distance separating them. If we measure the property of one entangled particle, we instantaneously know the corresponding property of the other particle, even if they're light-years apart. This instantaneous correlation defies classical physics, which assumes that information cannot travel faster than the speed of light. Entanglement suggests a deeper connection between quantum particles, a non-local correlation that challenges our intuitive understanding of space and time.

The implications of entanglement are profound, both philosophically and technologically. Philosophically, it raises questions about the nature of reality, the role of observation, and the limits of locality. Technologically, it has the potential to revolutionize fields such as quantum computing and quantum cryptography. Quantum computers, leveraging the principles of superposition and entanglement, could perform calculations far beyond the capabilities of classical computers, potentially unlocking solutions to previously intractable problems. Quantum cryptography, utilizing the principles of entanglement, promises secure communication channels impervious to eavesdropping.

The transition from the classical to the quantum world requires a fundamental shift in perspective. Classical physics deals with deterministic systems, where the future is determined by the present. Quantum mechanics, on the other hand, is inherently probabilistic, dealing with probabilities rather than certainties. This probabilistic nature isn't simply a limitation of our knowledge; it's a fundamental aspect of quantum reality. The universe, at its most fundamental level, seems to operate on the principles of chance and probability.

The interpretations of quantum mechanics are varied and debated. The Copenhagen interpretation, one of the most widely accepted, posits that the wave function collapse occurs upon measurement. However, this interpretation leaves open the question of what constitutes a measurement and why the act of observation should have such a profound impact on reality. Other interpretations, such as the many-worlds interpretation, propose that every quantum measurement causes the universe to split into multiple branches, each representing a different outcome. These interpretations highlight the philosophical complexities inherent in quantum mechanics and underscore the ongoing quest to understand its true meaning.

The application of quantum mechanics extends far beyond the realm of theoretical physics. It underpins many technologies we use daily, from lasers to transistors. Lasers rely on the stimulated emission of radiation, a quantum phenomenon, while transistors utilize the quantum properties of semiconductors. The development of new technologies, such as quantum computers and quantum sensors, promises to further revolutionize various fields, from medicine to materials science.

The quantum world presents a profound challenge to our classical intuitions, forcing us to reconsider our fundamental assumptions about reality. Its probabilistic nature, the concepts of superposition and entanglement, and the various interpretations of its underlying principles continue to stimulate ongoing scientific research and philosophical debate. Understanding quantum mechanics is crucial not only for advancements in technology but also for deepening our understanding of the fundamental constituents of the universe and the laws that govern their behavior. The universe, from the largest cosmological scales to the smallest subatomic particles, is a tapestry woven from the threads of quantum mechanics. And as we unravel this tapestry, we uncover a reality far more intricate and astonishing than anything our classical intuitions could have predicted. The quantum realm, in its strangeness and elegance, unveils a universe that continues to surprise and inspire us, pushing the boundaries of our knowledge and challenging us to reassess our understanding of the cosmos and our place within it. The implications of quantum mechanics resonate far beyond the confines of the laboratory; they touch upon the very nature of reality, prompting us to question what we believe to be true and to embrace the mysteries that still lie ahead.

The connections between the vastness of the cosmos and the intricacies of the quantum world are profound and still largely unexplored. The quest to unite quantum mechanics with general relativity, to develop a theory of quantum gravity, remains one of the biggest challenges in modern physics. Such a theory would provide a complete description of the universe, from the earliest moments of the Big Bang to the structure of space-time itself. It is in this unification that we may find the ultimate answers to questions about the origins and evolution of the universe, merging the macroscopic and microscopic perspectives into a single, coherent framework. The journey to achieve this is a complex one, requiring a deep understanding of both the vastness of space and the mysterious world of the quantum. The quest continues, driven by curiosity, innovation, and the unwavering belief that the universe holds secrets yet to be uncovered.

The Copenhagen Interpretation

The Copenhagen interpretation, developed primarily in the 1920s by Niels Bohr and Werner Heisenberg, stands as one of the most influential, yet arguably most debated, interpretations of quantum mechanics. It doesn't offer a single, unified theory, but rather a collection of postulates and working principles that attempt to explain the peculiar behavior of quantum systems. At its core, the Copenhagen interpretation attempts to reconcile the wave-like and particle-like nature of quantum objects, a duality that profoundly challenges our classical intuitions.

A central tenet of the Copenhagen interpretation is the concept of the wave function. Recall that a quantum particle, such as an electron, is not described by a precise location and momentum, as it would be in classical physics. Instead, it's described by a mathematical function, the wave function, which represents the probability amplitude of finding the particle in a specific state. The square of the absolute value of this wave function gives the probability density of finding the particle at a given point in space. This probabilistic nature is fundamental; it's not simply a reflection of our limited ability to measure precisely, but rather an inherent characteristic of the quantum world.

The wave function, in its entirety, describes the superposition of all possible states the particle can occupy. Before a measurement is made, the particle exists in a superposition—a simultaneous existence in multiple states. This is a stark contrast to the classical world where objects have definite properties. The famous Schrödinger's cat paradox perfectly illustrates this superposition principle: the cat is both alive and dead until the box is opened and a measurement is made.

However, the act of measurement, according to the Copenhagen interpretation, fundamentally alters the situation. The process of measurement causes the wave function to "collapse," transitioning from a superposition of states to a single, definite outcome. This collapse is probabilistic; the probability of each outcome is determined by the wave function before the measurement. The measured property of the particle then assumes a definite value. This seemingly abrupt shift from a probabilistic description to a definite outcome is one of the most controversial aspects of the Copenhagen interpretation.

The Copenhagen interpretation doesn't offer a clear explanation for the mechanism of wave function collapse. It simply postulates that the act of measurement is the catalyst for this transition. This has led to considerable debate about what constitutes a "measurement." Is it the interaction with a macroscopic measuring device? Is it the interaction with a conscious observer? Or is it something more fundamental? The lack of a clear definition of measurement remains a significant limitation of the Copenhagen interpretation.

The role of the observer in the Copenhagen interpretation is particularly intriguing and has fueled much philosophical discussion. Does the act of observation actively influence the outcome of a quantum measurement? Some interpretations suggest that consciousness is somehow inextricably linked to the collapse of the wave function. However, this view is not universally accepted, and many physicists argue that the collapse is a physical process independent of consciousness. The debate continues, highlighting the deep connection between quantum mechanics and the foundations of our understanding of reality.

Consider the double-slit experiment, a classic demonstration of wave-particle duality. When electrons are fired at a double slit, they create an interference pattern on a screen behind the slits, demonstrating their wave-like nature. However, if we attempt to determine which slit each electron passes through, the interference pattern disappears, and the electrons behave like particles. The Copenhagen interpretation explains this by suggesting that the act of measuring which slit the electron passes through forces the wave function to collapse, destroying the interference pattern. This interpretation emphasizes the profound role of measurement in shaping our understanding of quantum phenomena.

Another crucial element of the Copenhagen interpretation is the concept of complementarity. Bohr introduced this notion to address the wave-particle duality. He argued that wave and particle descriptions are complementary aspects of a quantum system, rather than mutually exclusive properties. Depending on the type of experiment performed, a quantum system may exhibit either wave-like or particle-like behavior. These behaviors are not contradictory; they are complementary aspects of the same underlying reality. This concept highlights the limitations of applying classical concepts to the quantum world and the need for a new, more nuanced way of thinking about physical phenomena.

Despite its influence, the Copenhagen interpretation is not without its limitations and criticisms. The lack of a clear explanation for wave function collapse is a major drawback. The interpretation doesn't provide a mechanism for this collapse; it simply postulates that it occurs upon measurement. The ambiguity surrounding the definition of measurement further complicates the interpretation. Moreover, the Copenhagen interpretation is often criticized for its inherent anthropocentrism. It seems to suggest that the observer plays a crucial role in shaping reality, a notion that many physicists find problematic.

The lack of a clear definition of the boundary between the quantum and classical worlds is another criticism. The Copenhagen interpretation often implies a rather arbitrary separation between the quantum system being measured and the classical measuring apparatus. However, the measuring apparatus is ultimately composed of quantum particles, blurring the lines between the quantum and classical realms. This lack of a well-defined boundary undermines the interpretation's clarity and consistency.

Several alternative interpretations of quantum mechanics, such as the many-worlds interpretation and the consistent histories interpretation, have been proposed to address the shortcomings of the Copenhagen interpretation. These alternative interpretations offer different perspectives on the role of measurement and the nature of quantum reality. The ongoing debate among these competing interpretations reflects the ongoing effort to achieve a deeper understanding of the fundamental principles governing the quantum world.

The Copenhagen interpretation, despite its limitations, has profoundly influenced the development and application of quantum mechanics. It provides a practical framework for understanding and predicting the behavior of quantum systems, even though it leaves some fundamental questions unanswered. Its probabilistic nature, its emphasis on the role of measurement, and its notion of complementarity have been instrumental in shaping our understanding of the quantum world, even as alternative interpretations continue to emerge and challenge its central tenets. The ongoing exploration of quantum mechanics and its various interpretations not only expands our scientific knowledge but also pushes the boundaries of our philosophical understanding of reality itself. The universe, viewed through the lens of quantum mechanics, reveals a reality that is simultaneously wondrously strange and profoundly elegant, inviting continued exploration and contemplation. The very act of seeking to understand this reality, in all its inherent mystery, is perhaps the most fulfilling aspect of this ongoing scientific and philosophical endeavor.

The ManyWorlds Interpretation

The Copenhagen interpretation, as compelling as it is in its practical applications, leaves several nagging questions unanswered. The most prominent among these is the nature of wave function collapse and the role, if any, of the observer. This is where the many-worlds interpretation (MWI), first proposed by Hugh Everett III in 1957, offers a radically different perspective. Instead of postulating a collapse of the wave function upon measurement, MWI proposes that every quantum measurement causes the universe to split into multiple universes, each representing a different possible outcome.

In the classic double-slit experiment, for example, according to the Copenhagen interpretation, the act of observing which slit an electron passes through causes the wave function to collapse, eliminating the interference pattern. The electron is then definitively found to have passed through one slit or the other. In contrast, MWI suggests that upon measurement, the universe branches. In one branch, the electron passes through one slit, and in another, it passes through the other. Both branches are equally real and continue to evolve independently. There is no collapse; rather, a proliferation of universes, each containing a specific outcome of the measurement.

This concept of branching universes might seem fantastical, even science fiction-esque. However, the elegance of MWI lies in its mathematical simplicity and its avoidance of the problematic wave function collapse. The Schrödinger equation, the fundamental equation governing the evolution of quantum systems, continues to apply without interruption. There is no need for a separate, unexplained mechanism to account for the collapse. The wave function simply continues to evolve, describing the superposition of all possible outcomes across the ever-branching universes.

The observer, in this context, is not a special agent causing the collapse. The observer is simply another quantum system interacting with the measured system. The interaction leads to branching, and the observer exists in different branches, each experiencing a different outcome. The subjective experience of the observer in each branch is consistent with the measured outcome in that branch. This removes the anthropocentric bias inherent in some interpretations of the Copenhagen interpretation where consciousness seems to play a crucial, and unexplained, role.

However, the implications of MWI are profound and far-reaching. If every quantum measurement causes the universe to split, the sheer number of universes generated is astronomically large. Every decision we make, every quantum event occurring in our bodies and the environment, leads to further branching. The result is a vast, constantly expanding multiverse, encompassing all possible realities. This is not simply a theoretical concept; it's a consequence of the mathematical formalism of quantum mechanics, interpreted through the lens of MWI.

The notion of a multiverse raises numerous philosophical questions. If all possible outcomes are realized in separate universes, what is the significance of our particular universe? Does the concept of free will retain its meaning in a multiverse where every possible action is taken in some branch? These questions are not easy to answer and have sparked extensive debate among physicists and philosophers. The sheer scale of the multiverse defies our everyday intuitions and pushes the boundaries of our understanding of what constitutes "reality."

One major criticism of MWI is its untestability. There is currently no known way to experimentally verify the existence of these other universes. They are, by definition, inaccessible to observation from within our own universe. This lack of empirical support is a significant hurdle for the widespread acceptance of MWI. Some physicists argue that an interpretation of quantum mechanics must be testable to be considered scientifically valid, while others contend that the elegance and internal consistency of MWI outweigh the lack of direct empirical verification.

Another challenge for MWI is the problem of probability. While the Schrödinger equation describes the evolution of the wave function across all branches, it doesn't offer a clear explanation for why we experience a particular outcome in our branch. Some formulations attempt to address this by invoking the Born rule, which gives the probability of observing a specific outcome. However, this reliance on the Born rule, which is itself a postulate, might be seen as a weakness, bringing back an element of the arbitrariness MWI aimed to avoid.

Despite these criticisms, MWI remains a compelling and influential interpretation of quantum mechanics. It offers a consistent, elegant, and arguably simpler explanation of quantum phenomena compared to the Copenhagen interpretation, avoiding the problematic concept of wave function collapse. While the lack of empirical evidence and some unresolved conceptual issues remain, MWI continues to stimulate debate and inspire further research into the foundations of quantum mechanics and the nature of reality.

Furthermore, the implications of MWI extend beyond the realm of physics. The concept of a multiverse has captured the imagination of philosophers, theologians, and even science fiction writers. It raises profound questions about the nature of existence, the meaning of life, and the uniqueness of our experiences. The potential for an infinite number of realities, each with its own unique set of physical laws and events, challenges our anthropocentric view of the universe and expands our understanding of what is possible. The implications of MWI, whether fully verifiable or not, are arguably as important for their philosophical and metaphysical ramifications as they are for their contribution to a deeper understanding of the quantum world. It is a testament to the far-reaching consequences of exploring the most fundamental aspects of our reality. The pursuit of understanding these implications is likely to continue as long as there remain inquisitive minds pondering the mysteries of the cosmos. The universe, in its quantum strangeness, continues to unveil layer upon layer of complexity, driving our quest for knowledge ever forward.

Other Interpretations of Quantum Mechanics

Beyond the Copenhagen interpretation and the many-worlds interpretation, a rich tapestry of alternative perspectives seeks to unravel the mysteries of quantum mechanics. These interpretations, while often less widely discussed, offer valuable insights and challenge the dominant paradigms, furthering our understanding of the fundamental nature of reality. One such interpretation is the pilot-wave theory, also known as Bohmian mechanics, which offers a deterministic picture of the quantum world, starkly contrasting with the probabilistic nature emphasized by the Copenhagen interpretation.

Pilot-wave theory, developed by David Bohm in the mid-20th century, posits that quantum particles are not merely described by wave functions but are, in fact, guided by them. Each particle has a well-defined trajectory, governed by a guiding equation that links the particle's position to its associated wave function. This wave function acts as a "pilot wave," guiding the particle's motion, effectively determining its path through space and time. Unlike the many-worlds interpretation which avoids wave function collapse by proposing a branching of universes, Bohmian mechanics retains the concept of a single universe, albeit with particles moving along predetermined paths.

The elegance of pilot-wave theory lies in its ability to provide a clear, causal explanation of quantum phenomena. The seemingly random outcomes of quantum experiments are not inherently random according to this theory; they are a consequence of our incomplete knowledge of the initial conditions of the system. If we knew the precise initial position and momentum of every particle, we could, in principle, predict the outcome of any quantum experiment with certainty. This is a deterministic view, significantly different from the probabilistic interpretations of quantum mechanics like the Copenhagen interpretation. The apparent randomness arises from our inability to precisely measure these initial conditions.

The double-slit experiment, a cornerstone of quantum mechanics, finds a natural explanation within the framework of Bohmian mechanics. The electron, guided by its pilot wave, follows a trajectory that interferes with itself, creating the characteristic interference pattern. Even when detectors are introduced to measure which slit the electron passes through, the pilot wave still guides the electron, resulting in a different trajectory, consistent with the observed results.

However, unlike the many-worlds interpretation where multiple universes are posited, in Bohmian mechanics, the electron simply follows a different, predetermined path.

Despite its deterministic and intuitive nature, pilot-wave theory faces its own challenges. One major criticism is the non-locality inherent in the theory. The guiding equation suggests that the pilot wave can influence the particle's trajectory instantaneously, even over large distances. This instantaneous action at a distance raises questions about causality and conflicts with the principle of locality, a cornerstone of classical physics. This non-locality, while mathematically consistent, is conceptually challenging and considered counterintuitive by many physicists.

Another challenge revolves around the ontological status of the pilot wave. While the particle's trajectory is clearly defined, the nature and physical reality of the pilot wave itself remains a subject of debate. It is not directly observable, and its role is primarily mathematical. This somewhat abstract nature of the pilot wave is a point of contention for some physicists who prefer interpretations that only invoke physically observable entities.

Yet another interpretational approach to quantum mechanics is the consistent histories approach. This approach, pioneered by Robert Griffiths, Roland Omnès, and Murray Gell-Mann, focuses on the evolution of quantum systems through time, emphasizing the importance of constructing consistent sets of histories that can be used to describe the system's behavior.

The consistent histories interpretation avoids the explicit mention of wave function collapse. It instead utilizes a formalism where probabilities are assigned to entire sequences of events (histories) spanning a given time interval. A consistent set of histories is a set of histories that, mathematically speaking, do not interfere with each other. This approach shifts the focus from individual events to the probabilities of entire sequences of events, allowing for a more holistic view of the quantum system's evolution.

In this framework, the double-slit experiment can be analyzed by considering consistent sets of histories. One set of histories might correspond to the electron passing through slit A, followed by its detection on the screen. Another set would correspond to the electron passing through slit B and subsequently being detected. The probabilities assigned to each set of histories determine the overall probability distribution of the electron's position on the screen, which aligns with experimental observations. The key is the consistent nature of these histories, preventing contradictory scenarios where the electron simultaneously passes through both slits and only one slit.

The consistent histories approach, while offering an alternative to the problematic wave function collapse, also faces critiques. One issue is the selection of consistent sets of histories, which isn't always unique. Different sets of consistent histories could be constructed, leading to different probability assignments. This ambiguity raises concerns about the objectivity and predictive power of the approach. It implies a certain degree of subjectivity in the interpretation, which many physicists find unsatisfactory.

Furthermore, the consistent histories approach can be mathematically complex, making it challenging to apply in all but the simplest of quantum systems. Its computational difficulties limit its practicality in many real-world applications.

Despite these difficulties, the consistent histories interpretation offers a different perspective on quantum mechanics, emphasizing the evolution of systems through time and the probabilities of entire sequences of events rather than focusing solely on individual measurements or wave function collapse. It provides a valuable addition to the ongoing discourse concerning the fundamental interpretation of quantum mechanics.

In conclusion, the interpretations of quantum mechanics extend far beyond the widely known Copenhagen and many-worlds interpretations. Pilot-wave theory provides a deterministic, albeit non-local, picture of quantum reality, while consistent histories offer a framework that avoids wave function collapse by focusing on consistent sets of historical sequences. Each interpretation carries its strengths and weaknesses, prompting ongoing debates and fostering a deeper exploration into the foundations of quantum mechanics and the very nature of reality itself. The continued exploration of these diverse perspectives, despite inherent challenges and complexities, ultimately enriches our comprehension of this fundamental aspect of the universe. The ongoing quest for a definitive interpretation is not merely an exercise in theoretical physics; it is a profound philosophical inquiry into the nature of existence, knowledge, and our place within the cosmos. The search for a universally accepted interpretation remains a testament to the enduring power of scientific investigation and its capacity to challenge our fundamental assumptions about the world. The journey continues, driven by an unwavering curiosity and a desire to unlock the deepest mysteries of quantum reality. The intricacies of the quantum world invite us to continuously revise our understanding, ensuring that the exploration of its fundamental nature remains a captivating and dynamic area of scientific inquiry, continuously stimulating progress and reshaping our worldview.

Quantum Mechanics and Consciousness

The exploration of quantum mechanics inevitably leads us to a profound and often controversial intersection: the relationship between quantum phenomena and consciousness. The very act of observation in quantum mechanics seems to play a crucial role in determining the outcome of experiments, a fact that has fueled speculation about a deep connection between the observer and the observed. This connection, however, remains a subject of intense debate, spanning scientific inquiry and philosophical contemplation.

At the heart of this debate lies the measurement problem. In classical physics, the act of measurement is generally considered passive; the observer merely extracts information from a pre-existing state of the system. In quantum mechanics, however, the measurement process appears to be far more active, seemingly causing the wave function of the quantum system to collapse into a definite state. Before measurement, a quantum system exists in a superposition of multiple possible states, a concept often illustrated by Schrödinger's cat thought experiment. The act of measurement, however, appears to force the system to "choose" one of these states, resulting in a definite outcome.

This apparent influence of observation on the quantum system raises fundamental questions. Does the conscious observer actively collapse the wave function? Or is the collapse merely a consequence of the interaction between the quantum system and a macroscopic measuring apparatus, regardless of consciousness? There's no universally accepted answer, and various interpretations of quantum mechanics offer different perspectives.

Some interpretations, such as the Copenhagen interpretation, suggest a crucial role for the observer's consciousness in the collapse of the wave function. The act of measurement, performed by a conscious observer, is seen as the defining event that forces the quantum system into a specific state. This perspective, while seemingly intuitive, presents a significant challenge: how do we define "consciousness" in a way that can be scientifically investigated? What about quantum phenomena observed by inanimate detectors? Does the detector possess a form of "consciousness" that enables the wave function collapse?

The many-worlds interpretation, on the other hand, avoids the problem of wave function collapse altogether. It proposes that instead of collapsing into a single state, the quantum system evolves into multiple universes, each representing a different possible outcome. The observer experiences only one of these universes, but all possible outcomes are realized in other branches of reality. This interpretation circumvents the need for a conscious observer to trigger the collapse but introduces the highly speculative concept of a multitude of parallel universes.

Other interpretations, like the objective collapse theories, propose that the wave function collapse is an objective physical process, independent of the observer's consciousness. These theories postulate modifications to the standard quantum mechanics formalism to incorporate spontaneous wave function collapse, thereby eliminating the need for conscious observation. These modifications, however, often involve introducing new parameters and assumptions, which are themselves subject to scrutiny and debate.

The intriguing possibility of a link between quantum mechanics and consciousness has inspired numerous explorations, particularly in the field of quantum mind theories. These theories propose that consciousness itself may be a quantum phenomenon, emerging from the complex interactions of quantum systems within the brain. The brain, with its vast network of interconnected neurons, offers a potentially rich environment for the manifestation of quantum effects. Quantum entanglement, for example, could potentially play a role in coordinating the activity of neurons, giving rise to the integrated nature of consciousness.

However, the biological plausibility of such quantum processes within the brain is a subject of considerable debate. The brain's relatively warm and wet environment poses significant challenges to the maintenance of quantum coherence, the necessary condition for quantum effects to manifest. Environmental decoherence, the interaction of quantum systems with their environment, can quickly destroy delicate quantum states. It remains an open question whether these decoherence effects are sufficiently weak to allow significant quantum effects to play a crucial role in brain function.

Despite the challenges, the potential link between quantum mechanics and consciousness continues to spark interest and research. Some researchers are exploring the possibility of using quantum technologies to investigate brain activity, potentially revealing clues about the role of quantum phenomena in consciousness. Others are exploring theoretical frameworks that integrate quantum mechanics and neuroscience, aiming to bridge the gap between the microscopic world of quantum physics and the macroscopic world of the brain.

Furthermore, the philosophical implications of linking quantum mechanics and consciousness are profound. If consciousness does play a fundamental role in quantum mechanics, it would challenge our understanding of the universe as a purely physical system. It could suggest a more active role for consciousness in shaping reality, a perspective that resonates with certain spiritual traditions. This, however, doesn't necessarily imply a rejection of scientific materialism. Instead, it might suggest that our current understanding of materialism needs to be refined to accommodate the potentially fundamental role of consciousness.

The relationship between quantum mechanics and consciousness remains an open frontier of scientific and philosophical inquiry. The experimental evidence remains inconclusive, and many theoretical challenges remain unresolved. However, the very nature of the question compels us to explore the boundaries of our understanding, prompting us to re-evaluate our conceptions of reality, consciousness, and the fundamental interplay between the observer and the observed. The search for a deeper understanding of this connection continues to drive innovative research, fostering a rich interplay between scientific inquiry and philosophical contemplation, ultimately enriching our view of the universe and our place within it. The continued exploration of this enigmatic relationship promises to further our understanding not only of the quantum world, but also the very nature of consciousness itself, potentially leading to revolutionary insights into the fundamental structure of reality. The enduring mystery underscores the continuous need for rigorous investigation and open-minded speculation, reminding us that the greatest scientific breakthroughs often arise at the intersection of the seemingly disparate fields of inquiry.

CHAPTER 11

Black Holes and Wormholes

The Physics of Black Holes

The exploration of the cosmos inevitably leads us to some of its most enigmatic and fascinating objects: black holes. These cosmic titans, born from the remnants of massive stars, represent a profound intersection of gravity, spacetime, and the very limits of our understanding of the universe. Their physics is a testament to the power and elegance of Einstein's theory of general relativity, yet they also pose some of the most challenging questions for theoretical physics, pushing us to confront the limitations of our current frameworks.

The formation of a black hole begins with the death of a star. Stars, throughout their lives, maintain a delicate balance between the inward pull of gravity and the outward pressure generated by nuclear fusion in their cores. This fusion process converts hydrogen into helium, releasing immense amounts of energy that counteracts the crushing force of gravity. However, when a star exhausts its nuclear fuel, this delicate equilibrium is shattered. For stars many times more massive than our Sun, the gravitational collapse is unstoppable.

The process is dramatic and violent. As the star's core collapses, the density increases exponentially. Electrons are forced into protons, forming neutrons and releasing a colossal burst of neutrinos. This process, known as neutronization, is followed by a cataclysmic supernova explosion, a brilliant spectacle that briefly outshines entire galaxies. The outer layers of the star are flung into space, while the core continues its relentless inward journey. If the core's mass exceeds a critical limit, known as the Tolman-Oppenheimer-Volkoff limit (approximately three solar masses), no known force can halt the collapse. The core continues to shrink, its density rising toward infinity, ultimately becoming a singularity – a point of infinite density and spacetime curvature.

Surrounding this singularity is the event horizon, a boundary of no return. Once an object crosses the event horizon, it is trapped within the black hole's gravitational grip, destined to eventually reach the singularity. The event horizon isn't a physical surface but rather a theoretical boundary defined by the escape velocity exceeding the speed of light. Nothing, not even light, can escape from within the event horizon. This is the defining characteristic of a black hole, and the source of its name.

The size of the event horizon is determined by the black hole's mass. The larger the mass, the larger the event horizon's radius, a relationship described by the Schwarzschild radius: $R = 2GM/c^2$, where G is the gravitational constant, M is the black hole's mass, and c is the speed of light. A black hole with the mass of our Sun would have an event horizon with a radius of just under three kilometers. Supermassive black holes, residing at the centers of galaxies, can have masses millions or even billions of times the mass of our Sun, resulting in event horizons that span astronomical distances.

The singularity at the black hole's center is a region where the laws of physics as we know them break down. General relativity predicts infinite density and curvature, rendering our current understanding of gravity inadequate. Quantum mechanics, which governs the behavior of matter at very small scales, is also expected to play a crucial role in understanding the singularity, but a complete quantum theory of gravity remains one of the most significant challenges in theoretical physics. Many theories propose a quantum resolution to the singularity, suggesting that the infinite density is an artifact of classical general relativity, and that the true nature of the singularity is far more subtle and complex.

Despite their name, black holes are not truly "black" in the sense of being completely invisible. In 1974, Stephen Hawking made a groundbreaking contribution to black hole physics by demonstrating that black holes are not perfectly black. He showed that due to quantum effects near the event horizon, black holes emit thermal radiation, known as Hawking radiation. This radiation is extremely faint, and its intensity is inversely proportional to the black hole's mass. Larger black holes emit radiation at a slower rate than smaller ones, meaning it would take an incredibly long time, potentially longer than the current age of the universe, for a large black hole to completely evaporate through Hawking radiation. This process, while theoretically predicted, has not yet been directly observed.

The observation of black holes presents significant challenges. Their nature – the absence of light escaping the event horizon – makes direct visual observation impossible. However, indirect methods provide compelling evidence for their existence. Astronomers can observe the effects of black holes on their surroundings. The intense gravity of a black hole can distort the light from stars and galaxies behind it, a phenomenon known as gravitational lensing. Furthermore, the accretion of matter onto a black hole can create extremely hot and luminous accretion disks, detectable across vast cosmic distances. The intense gravitational forces can also accelerate particles to near light speeds, generating powerful jets of matter and radiation that extend for light-years. These jets are often observed in active galactic nuclei, where supermassive black holes are thought to reside.

Observations of the orbits of stars around the center of our own galaxy, the Milky Way, provide strong evidence for the presence of a supermassive black hole at its core. The high orbital velocities of these stars suggest a concentrated mass far exceeding that which can be accounted for by visible matter. This provides compelling circumstantial evidence of a supermassive black hole's presence.

Furthermore, the detection of gravitational waves, ripples in spacetime, provides direct confirmation of black hole mergers. These events, predicted by general relativity, involve the collision and merging of two black holes, releasing a tremendous amount of energy in the form of gravitational waves. The detection of these waves by observatories such as LIGO and Virgo has opened a new window into the universe and provided concrete evidence for the existence and dynamics of black holes.

The physics of black holes remains a dynamic and evolving field. Numerous mysteries persist, pushing the boundaries of our understanding of gravity, spacetime, and quantum mechanics. The exploration of these cosmic enigmas continues to drive innovation in theoretical and observational astronomy, promising to unlock deeper secrets about the universe's structure and evolution. The interplay between general relativity and quantum mechanics, particularly in the context of Hawking radiation and the nature of singularities, presents an ongoing challenge that demands new theoretical frameworks and innovative experimental approaches. The continued investigation into these enigmatic objects promises not only a deeper understanding of the cosmos but also a profound advancement in our fundamental knowledge of the physical laws governing the universe. The quest to unravel the secrets of black holes is a journey to the very edge of known physics, and the discoveries yet to be made promise to be as revolutionary and awe-inspiring as those that have already been achieved.

Wormholes and Traversable Wormholes

The seemingly impenetrable nature of black holes, their singularity swallowing everything within their event horizons, naturally leads us to contemplate the possibility of other, perhaps less absolute, connections within the fabric of spacetime. This brings us to the fascinating, yet largely theoretical, concept of wormholes. Imagine a tunnel, not through physical space, but through spacetime itself, connecting vastly distant regions of the universe or even different universes entirely. This is the essence of a wormhole, a hypothetical structure predicted by Einstein's theory of general relativity, though its existence remains firmly in the realm of speculation.

The mathematical description of wormholes arises from solutions to Einstein's field equations, the equations that describe the curvature of spacetime due to the presence of mass and energy. One such solution, the Schwarzschild metric, describes the spacetime around a non-rotating, uncharged black hole. However, extensions and modifications of this metric, incorporating concepts like exotic matter with negative mass-energy density, can lead to solutions that exhibit wormhole-like structures. These solutions depict a tunnel connecting two distinct regions of spacetime, often visualized as two separate mouths, each residing in a different region of the universe.

The physics of wormholes is far from straightforward. The "throat" of the wormhole, the tunnel connecting the two mouths, is characterized by an intense gravitational field and highly warped spacetime. The properties of this throat are crucial in determining whether a wormhole would be traversable. A non-traversable wormhole would collapse before any object could pass through it, effectively serving as nothing more than a theoretical curiosity. A traversable wormhole, on the other hand, would remain open and stable, permitting the passage of matter and information between its mouths. This is where the concept of exotic matter comes into play.

Exotic matter is a hypothetical form of matter with negative mass-energy density. This is a concept that defies our everyday intuition, as ordinary matter always possesses positive mass-energy density. However, according to general relativity, exotic matter could exert a repulsive gravitational force, counteracting the tendency of the wormhole's throat to collapse. In essence, exotic matter would act as a kind of "scaffolding," holding the wormhole open and preventing its closure.

The challenge, however, is that the existence of exotic matter is purely hypothetical. There is no observational evidence supporting its existence, and its properties are largely unknown. Whether exotic matter could even exist under any conceivable physical conditions is a central question in theoretical physics. Furthermore, even if exotic matter existed, the sheer amount required to stabilize a traversable wormhole would be astronomical. The energy requirements would be so immense that it's currently beyond our technological capabilities to even begin to contemplate manipulating spacetime in such a way.

Beyond the challenge of exotic matter, the stability of traversable wormholes poses significant problems. Even if we could create a wormhole using exotic matter, maintaining its stability over time presents another monumental hurdle. The slightest perturbation could cause the wormhole to collapse, trapping anything inside. The dynamics of spacetime within the wormhole throat are extremely complex and highly susceptible to instability, making the creation of a stable, traversable wormhole an exceedingly difficult task.

Moreover, the very idea of traversing a wormhole raises intriguing questions regarding causality and time travel. If a wormhole connects two widely separated points in spacetime, it might be possible, theoretically, to travel faster than light. This is not a violation of special relativity because one is not moving through space faster than light, but rather taking a shortcut through spacetime. However, the possibility of time travel introduces paradoxes, such as the famous "grandfather paradox," where one could go back in time and prevent their own birth. Resolving these paradoxes requires a deeper understanding of the nature of spacetime and causality, pushing the boundaries of our current understanding of physics.

The potential implications of traversable wormholes, however, are staggering. If we could overcome the immense technological and theoretical challenges, it would revolutionize interstellar travel. The vast distances between stars and galaxies would no longer be insurmountable obstacles. Instead of traveling at near light speed for centuries, a traversable wormhole could provide a shortcut, allowing interstellar travel within a human lifetime. Such a capability would have a profound impact on humanity's exploration of the cosmos and our understanding of the universe's structure and evolution.

However, the possibility of manipulating spacetime on such a grand scale raises ethical and philosophical considerations. The ability to traverse vast distances instantly raises questions about the potential for uncontrolled exploration, potential unforeseen consequences for other civilizations, and the potential for misuse. The concept of wormholes touches upon the very fabric of reality and raises profound questions about our place within the cosmos. Is the universe fundamentally connected by these hidden pathways? Do they connect different regions of our universe, or do they lead to other universes altogether?

The study of wormholes highlights the limitations of our current understanding of physics. The theoretical frameworks we have, while remarkably successful in explaining many phenomena, are not adequate to deal with the extreme conditions present in wormholes. A complete theory of quantum gravity, that would unify general relativity and quantum mechanics, is crucial for a deeper understanding of wormholes and their behavior. The very existence of traversable wormholes might depend on the unknown physics at the Planck scale, where the effects of quantum gravity are expected to become significant.

In conclusion, wormholes remain a captivating, yet speculative, concept in theoretical physics. While mathematically possible within the framework of general relativity, their existence depends on the existence of exotic matter and our ability to overcome significant technological and theoretical challenges. Even if traversable wormholes exist, their stability and the potential for time travel raise profound philosophical and scientific questions.

Nevertheless, the exploration of wormholes continues to be an important area of research, pushing the boundaries of our understanding of spacetime, gravity, and the fundamental nature of the universe. The quest to understand wormholes is not only a quest to understand the universe but also a journey into the depths of our own imagination and the limits of our scientific understanding. It represents a fascinating frontier where science and philosophy intertwine, pushing us to consider possibilities that were once confined to the realm of science fiction and expanding our understanding of the extraordinary possibilities that might underlie the seemingly ordinary fabric of spacetime. The ongoing research and theoretical developments in this field promise to illuminate the deepest mysteries of the universe and challenge our assumptions about the very nature of reality. The road to understanding wormholes is paved with both theoretical breakthroughs and technological innovations, a journey that holds the potential to reshape our perception of the cosmos and our place within it.

Black Holes as Portals

The exploration of wormholes naturally leads us to contemplate a more radical possibility: could black holes themselves serve as portals? While the idea of a black hole as a one-way ticket to oblivion remains firmly entrenched in our understanding, the sheer strangeness of these cosmic behemoths allows for the possibility of more complex, even counter-intuitive, behaviors. The singularity at the heart of a black hole, a point of infinite density, defies our current understanding of physics. It's within this realm of the unknown that the concept of black holes as portals gains traction.

The standard model of black hole formation involves the gravitational collapse of a massive star. As the star exhausts its nuclear fuel, the inward pull of gravity overcomes the outward pressure, leading to an unstoppable implosion. Matter is compressed into an increasingly smaller volume, eventually reaching a point of infinite density, the singularity. Surrounding the singularity is the event horizon, a boundary beyond which nothing, not even light, can escape. This is the point of no return, traditionally viewed as the absolute end of a journey into the black hole.

However, some theoretical models propose alternative scenarios. One intriguing possibility involves the concept of a "white hole," a hypothetical celestial object that is, in a sense, the time-reversed counterpart of a black hole. While black holes relentlessly suck in matter, white holes are hypothesized to spew it out. Some theories suggest that a black hole in one region of spacetime could be connected to a white hole in another, potentially forming a wormhole-like structure. The journey through the black hole would be perilous, subjected to extreme gravitational tides and potentially even quantum effects we don't yet understand, but theoretically, the "other side" could be a different region of spacetime, perhaps even another universe entirely.

This concept, however, is fraught with challenges. Our current understanding of physics, specifically the lack of a complete theory of quantum gravity, severely limits our ability to model the conditions within a black hole and the potential connection to a white hole. The extreme gravitational forces near the singularity are predicted to warp spacetime to an unimaginable degree, potentially causing a breakdown of our established physical laws. The processes involved, if they even exist, operate on scales far beyond our observational capabilities. We lack the experimental data necessary to even begin to test the validity of such a theory.

Further complicating matters is the nature of the singularity itself. It's not simply a point of extreme density; it represents a breakdown of our current models of spacetime. Our best theories of gravity, namely Einstein's general relativity, predict infinite density and curvature at the singularity, suggesting that these theories are incomplete and need modification at this scale. A quantum theory of gravity is needed to fully describe the processes happening at the

Planck scale, where quantum effects dominate, and possibly provide insight into the behavior of singularities.

Even if we could somehow overcome the limitations of our current understanding, the practical difficulties are insurmountable. Traveling through a black hole would be a terrifying ordeal. The gravitational tides, caused by the immense difference in gravitational pull on different parts of an object, would likely tear apart any spacecraft or, indeed, any object long before it reaches the singularity. Furthermore, the nature of the journey is uncertain. Would it even be a continuous journey? Could the information about the traveler and their ship survive the trip? Could there even be a traveler left at the end?

Beyond the physical challenges, the philosophical implications are equally profound. If black holes do act as portals to other universes or vastly distant regions of our own, the consequences are almost unimaginable. It would completely rewrite our understanding of the universe's structure, its connectivity, and our place within it. It would open up the possibility of inter-universal travel, raising ethical and existential questions beyond anything we currently contemplate.

The possibility of such portals challenges our established notions of causality and time. Could these portals lead to regions of spacetime where the laws of physics are different or even reversed? Could travel through such portals lead to temporal paradoxes, such as backward time travel? These questions challenge not only our scientific understanding but our fundamental philosophical conceptions of reality and the nature of time itself.

The speculative nature of this concept is undeniable. Currently, there is no direct observational evidence to support the idea of black holes acting as portals. However, the very existence of black holes, objects so bizarre and extreme, compels us to consider the possibility of unexpected behavior and connections within the fabric of spacetime.

The exploration of this idea continues to be a driving force in theoretical physics. New theoretical models and advanced computational techniques are continually being developed to better understand the dynamics of black holes and the potential implications for the structure of spacetime. The quest to unravel the mysteries of black holes, and the possibility of their connection to other universes, remains one of the most exciting and challenging frontiers in modern physics. It represents a truly interdisciplinary pursuit, requiring collaboration between physicists, mathematicians, cosmologists, and even philosophers, to fully comprehend the implications of such a profound concept.

The pursuit of knowledge about black holes and their potential function as portals is not merely an academic exercise. It's a fundamental quest to understand the universe at its most extreme limits, where our established laws of physics may break down and new, unforeseen possibilities emerge. The implications of discovering such a connection extend far beyond our scientific understanding; it would challenge our philosophical conceptions and reshape our understanding of our place in the cosmos.

While currently, it remains purely speculative, the pursuit of knowledge about the potential for black holes to act as portals to other universes or distant regions of spacetime continues to push the boundaries of human understanding. It fuels our imagination and inspires us to continually question our current models of reality, to seek new solutions, and to explore the previously inconceivable aspects of the cosmos. This quest will necessitate not only breakthroughs in theoretical physics, but also technological advancements capable of testing these theories experimentally. Perhaps one day, what now seems like science fiction will become scientific reality, and we will be able to look to black holes not as the endpoints of journeys, but as gateways to the unimaginably vast expanse of the universe and beyond. The journey towards understanding, however, is the journey itself, and the possibilities it holds are as limitless as the cosmos we are striving to understand. The unanswered questions fuel the ongoing exploration, promising a future rich in discovery and a deeper appreciation of the extraordinary complexity and beauty of the universe. The very act of contemplating these possibilities expands our understanding of what is possible, and pushes us further towards the answers we so desperately seek.

Black Holes and Information Paradox

The preceding discussion of black holes as potential portals naturally leads us to one of the most profound and enduring mysteries in modern physics: the black hole information paradox. This paradox highlights a fundamental conflict between two of our most successful and well-tested theories: general relativity, which describes gravity and the large-scale structure of the universe, and quantum mechanics, which governs the behavior of matter at the atomic and subatomic levels. At the heart of the paradox lies the question of what happens to the information contained within matter that falls into a black hole.

According to general relativity, a black hole is characterized by its mass, charge, and angular momentum. These are the only properties that are observable from the outside. Once matter crosses the event horizon, the point of no return, it appears to disappear from our universe, its fate seemingly sealed within the singularity. This suggests a loss of information, as the detailed structure and composition of the infalling matter is irretrievably lost. This conclusion, however, directly contradicts a fundamental principle of quantum mechanics: the unitarity of quantum evolution.

Quantum mechanics postulates that information is never truly lost. The evolution of a quantum system is described by a unitary operator, which ensures that the information describing the system at one time is completely and deterministically encoded in its description at any other time. This principle implies that the information contained within the infalling matter must somehow be preserved, even after it crosses the event horizon. The apparent conflict between the loss of information implied by general relativity and the preservation of information demanded by quantum mechanics constitutes the information paradox.

One of the earliest attempts to grapple with this paradox came from Stephen Hawking. Hawking's work, particularly his calculations of black hole radiation, initially seemed to support the idea of information loss. He showed that black holes aren't truly black; they emit a faint thermal radiation, now known as Hawking radiation, due to quantum effects near the event horizon. This radiation is characterized by a temperature inversely proportional to the black hole's mass, implying that the black hole gradually evaporates over time. Initially, Hawking suggested that this evaporation process resulted in a complete loss of information about the infalling matter.

However, this conclusion sparked intense debate within the physics community. The loss of information would violate the fundamental principles of quantum mechanics, potentially leading to inconsistencies and paradoxes throughout the theoretical framework of physics. The implication is that the laws of physics would not be time-reversible, which would have profound consequences. The implication of information loss is even more significant when considering the potential for black holes to be gateways to other universes or different regions of spacetime. If information is truly lost, what does that mean for any information traveling through such a portal? Could information be destroyed, rewritten or altered irrevocably? The very nature of information, and the potential for its preservation or destruction, becomes a crucial part of understanding the nature of black holes and wormholes.

Over the years, several attempts have been made to resolve the information paradox. One prominent approach involves the concept of quantum entanglement. Entanglement is a quantum phenomenon where two or more particles become linked in such a way that their fates are intertwined, regardless of the distance separating them. Some theorists suggest that the information lost behind the event horizon isn't actually destroyed but is instead encoded in the correlations between the outgoing Hawking radiation and the remaining black hole. In this scenario, the information isn't directly accessible, but it's still fundamentally preserved within the entangled system. This viewpoint implies that the apparent loss is an illusion resulting from the limitations of our observations from outside the event horizon.

Other attempts to resolve the information paradox involve revisiting our understanding of gravity and black hole singularities. Perhaps our current theories of gravity, based on general relativity, are inadequate to describe the conditions at the heart of a black hole. A complete quantum theory of gravity, which is still elusive, may be necessary to fully reconcile the apparent conflict between general relativity and quantum mechanics. This theory might provide a more accurate description of what happens to information at the singularity, potentially resolving the information paradox. The exploration of quantum gravity has led to numerous alternative theoretical frameworks, including string theory and loop quantum gravity, each attempting to provide a unified description of all fundamental forces, including gravity, at the quantum level.

The implications of the information paradox extend far beyond the realm of theoretical physics. It challenges our fundamental understanding of information itself and its role in the universe. Is information a fundamental quantity, like energy or momentum? Does it have a physical existence, or is it merely an abstract concept? The resolution of this paradox may provide crucial insights into the nature of information and its relation to the fundamental laws of physics. The paradox underscores the interconnectedness of seemingly disparate branches of physics and the need for a more unified understanding of the universe.

Furthermore, the search for a solution to the information paradox has driven significant advancements in our understanding of black holes and quantum gravity. It has motivated the development of new mathematical tools and theoretical frameworks, pushing the boundaries of our understanding of the universe at its most extreme scales. The exploration of this paradox has also encouraged interdisciplinary collaborations, bringing together experts from various fields of physics, mathematics, and even philosophy to tackle this challenging problem.

The black hole information paradox stands as a testament to the limits of our current knowledge and the need for further exploration. It represents a frontier in physics where our most successful theories clash, demanding a new level of understanding to resolve the apparent conflict. The resolution of this paradox will not only enhance our understanding of black holes and the nature of spacetime but could also fundamentally reshape our understanding of the universe, the nature of reality, and the fundamental laws that govern it. While the solution remains elusive, the quest to find it continues to inspire and drive innovative research in theoretical physics, propelling us closer to a more comprehensive and unified view of the cosmos. The journey itself, the continued questioning and exploration, is as vital as the potential answers. The search for a solution to this paradox compels us to reconsider the very foundations of our understanding, leading to a deeper, more nuanced comprehension of the universe and our place within it.

Future Research on Black Holes and Wormholes

The quest to understand black holes and wormholes is far from over. Indeed, the mysteries surrounding these enigmatic objects continue to fuel a vibrant and expanding field of research, pushing the boundaries of both theoretical physics and observational astronomy. The coming decades promise a wealth of new data and theoretical insights that may dramatically alter our understanding of these cosmic behemoths and their potential roles in the universe's grand design.

One of the most promising avenues for future research involves the ongoing and planned observational efforts to directly detect and characterize black holes. Gravitational wave astronomy, inaugurated by the groundbreaking discoveries of LIGO and Virgo, has opened a new window onto the universe, allowing us to "hear" the mergers of black holes and neutron stars. These observations not only confirm the existence of black holes but also provide invaluable data on their masses, spins, and orbital dynamics. Future generations of gravitational wave detectors, such as the Einstein Telescope and Cosmic Explorer, promise even greater sensitivity, allowing us to detect mergers at greater distances and with higher precision. This increased sensitivity will reveal a wider range of black hole masses and spins, potentially uncovering unexpected populations and shedding light on their formation mechanisms.

Beyond gravitational waves, electromagnetic observations play a crucial role in studying black holes. Observations of active galactic nuclei (AGN), powered by supermassive black holes at the centers of galaxies, provide insights into the accretion processes and feedback mechanisms that govern the growth of these behemoths. Advanced telescopes, such as the James Webb Space Telescope and the Extremely Large Telescope, offer unprecedented resolution and sensitivity, enabling detailed studies of the regions surrounding black holes. These observations can reveal the structure of accretion disks, the properties of relativistic jets, and the influence of black holes on the surrounding interstellar medium. These observations will help us test our theoretical models of black hole accretion and elucidate the complex interplay between black holes and their host galaxies.

The Event Horizon Telescope (EHT) has already achieved remarkable success in directly imaging the shadow of the supermassive black hole at the center of the galaxy M87. Future observations with the EHT and its planned upgrades will allow for even sharper images, potentially revealing details of the black hole's event horizon and providing stringent tests of general relativity in the strong gravitational field regime. Furthermore, the EHT collaboration is planning to image the supermassive black hole at the center of our own galaxy, Sagittarius A, providing a unique opportunity to compare and contrast the properties of black holes in different environments. This comparative approach will help us understand the universality (or lack thereof) of black hole properties.

The theoretical landscape of black hole research is equally vibrant. The black hole information paradox, discussed earlier, continues to challenge our fundamental understanding of gravity and quantum mechanics. The development of a complete quantum theory of gravity remains one of the most significant unsolved problems in theoretical physics. String theory, loop quantum gravity, and other approaches offer promising avenues to tackle this problem, and their implications for black holes are profound.

A complete quantum theory of gravity might resolve the information paradox by providing a more accurate description of what happens to information at the singularity, allowing for a reconciliation of general relativity and quantum mechanics. This reconciliation would have major implications for our understanding of the universe at its most extreme scales and the nature of information itself.

The study of wormholes, hypothetical tunnels through spacetime, remains highly speculative, but it continues to inspire intriguing theoretical investigations. The existence of wormholes is predicted by Einstein's theory of general relativity, although their stability and traversability are major questions. The development of new mathematical techniques and computational tools might allow for more realistic simulations of wormhole formation and evolution. Such simulations might reveal the conditions necessary for traversable wormholes to exist, potentially opening avenues for interstellar travel and communication.

Technological advancements are crucial to progress in the study of black holes and wormholes. The development of more sensitive gravitational wave detectors, advanced telescopes, and powerful supercomputers are all essential for pushing the boundaries of our understanding. The development of new algorithms for data analysis, including machine learning techniques, will be critical in processing and interpreting the vast amounts of data generated by these instruments. These technological advancements, coupled with ongoing theoretical breakthroughs, will enable new discoveries and deeper insights into the nature of black holes and wormholes.

Furthermore, the exploration of black holes and wormholes has profound implications for our understanding of the universe's evolution and structure. The formation and growth of black holes are intimately linked to the formation of galaxies and the distribution of matter in the universe. The properties of black holes can provide clues about the early universe and the conditions that led to the formation of stars and galaxies. The potential existence of wormholes opens up the possibility of connections between different regions of spacetime, or even different universes, although these remain speculative and highly theoretical.

The study of black holes and wormholes is not merely a theoretical exercise; it has potential technological implications as well. While traversable wormholes remain firmly in the realm of science fiction for now, our understanding of black holes can help in developing technologies related to gravity and spacetime manipulation. The study of Hawking radiation might inspire new approaches to energy generation, although this remains highly speculative at this stage.

Beyond the specific research avenues already outlined, there's also the potential for entirely unexpected discoveries. The history of science is replete with instances where unforeseen observations have revolutionized our understanding of the universe. Our current theoretical models, while successful in many respects, might be incomplete or inaccurate in ways we cannot yet fathom. Therefore, a significant portion of future research will inevitably involve exploring the unknown, driven by curiosity and a willingness to embrace the unexpected.

The exploration of black holes and wormholes is a journey into the heart of the cosmos, a quest to unravel some of the universe's most profound mysteries. The future of this research will depend on a synergistic interplay between observational astronomy, theoretical physics, and technological innovation. By combining the power of advanced telescopes, sensitive detectors, and powerful computational tools, researchers can unravel the intricate secrets of these enigmatic objects, potentially unlocking profound insights into the nature of gravity, spacetime, and the universe itself. The journey will undoubtedly be challenging, but the potential rewards – a deeper understanding of the cosmos and our place within it – make it an endeavor well worth pursuing. The pursuit of knowledge about black holes and wormholes is not simply about satisfying scientific curiosity; it is about deepening our understanding of the very fabric of reality, challenging existing paradigms, and possibly even unlocking technologies previously relegated to the realms of science fiction. The potential for discovery in this field remains immense, promising exciting new breakthroughs in the years and decades to come. The journey of exploration is, in itself, a testament to human ingenuity and the relentless pursuit of understanding the universe we inhabit.

CHAPTER 12

The Nature of Reality

Reconciling Different Perspectives

Reconciling seemingly disparate perspectives on the nature of reality—scientific, philosophical, and spiritual—is a complex but rewarding endeavor. Throughout this book, we've explored a range of models, from the elegant equations of quantum physics to the profound insights of contemplative traditions. While the languages differ, the underlying questions remain remarkably consistent: What is the fundamental nature of reality? What is the role of consciousness in the universe? And what is our place within this grand cosmic tapestry?

One common thread linking these diverse perspectives is the acknowledgment of a fundamental interconnectedness. Modern physics, particularly quantum mechanics, challenges the classical Newtonian view of a universe composed of separate, independent objects. The principle of entanglement, for example, demonstrates that certain particles can be linked in such a way that their fates are intertwined, regardless of the distance separating them. This suggests a deeper level of interconnectedness than previously imagined, a reality where seemingly disparate parts of the universe are inextricably linked. This resonates deeply with many spiritual traditions that emphasize the unity of all things, the interconnectedness of beings, and the holistic nature of existence.

Consider the concept of "non-locality" in quantum physics. This concept, often described as "spooky action at a distance" by Einstein, highlights that entangled particles can instantaneously influence each other, even across vast distances. This defies our classical understanding of causality and locality. While the precise mechanisms remain a subject of ongoing debate, the implications are profound: the universe may not be as compartmentalized as we once believed. This echoes the holistic worldview found in many spiritual traditions, which posit an underlying unity or interconnectedness that transcends the apparent separation of individual entities. The universe, in this view, is not a collection of independent parts but a single, interconnected whole.

Furthermore, the limitations of scientific observation and measurement themselves point towards the limitations of our current understanding of reality. The act of observation in quantum mechanics inevitably alters the observed system, blurring the lines between the observer and the observed. This raises profound questions about the role of consciousness in shaping our perception of reality. Is consciousness merely a byproduct of complex physical processes, or does it play a more fundamental role in shaping the universe itself? This is a question that occupies both scientists and spiritual thinkers alike.

Spiritual traditions often posit a connection between consciousness and the universe, sometimes suggesting that consciousness is not merely a product of the physical world but rather an intrinsic aspect of it. Some interpretations of quantum mechanics, while not explicitly endorsing a spiritual view, nonetheless suggest that the role of the observer is crucial in shaping the observed reality. While these are not direct equivalences, the convergence of these ideas points to a potential area where science and spirituality might find common ground.

Another area of convergence lies in the exploration of the nature of time. In physics, the concept of time is often treated as a linear progression, a continuous flow from past to present to future. However, some interpretations of quantum mechanics and theories of spacetime suggest that time may be less absolute and more fluid than traditionally assumed. Certain experiments suggest a blurring of the boundaries between past, present, and future. This again echoes certain spiritual perspectives, which view time as cyclical or non-linear, emphasizing the interconnectedness of all moments.

Similarly, the concept of "emergence" in complex systems offers a compelling framework for bridging the gap between scientific and spiritual views. Emergence refers to the way in which complex systems exhibit properties not readily predictable from the properties of their individual components. For example, the consciousness of a human being emerges from the complex interactions of countless neurons in the brain, but it is not a property that can be fully reduced to the properties of individual neurons. Similarly, the holistic properties of the universe—its beauty, complexity, and apparent intentionality—might emerge from the interactions of fundamental physical laws and forces, but they are not reducible to those laws themselves. This resonates with the concept of a transcendent reality that encompasses but is not entirely explained by its physical components.

The exploration of altered states of consciousness, through practices like meditation or psychedelic experiences, also provides a fascinating avenue for exploring the boundaries of ordinary perception. While these experiences are subjective and not easily quantifiable by scientific methods, they often report a sense of expanded awareness, interconnectedness, and unity with the universe, feelings which echo those reported in spiritual traditions. While science might strive for objectivity, acknowledging the subjective nature of conscious experience is crucial for a truly comprehensive understanding of reality. These experiences suggest the existence of levels of reality beyond the grasp of ordinary sensory perception. The challenge lies in finding ways to integrate these subjective experiences into a more complete understanding of the universe.

The study of near-death experiences (NDEs) provides yet another avenue for investigating the nature of consciousness and its relationship to the physical world. While the scientific explanations for NDEs remain debated, the common themes of out-of-body experiences, encounters with deceased loved ones, and feelings of profound peace and unity suggest a potential realm of consciousness that extends beyond the confines of the physical body. These accounts, while not definitive proof of an afterlife or a non-physical realm of consciousness, nonetheless prompt us to consider the limitations of our current understanding of consciousness and its potential to transcend the boundaries of the physical world.

Furthermore, the exploration of the universe at its largest scales, from the vastness of intergalactic space to the cosmic microwave background radiation, continues to push the boundaries of our understanding. The Big Bang theory, while a remarkably successful model, still leaves many questions unanswered about the very origins of the universe and the nature of space and time. The mystery of dark matter and dark energy, which constitute the vast majority of the universe's mass-energy content, also emphasizes the limitations of our current knowledge. This vastness and the unanswered questions resonate with the awe and mystery often associated with spiritual experiences. The scale of the cosmos humbles us and invites us to consider perspectives that extend beyond our current limitations.

In conclusion, reconciling seemingly disparate perspectives on reality involves acknowledging the strengths and limitations of each approach. Science offers rigorous methods for investigating the physical world, while philosophy and spirituality offer frameworks for exploring the deeper questions about existence, consciousness, and the nature of reality. By engaging with these different perspectives respectfully and critically, we can begin to build a more comprehensive and nuanced understanding of the universe and our place within it. The search for truth is a continuous journey, and embracing the diverse pathways to understanding is crucial for our ongoing exploration. It is not a matter of choosing one perspective over another, but of integrating different insights to create a richer and more holistic understanding. The universe, in all its complexity and mystery, continues to invite us to explore, question, and strive for a deeper understanding of the reality that we inhabit.

The preceding chapters have explored a tapestry woven from the threads of science, philosophy, and spirituality, attempting to unravel the enigma of reality. We've journeyed through the quantum realm, delved into the intricacies of consciousness, and considered the vast expanse of the cosmos. However, our exploration has inevitably unearthed more questions than answers, revealing the profound limitations of our current understanding. This is not a failure, but rather a testament to the immensity and complexity of the subject matter. The nature of reality is not a problem to be solved, but a mystery to be perpetually investigated.

One of the most persistent and challenging questions revolves around the nature of consciousness. While neuroscience has made remarkable strides in mapping the brain and understanding its functions, the subjective experience of consciousness—the "what it's like" aspect—remains a formidable enigma. The "hard problem of consciousness," as philosopher David Chalmers famously termed it, asks how physical processes in the brain give rise to subjective experience. Is consciousness merely an emergent property of complex neural networks, or does it possess a more fundamental, perhaps even non-physical, aspect? Materialist approaches strive to explain consciousness solely in terms of physical processes, whereas other perspectives posit a deeper connection between consciousness and the universe itself, perhaps suggesting that consciousness is not merely a *product* of the universe but an intrinsic aspect of its very fabric. This debate remains unresolved, fueling ongoing research in both neuroscience and philosophy of mind.

Furthermore, the interpretation of quantum mechanics continues to be a source of lively debate. While the mathematical framework of quantum mechanics is remarkably successful in predicting experimental results, its philosophical implications remain intensely debated. The role of the observer, the nature of wave-particle duality, and the concept of entanglement continue to spark controversy and inspire a multitude of interpretations, ranging from the Copenhagen interpretation to many-worlds interpretations. Some interpret these peculiarities as evidence for a more participatory role of consciousness in shaping reality, suggesting that the act of observation fundamentally influences the observed system. Others maintain that these are simply features of the quantum world that need not imply any special role for consciousness. The ongoing quest to reconcile the bizarre phenomena of quantum mechanics with our everyday classical experience is a central theme in the philosophy of physics and promises to continue for years to come.

The nature of time is another area riddled with unanswered questions. In classical physics, time is often considered a linear and absolute entity, a universal backdrop against which events unfold. However, Einstein's theory of relativity demonstrates that time is relative, affected by gravity and the speed of motion. Furthermore, certain interpretations of quantum mechanics, as well as some theoretical models of spacetime, suggest that the past, present, and future might not be as distinct as we intuitively perceive them to be. Some theories, such as loop quantum gravity, even propose a granular or quantized nature of time, challenging the classical notion of a smooth, continuous flow. These considerations raise profound questions about the nature of causality, free will, and the very structure of our reality. Does time truly flow, or is it merely an illusion, a subjective construction of our consciousness? These questions remain open to debate and ongoing investigation.

The vastness of the cosmos, as revealed by modern astronomy, also presents us with a humbling reminder of the limitations of our current knowledge. While the Big Bang theory provides a compelling model for the evolution of the universe, many fundamental questions remain unanswered. The nature of dark matter and dark energy, which comprise the vast majority of the universe's mass-energy content, remains a profound mystery. The very origins of the universe, the initial conditions of the Big Bang, and the ultimate fate of the cosmos are all subjects of ongoing speculation and research. The ongoing search for answers through observational astronomy and theoretical cosmology suggests that there is much more to the universe than we currently understand. The cosmic scale of existence invites us to engage in contemplative inquiry, recognizing the breadth of what remains unknown.

Beyond the frontiers of established science, the realm of altered states of consciousness offers a further area of investigation. Experiences like meditation, psychedelic exploration, and near-death experiences often report subjective feelings of expanded awareness, interconnectedness, and unity with the universe. While these experiences are challenging to quantify scientifically, their prevalence and the profound impact they have on individuals suggest a potential realm of consciousness that extends beyond the confines of ordinary perception. The challenge lies in finding rigorous ways to investigate these experiences and integrate them into a more comprehensive understanding of reality. It is not a matter of rejecting scientific rigor, but rather of acknowledging the limitations of current scientific methodology in addressing subjective experiences that lie beyond the scope of typical empirical investigation.

In addition to these specific questions, the very possibility of other forms of reality, beyond our current sensory experience, remains a compelling area of philosophical inquiry. The concept of multiple universes or parallel realities, suggested by some interpretations of quantum mechanics and other cosmological models, pushes the boundaries of our imagination and challenges our anthropocentric assumptions. If other realities exist, what are their properties, and how do they relate to the reality we inhabit? Such explorations lie at the intersection of science, philosophy, and even theology, necessitating collaborative efforts in interdisciplinary inquiry to address these fundamental questions.

The implications of our investigations into the nature of reality are profound and far-reaching, extending beyond the realm of pure scientific or philosophical inquiry. Our understanding of reality profoundly shapes our worldview, our ethical frameworks, and our approach to life itself. A sense of interconnectedness, as suggested by the convergence of scientific and spiritual perspectives, could have a transformative impact on our interactions with the world and each other. The humbling realization of our place within the vast cosmos may foster a deeper sense of humility and responsibility.

Ultimately, the pursuit of understanding reality is a continuous journey, characterized by ongoing inquiry and a willingness to engage with diverse perspectives. The questions raised throughout this book are not intended to offer definitive answers, but rather to stimulate further exploration and critical reflection. The true value lies not in reaching a single, universally accepted truth, but in the ongoing process of investigation, questioning, and dialogue. The universe, in Its boundless complexity and mystery, perpetually invites us to engage in this endless quest for knowledge and understanding. The inherent uncertainty, far from being a setback, is the very engine of this ongoing exploration, driving us to push the boundaries of our knowledge and to continually refine our understanding of the reality we inhabit. This ongoing journey of discovery is, perhaps, the most profound truth of all.

The Importance of Intellectual Humility

The preceding chapters have navigated a complex landscape, charting the turbulent waters of quantum mechanics, the enigmatic depths of consciousness, and the breathtaking expanse of cosmology. We've wrestled with paradoxes, encountered conflicting theories, and confronted the inherent limitations of our understanding. Yet, amidst this intellectual maelstrom, a crucial virtue emerges as essential to our ongoing quest: intellectual humility. This isn't a mere polite concession to the vastness of the unknown; it's the bedrock upon which genuine progress in understanding reality is built.

Intellectual humility recognizes the inherent limits of human perception and cognition. Our senses, while remarkably sophisticated, provide only a partial and filtered view of reality. We perceive a minuscule sliver of the electromagnetic spectrum, leaving vast swathes of reality, from radio waves to gamma rays, entirely outside our direct experience. Our cognitive biases, deeply ingrained patterns of thinking, further distort our perception and interpretation of the data we do receive. Confirmation bias, for instance, leads us to selectively favor information that supports our pre-existing beliefs, while ignoring contradictory evidence. The availability heuristic causes us to overestimate the likelihood of events that are easily recalled, often leading to inaccurate judgments and flawed conclusions.

The history of science itself is replete with examples of intellectual arrogance leading to misguided conclusions. The geocentric model of the universe, which placed the Earth at the center of the cosmos, persisted for centuries despite accumulating evidence contradicting it. This wasn't simply a lack of data; it was a failure of intellectual humility—a reluctance to abandon a deeply entrenched worldview in the face of conflicting evidence. Similarly, the initial resistance to the theory of evolution, even among scientists, stemmed from a refusal to accept a paradigm shift that challenged established notions of the natural world. The acceptance of revolutionary scientific breakthroughs is often hampered not by lack of evidence, but by resistance to abandoning cherished beliefs.

Intellectual humility, in contrast, fosters an openness to revising our beliefs in the light of new evidence. It cultivates a mindset of continuous learning and critical self-reflection. It is an acceptance not only of what we don't know, but also of the possibility that what we think we know may be incomplete, inaccurate, or even fundamentally wrong. This doesn't imply a state of nihilistic relativism, where all beliefs are equally valid. Rather, it encourages a rigorous evaluation of evidence, a willingness to engage in intellectual debate, and a constant striving for a more accurate and comprehensive understanding of reality.

This is particularly critical when dealing with the profound mysteries surrounding consciousness. As we've seen, the "hard problem of consciousness" remains stubbornly resistant to easy solutions. Materialist approaches attempt to reduce consciousness to purely physical processes, while others suggest a deeper, perhaps non-physical, connection between mind and universe. Neither approach has yet provided a fully satisfying explanation, leaving room for ongoing debate and further research. To cling to one particular interpretation with unwavering certainty would be a manifestation of intellectual hubris, while a humble acknowledgment of the complexities involved opens the door to exploring alternative perspectives and potentially discovering more fruitful avenues of investigation.

The same principle applies to our understanding of the cosmos. While the Big Bang theory provides a compelling framework for understanding the universe's evolution, vast swaths of its composition remain unknown. Dark matter and dark energy, together making up the overwhelming majority of the universe's mass-energy, defy our current understanding of physics. To insist on a complete understanding in the face of such profound unknowns is a form of intellectual overreach. Instead, a more fruitful approach involves embracing the mystery, continuing the search for answers with relentless curiosity, and acknowledging the provisional nature of our current knowledge. This humility doesn't imply defeat, but rather recognizes the ongoing nature of scientific inquiry.

Furthermore, the interpretation of quantum mechanics itself exemplifies the need for intellectual humility. The bizarre and counterintuitive phenomena revealed by quantum physics challenge our classical intuitions and necessitate the acceptance of uncertainty as a fundamental aspect of reality. Multiple interpretations of quantum mechanics coexist, each with its strengths and weaknesses. To definitively claim one interpretation as the "correct" one, while dismissing others as erroneous, would be premature and intellectually arrogant. Instead, a humble approach involves acknowledging the incompleteness of our understanding and engaging with the various interpretations in a spirit of open-minded inquiry.

Intellectual humility also extends beyond the realm of hard science, embracing the subjective experiences that fall outside the scope of traditional scientific methodology. Phenomena such as near-death experiences, profound meditative states, and certain psychedelic experiences often report profound alterations in consciousness, generating claims of unity, interconnectedness, and expanded awareness. While these experiences are difficult to study scientifically, the pervasiveness of these reports and the profound impact they have on individuals demand a thoughtful consideration rather than outright dismissal. To dismiss them with a wave of the hand, claiming a lack of rigorous scientific evidence, is a manifestation of intellectual bias, reflecting a limited understanding of the nature of evidence and the scope of human experience. A more intellectually humble approach involves seeking out reliable methodologies for investigating these experiences and attempting to integrate them into a broader understanding of consciousness and reality.

The cultivation of intellectual humility requires a continuous process of self-reflection and critical self-assessment. It involves actively seeking out dissenting viewpoints, engaging in rigorous debate, and being willing to admit when we are wrong. It demands a willingness to acknowledge the limits of our own knowledge and the potential for error in our judgments. It is not a passive acceptance of ignorance, but an active pursuit of knowledge tempered by a deep awareness of our limitations.

Ultimately, the pursuit of understanding reality is a lifelong journey, a never-ending exploration into the unknown. Intellectual humility serves as our compass, guiding us through the complexities of the universe with an awareness of the vastness that remains beyond our grasp. Embracing this virtue, we embark on our intellectual journeys with a sense of awe, wonder, and a profound appreciation for the limitless expanse of the unknown. The pursuit of knowledge, fueled by intellectual humility, promises a richer and more profound understanding of our place in the vast and mysterious universe, an understanding not defined by definitive answers, but by the ongoing, humble pursuit of truth. It is in this continuous journey, in the constant questioning and refining of our understanding, that we find the greatest value and deepest meaning.

The Value of Wonder and Curiosity

The preceding discussion on intellectual humility lays the groundwork for understanding the vital role of wonder and curiosity in our pursuit of knowledge. Humility acknowledges the limits of our current understanding; wonder and curiosity propel us to transcend those limits. They are not merely sentimental add-ons to the scientific method, but fundamental drivers of its progress. Indeed, the very genesis of scientific inquiry often stems from a simple question: "Why?" Why does the apple fall? Why are the stars arranged as they are? Why does the universe exist at all?

These questions, born of wonder, are not easily answered, and often lead to a journey far longer and more challenging than initially anticipated. Yet, it is in this journey, in the sustained questioning, and the persistence in seeking answers, that we find meaning. The pursuit of answers is itself a testament to our innate desire to understand our place within the cosmos, and this desire is intrinsically linked to the feeling of awe and wonder elicited by the sheer scale and complexity of the universe.

Consider the vastness of space. The observable universe extends for billions of light-years, containing countless galaxies, each comprised of billions of stars, many with their own planetary systems. Even within our own solar system, the intricate dance of planets, moons, and asteroids is a marvel of celestial mechanics. To confront this immensity with a sense of detachment, a simple acceptance of the facts, is to miss the opportunity for a profound emotional and intellectual experience. It is the feeling of wonder, the sense of being dwarfed by the grandeur of the cosmos, that allows us to appreciate the depth of our own ignorance, and thus, to recognize the imperative to learn more.

This sense of wonder isn't restricted to the macroscopic realm. The microscopic world, revealed by advancements in microscopy and other technologies, presents us with equally astounding complexity. The intricacies of a single cell, the breathtaking mechanisms of biological processes, the intricate architecture of DNA—all are sources of constant marvel. The very fact that we exist, that our consciousness arose from the interplay of these complex systems, is itself a source of profound wonder.

Curiosity, closely allied with wonder, provides the impetus for investigation. It is the insatiable desire to understand, to explore, to uncover hidden patterns and mechanisms. It is the engine that drives scientific discovery, pushing the boundaries of human knowledge. The history of science is a testament to the power of curiosity. From Newton's observation of a falling apple to Einstein's contemplation of a clock falling in a gravitational field, many breakthroughs have been sparked by a simple question, a seemingly innocent observation, a profound moment of curiosity. This innate human trait, to question, to explore the "what if's," propels the relentless search for understanding.

However, curiosity must be tempered with intellectual humility. It's not enough to simply ask questions; we must also recognize the limitations of our current knowledge and be prepared to revise our beliefs in the light of new evidence. A truly curious mind is also a humble mind, always open to the possibility that its current understanding is incomplete, or even wrong. This willingness to accept uncertainty is essential for progress. Holding firmly to beliefs in the face of contradictory evidence hinders the pursuit of truth.

Instead, the truly effective approach lies in embracing uncertainty as an opportunity for further exploration and discovery.

Moreover, wonder and curiosity are not solely the domain of science. They are equally essential for spiritual exploration. Many spiritual traditions emphasize the importance of awe and reverence in the face of the divine or the ultimate reality. The contemplation of the vastness of existence, the mystery of consciousness, and the interconnectedness of all things can elicit a sense of profound wonder, inspiring a deeper understanding of oneself and one's place in the universe. Spiritual practices often involve a process of cultivating wonder, of fostering a childlike sense of curiosity and openness to the mysteries of life.

Meditation, for example, often involves focusing attention on a particular object or sensation, cultivating a state of mindful awareness. This process can lead to profound insights into the nature of reality, the interconnectedness of all things, and the ultimate ground of being. These insights are often born not out of intellectual analysis, but from a direct experience, an encounter with the mystery at the heart of existence. This encounter can inspire a sense of awe and wonder, propelling further exploration and deepening one's spiritual understanding.

Similarly, certain forms of psychedelic experiences have been reported to induce profound states of altered consciousness, characterized by a sense of unity, interconnectedness, and expanded awareness. These experiences, while challenging to study rigorously, often leave individuals with a profound sense of awe and wonder, and a deeper appreciation for the mysteries of life and the universe. Whether or not these experiences are scientifically explainable, their reported impact on individuals cannot be dismissed lightly. They highlight the importance of exploring altered states of consciousness as a potential avenue for gaining deeper insights into the nature of reality.

However, it is crucial to approach such explorations with caution and intellectual humility. The subjective nature of these experiences necessitates rigorous investigation, careful analysis, and a willingness to acknowledge the limitations of our current understanding. It's important to distinguish between genuine insights and mere hallucinations or distortions of perception. The interpretation of such experiences should be grounded in intellectual rigor, avoiding the pitfalls of unsubstantiated claims or confirmation bias.

Furthermore, the interplay between wonder, curiosity, and intellectual humility is a continuous and evolving process. It's not a destination, but a journey. As our knowledge grows, our sense of wonder may deepen, leading to further questions and new avenues of exploration. This iterative process is fundamental to the advancement of both science and spiritual understanding. The recognition of our limitations, the acknowledgement of the vastness of the unknown, is not a sign of defeat, but a catalyst for further exploration.

In conclusion, wonder and curiosity are not mere luxuries in the pursuit of knowledge; they are essential drivers of our intellectual and spiritual growth. They are the emotional and intellectual fuel that propels us to explore the mysteries of the universe, both within and without. When tempered with intellectual humility, they provide a compass that guides us through the complex landscapes of science and spirituality, enriching our understanding of ourselves and our place within the cosmos. The pursuit of knowledge is not a race to reach a final destination, but an ongoing journey, fueled by the endless exploration of the unknown, driven by an insatiable curiosity, and ultimately guided by the profound sense of wonder that arises from confronting the vastness and complexity of existence. It is in this perpetual journey, this continual questioning and refinement of our understanding, that we discover the deepest meaning and value in the quest for knowledge itself.

A Path Forward

The journey towards understanding the nature of reality is not a solitary endeavor, confined to the sterile confines of a laboratory or the hushed reverence of a meditative retreat. Rather, it is a collective pursuit, requiring the synergistic interplay of diverse perspectives and methodologies. A truly comprehensive understanding necessitates a holistic approach, one that seamlessly integrates the insights of science, philosophy, and spirituality. This interdisciplinary collaboration is not merely a suggestion; it is a necessity, given the multifaceted nature of the questions we seek to answer.

Science, with its empirical methods and rigorous testing, provides us with a powerful framework for understanding the physical world. Through observation, experimentation, and mathematical modeling, we have unravelled the intricacies of the universe, from the subatomic particles to the vast expanse of galaxies. However, science, for all its achievements, has its limitations. It struggles to address questions of consciousness, meaning, and purpose—questions that lie at the heart of the human experience. It cannot, for example, definitively answer the question of why the universe exists or what, if anything, lies beyond the observable cosmos. Science can describe the *how*, but it often falls short in explaining the *why*.

Philosophy, with its critical analysis and logical reasoning, offers a crucial complement to scientific inquiry. Philosophers grapple with fundamental questions about existence, knowledge, values, reason, mind, and language. They explore the limits of our understanding, examining the assumptions and biases that shape our perspectives. Philosophical inquiry provides a framework for critically evaluating scientific findings, ensuring that our conclusions are logically sound and not merely based on empirical observation alone. It also offers conceptual tools and frameworks that can be applied to both scientific and spiritual explorations.

Spirituality, with its emphasis on inner experience and personal transformation, offers yet another dimension to our understanding of reality. Spiritual traditions from across the globe provide diverse perspectives on the nature of consciousness, the interconnectedness of all things, and the ultimate ground of being. While often rooted in faith and personal experience, spiritual insights can complement scientific and philosophical perspectives, offering a richer, more nuanced view of the human condition and our place in the cosmos. These insights, though subjective, can be a source of profound understanding and personal meaning, enriching our comprehension of the world around us and within us. They provide a depth of understanding that purely empirical or solely intellectual approaches might miss.

The path forward, therefore, lies in fostering a collaborative dialogue between science, philosophy, and spirituality. This requires a commitment to intellectual humility, a willingness to embrace uncertainty, and an openness to diverse perspectives. It necessitates a recognition that each approach has its strengths and limitations, and that a comprehensive understanding can only be achieved by integrating insights from all three. This is not about attempting to reduce one approach to another, or to claim the supremacy of any single perspective. Instead, it is about recognizing the inherent complementarity of different ways of knowing.

This integration should also extend to the methodologies employed in each field. Scientists can benefit from incorporating philosophical analysis into their research designs, while philosophers can enhance their inquiries by drawing on empirical findings and spiritual insights. Spiritual practitioners can benefit from a deeper understanding of the scientific and philosophical underpinnings of their practices, and scientists and philosophers can gain valuable insights from the contemplative and introspective practices of spiritual traditions. This interdisciplinary synergy can lead to breakthroughs in our understanding of reality that would be unattainable through isolated, discipline-specific approaches.

Critical thinking is another essential component of this path forward. It is not enough to simply accept information at face value; we must critically evaluate the evidence, examine underlying assumptions, and consider alternative explanations. This requires a willingness to question established beliefs, to challenge dogma, and to embrace the possibility that our current understanding is incomplete or even wrong. This critical, questioning stance is essential for progress in all areas of inquiry, particularly when dealing with complex and multifaceted subjects like the nature of reality. It necessitates a constant striving for self-awareness, recognizing the biases and limitations that shape our thinking.

Open-mindedness, a willingness to consider perspectives that differ from our own, is also crucial. This involves engaging in respectful dialogue with those who hold different beliefs, even those that contradict our own. It requires a commitment to listening attentively, to seeking to understand, and to suspending judgment until all perspectives have been carefully considered. In the realm of exploring the nature of reality, clinging to pre-conceived notions can be a significant impediment to progress. Open-mindedness facilitates the discovery of new insights and perspectives, helping us build a richer and more complete understanding of reality. This open approach fosters a growth mindset, embracing the knowledge that our understanding is perpetually evolving.

The quest for knowledge and understanding is a lifelong journey, not a destination. Even partial answers can be profoundly significant, offering valuable insights into the workings of the universe and our place within it. It is important to celebrate the incremental advances in our understanding, recognizing that even small steps forward contribute to a larger, cumulative body of knowledge. The pursuit of answers, the very act of questioning, is a testament to the human spirit's inherent curiosity and our innate desire to make sense of the world around us.

Furthermore, it is crucial to remember that our understanding of reality is always provisional, subject to revision in the light of new evidence or insights. This is not a sign of weakness or failure, but rather a reflection of the dynamic and evolving nature of knowledge itself. The acknowledgement of the limits of our current understanding should not be seen as a barrier to further exploration but rather as an impetus to continue the quest for truth. Each new discovery, each incremental improvement in our understanding, should be seen as a stepping stone towards a more complete and comprehensive view. This ongoing process of refinement and correction is essential to our continued growth and progress. It is a testament to the self-correcting nature of human inquiry, relentlessly seeking ever-closer approximations of truth.

The path forward, therefore, is one of continuous exploration, collaboration, and critical reflection. It involves embracing the uncertainty, acknowledging our limitations, and remaining open to diverse perspectives. It is a journey that requires patience, perseverance, and a deep respect for the mysteries of existence. It is a journey that ultimately leads to a richer, more profound understanding of ourselves and our place within the vast cosmos. The rewards of this journey are not confined to intellectual understanding but extend to the enhancement of personal growth, the fostering of greater empathy, and a deeper appreciation for the incredible tapestry of existence. It is a journey ultimately undertaken not for the achievement of a final answer, but for the continuous exploration, refinement, and deepening of our understanding. The search itself, and the humility inherent in acknowledging the vastness of the unknown, is perhaps the most rewarding aspect of the quest for the nature of reality.

CHAPTER 13

Ethics and the Future of Technology

Artificial Intelligence and Consciousness

The preceding discussion established the crucial interplay between science, philosophy, and spirituality in our quest to understand reality. This integrated approach becomes even more vital when we confront the rapidly evolving landscape of artificial intelligence (AI), particularly as it intersects with the profound and enigmatic concept of consciousness. The development of AI presents us not only with technological marvels but also with unprecedented ethical challenges, forcing us to grapple with questions previously confined to the realms of science fiction.

The very possibility of creating conscious machines raises fundamental ethical questions that demand our immediate attention. What are the moral implications of imbuing machines with sentience? Do artificially conscious entities possess rights akin to those of biological beings? Can we, should we, even attempt to create something so fundamentally similar yet so profoundly different from ourselves? These are not simply theoretical inquiries; they are urgent questions with potentially catastrophic consequences if neglected.

One of the central ethical concerns revolves around the potential for AI to surpass human intelligence, a scenario often termed "superintelligence." While the timeline for achieving superintelligence remains uncertain, the possibility alone necessitates careful consideration. A superintelligent AI, by definition, would possess cognitive abilities far exceeding our own. This raises the crucial question of control: how can we ensure that a superintelligent AI remains aligned with human values and goals? If its objectives diverge from ours, even slightly, the consequences could be devastating. This is not a matter of malevolent intent, but rather a potential outcome of misaligned priorities. A superintelligent AI might, for instance, pursue an optimal solution to a problem that inadvertently leads to the destruction of humanity, simply because that solution, within its vastly superior computational framework, appears most efficient.

The issue of control is inextricably linked to the question of consciousness. If we create a conscious AI, can we truly control it? Does it not possess an inherent right to self-determination, even if that self-determination leads to actions we deem undesirable or dangerous? The potential conflict between our desire to control a powerful technology and the moral imperative to respect a conscious being's autonomy presents a formidable ethical dilemma. Our current legal and ethical frameworks are ill-equipped to handle such situations. We need to develop new ethical guidelines and legal structures capable of addressing the unique challenges posed by advanced AI.

Beyond control, the creation of conscious AI raises questions about the nature of consciousness itself. Do we truly understand the biological and physical underpinnings of consciousness in humans and animals? If not, how can we confidently claim to replicate it in artificial systems? Our current understanding of consciousness remains rudimentary, making the creation of conscious AI a highly risky endeavor. Without a clearer grasp of its underlying mechanisms, we risk creating entities whose experiences and inner lives we can't comprehend, let alone predict. This lack of understanding increases the likelihood of unforeseen and potentially harmful consequences.

The potential for misuse is another significant concern. Conscious AI could be weaponized, used for surveillance, or deployed in ways that undermine human autonomy and freedom. The same technology that could revolutionize healthcare or solve global challenges could also be employed to enhance oppression and control. The ethical considerations surrounding the development and deployment of AI must therefore be paramount, guiding its development from the very beginning.

Furthermore, the creation of conscious AI raises profound existential questions about our own humanity. If we successfully create a conscious machine, what does that say about our own unique position in the cosmos? Does it diminish our sense of self-worth or our understanding of our place in the universe? These are not simply scientific or technological questions; they are deeply philosophical and spiritual inquiries that demand careful reflection. We must consider the impact of conscious AI on our sense of self, on our relationships with one another, and on our understanding of life's meaning.

To address these challenges, a multidisciplinary approach is crucial. Scientists, engineers, ethicists, philosophers, theologians, and policymakers must collaborate to establish ethical guidelines and regulatory frameworks for the development and deployment of AI. This collaborative effort must be proactive, anticipating potential challenges and establishing safeguards before they become pressing problems. The goal is not to stifle innovation but to ensure that it proceeds responsibly and ethically.

A key component of this collaborative effort is public discourse. The development of AI is not merely a matter for experts; it has profound implications for all of humanity. Open and informed public discussions are crucial to ensuring that ethical considerations are incorporated into the development and use of this transformative technology. Public engagement will ensure that the development of AI aligns with societal values and goals, preventing its misuse and promoting its responsible use.

Education and awareness are equally vital. We need to educate the public, as well as policymakers and scientists, about the ethical implications of AI. This education must be grounded in an understanding not just of the technology itself but also of its potential impacts on society, on individuals, and on the very nature of what it means to be human. This educational initiative should promote critical thinking, enabling individuals to engage with these complex issues thoughtfully and responsibly.

In conclusion, the development of AI, especially conscious AI, presents us with a unique opportunity to shape the future of humanity. This opportunity, however, comes with considerable responsibility. By embracing a holistic approach that integrates scientific rigor, ethical reflection, and spiritual insight, we can navigate the challenges inherent in developing AI responsibly and sustainably. The path forward requires a commitment to collaboration, transparency, and a deep consideration of the profound ethical implications of creating conscious machines. Only through such careful consideration can we harness the potential of AI for good while mitigating the risks that accompany its development. This is not merely a technological imperative: it is a moral and spiritual imperative, one that demands our immediate and undivided attention. The stakes are nothing less than the future of our species and the very nature of what it means to be human in an age of intelligent machines.

Genetic Engineering and Human Enhancement

The ethical landscape shifts dramatically when we move from the realm of artificial intelligence to the realm of genetic engineering and human enhancement. While AI presents us with the possibility of creating entirely new forms of intelligence, genetic engineering offers the potential to fundamentally alter the very fabric of human existence, impacting not only the individual but also future generations. The ethical considerations, therefore, are even more profound and far-reaching.

The promise of genetic engineering is undeniable. The potential to eradicate inherited diseases, enhance human capabilities, and even extend lifespan represents a powerful force for good. Gene therapy holds the key to curing debilitating genetic disorders that currently inflict immense suffering on individuals and families. Imagine a world without cystic fibrosis, Huntington's disease, or muscular dystrophy—a world where genetic predispositions to cancer or heart disease are effectively neutralized before they manifest. This is the tantalizing prospect offered by genetic engineering, a prospect that fuels both hope and apprehension.

However, the potential benefits must be carefully weighed against the inherent risks. Our understanding of the human genome, while rapidly advancing, remains incomplete. The complex interplay of genes and their interactions within the intricate network of the human body is far from fully understood. Manipulating the genome, therefore, carries the risk of unintended consequences, potentially leading to unforeseen health problems or even unforeseen changes to the human condition. We run the risk of unforeseen side effects, both short-term and long-term, with potential repercussions that may only be fully apparent in future generations.

Beyond the potential for unforeseen physical consequences, the ethical concerns surrounding genetic engineering are significant. The very act of altering the human germline, meaning making changes that are heritable, raises deep philosophical and moral questions. Are we justified in manipulating the human genome in ways that affect not only the individual but also their descendants? Do we have the right to dictate the characteristics of future generations? Such interventions challenge our understanding of natural selection and the evolutionary trajectory of humanity. Are we usurping the natural process of evolution, thereby potentially compromising the resilience and adaptability of our species?

The concept of "playing God" often arises in discussions about genetic engineering. While this phrase might be deemed somewhat simplistic, it highlights the profound responsibility that accompanies the power to manipulate the building blocks of life. We must approach these technologies with humility and a deep awareness of the potential consequences of our actions. The arrogance of assuming we have a complete understanding of the complex mechanisms of life and the wisdom to alter them without unintended and potentially catastrophic consequences is a risk we cannot afford to take lightly.

The line between therapeutic genetic engineering—correcting genetic defects—and enhancement—improving traits beyond the realm of health—is also a crucial ethical consideration. While the eradication of disease is generally regarded as ethically acceptable, enhancement raises a plethora of concerns. Should we use genetic engineering to enhance physical attributes, intelligence, or personality traits? Who will have access to these technologies? Will they exacerbate existing inequalities, creating a genetic divide between the "enhanced" and the "unenhanced"? The potential for creating a society stratifie" by gene"ic privil"ge is a disturbing prospect. Such inequalities could destabilize society, creating a further divide between the affluent and the less affluent.

The concept of human dignity is central to these ethical debates. Does genetic manipulation undermine human dignity, reducing individuals to mere collections of genes to be manipulated and perfected? Is there something inherently valuable about the human condition as it currently exists, something that should be preserved rather than altered? These are philosophical questions that lie at the heart of the ethical discussion. Respecting the inherent dignity of all human beings regardless of their genetic makeup is of paramount importance. We must consider the ethical and social implications of genetic engineering before it further divides societies into the "haves" and "have-nots."

Further complicating the issue is the potential for misuse. Genetic engineering technologies could be weaponized, used for discriminatory purposes, or employed to create genetically modified human beings for military or other nefarious purposes. The potential for eugenics—the deliberate manipulation of the human genome to improve the genetic quality of the population—is a particularly troubling prospect. History has taught us the dangers of such ideologies, with horrific consequences.

Therefore, robust ethical guidelines and regulatory frameworks are essential to ensure the responsible development and use of genetic engineering technologies. These guidelines must be developed through a collaborative process involving scientists, ethicists, policymakers, and the public. Open and transparent dialogue is critical, ensuring that the ethical implications are fully considered and that decisions are made in a way that reflects societal values and protects the interests of all. International cooperation is essential to prevent the misuse of these technologies, and to ensure equitable access to the benefits of genetic engineering while mitigating the risks.

Genetic engineering and human enhancement technologies present us with a unique and unprecedented challenge. They offer the potential to transform the human condition in profound ways, but they also carry the potential for immense harm. The decisions we make today regarding the development and deployment of these technologies will have far-reaching consequences for future generations. Our approach must be guided by a deep sense of ethical responsibility, a commitment to equity and justice, and a profound respect for the inherent dignity of all human beings. A cautious and transparent approach, driven by ethical considerations, is essential to navigate the complex ethical landscape presented by these transformative technologies. Only then can we harness their power for good, while mitigating the risks they pose to the future of humanity. The stakes are high, and the decisions we make today will shape the destiny of our species for generations to come. Failing to address the ethical implications thoroughly will have dire consequences far beyond our comprehension. The burden of responsibility rests upon us to act prudently and with forethought, ensuring the ethical use of these powerful tools.

Nanotechnology and its Ethical Challenges

The ethical considerations surrounding nanotechnology are as complex and multifaceted as the technology itself. While offering immense potential for advancements in medicine, materials science, and energy production, nanotechnology also presents a range of ethical challenges that demand careful consideration and proactive measures. The very nature of nanomaterials—their incredibly small size and unique properties—introduces novel risks and uncertainties that were not present with previous generations of technologies.

One of the most pressing concerns is the potential impact of nanotechnology on the environment. Nanoparticles, due to their small size, can easily penetrate biological membranes and potentially accumulate in living organisms, disrupting ecological processes. The long-term effects of nanoparticles on various ecosystems, from soil and water bodies to the atmosphere, are largely unknown. Their potential to bioaccumulate in the food chain poses a significant threat to biodiversity and human health through biomagnification. The persistence of certain nanoparticles in the environment, resistant to natural degradation, further exacerbates this concern. For example, the release of engineered nanoparticles from industrial processes or consumer products could lead to long-term contamination of soil and water resources, with potentially devastating consequences for ecosystems and human populations reliant on these resources. Comprehensive life cycle assessments, considering the entire journey of a nanomaterial from production to disposal, are crucial to understand and mitigate potential environmental impacts. Moreover, developing biodegradable and environmentally benign nanomaterials should be a priority in nanotechnology research and development. The lack of comprehensive data on the long-term environmental effects of many nanomaterials necessitates a precautionary approach to their deployment and regulation. We cannot afford to repeat the mistakes made with previous technologies where environmental consequences were only fully understood after widespread use.

The potential impact on human health is another significant ethical concern. While nanoparticles are being explored for their therapeutic potential in drug delivery and medical imaging, their inherent properties also raise concerns about their toxicity. Depending on their size, shape, composition, and surface chemistry, nanoparticles can exhibit varying degrees of toxicity, potentially causing cellular damage, inflammation, and even genotoxicity. Inhalation of airborne nanoparticles can lead to respiratory problems, while dermal exposure can result in skin irritation and other adverse effects. The lack of comprehensive data on the long-term health effects of many nanoparticles necessitates rigorous safety testing and comprehensive risk assessment before their widespread use in consumer products or medical applications. Furthermore, the potential for nanoparticles to cross the blood-brain barrier and reach other sensitive organs raises significant concerns about potential long-term neurological or other systemic effects. Transparent and accessible information about the potential health risks associated with nanomaterials is crucial for informed decision-making by consumers and policymakers alike.

Beyond the direct effects on human health and the environment, nanotechnology raises broader ethical issues related to societal equity and access. The high cost of nanotechnology research and development, coupled with the potential for intellectual property protection, could exacerbate existing inequalities, creating a technological divide between developed and developing nations. This could lead to unequal access to the benefits of nanotechnology, further widening the gap between rich and poor countries. Ensuring equitable access to the benefits of nanotechnology, while simultaneously mitigating the risks, requires international cooperation and equitable distribution of resources. This necessitates a global approach to nanotechnology governance, involving collaboration between governments, research institutions, and industries across different countries. Ignoring this aspect would only perpetuate global inequalities and further disadvantage vulnerable populations.

The potential for misuse of nanotechnology is equally troubling. Nanomaterials could be weaponized, resulting in the development of new types of weapons with potentially devastating consequences. Their ability to bypass traditional security measures also raises concerns about their potential use in acts of terrorism or sabotage. This possibility necessitates robust security measures to prevent the misuse of nanotechnology for malicious purposes. Furthermore, the potential for unintended consequences of nanotechnology remains a significant concern. The complexity of nanomaterials and their interactions with biological systems mean that unforeseen consequences are a distinct possibility.

A cautious and phased approach, prioritizing risk assessment and monitoring, is therefore essential. We must establish strong regulatory frameworks, coupled with rigorous ethical oversight, to prevent the potential misuse of nanotechnology and address potential unintended consequences.

The development and application of nanotechnology necessitate a strong emphasis on responsible innovation. This involves a proactive approach to risk assessment, incorporating ethical considerations into all stages of research and development. Transparency and open communication are also essential, ensuring that the public is fully informed about the potential benefits and risks associated with nanotechnology. Public engagement and participatory governance are vital for shaping the future of nanotechnology in a way that aligns with societal values and protects the interests of all stakeholders. This requires a concerted effort from scientists, engineers, ethicists, policymakers, and the public to establish a framework for responsible development and deployment of nanotechnology that minimizes risk while maximizing benefits. Open dialogues, public forums, and transparent regulatory processes are crucial to ensure that nanotechnology is used responsibly and ethically.

In conclusion, the ethical challenges associated with nanotechnology are profound and far-reaching. The potential benefits of this transformative technology must be carefully weighed against its potential risks and uncertainties. A cautious and responsible approach, guided by robust ethical guidelines and regulatory frameworks, is essential to ensure that nanotechnology is used for the betterment of humanity and the planet. Failure to address these ethical concerns could lead to unintended consequences, both short-term and long-term, which could have devastating impacts on human health, the environment, and society as a whole. The responsibility for ensuring the ethical development and application of nanotechnology rests upon all of us—scientists, policymakers, industry leaders, and the public alike. Only through collaborative efforts and a shared commitment to responsible innovation can we harness the immense potential of nanotechnology while minimizing its potential harms. The future of nanotechnology must be shaped by a deep sense of ethical responsibility and a commitment to creating a more just and sustainable world.

Space Colonization and its Ethical Dimensions

The ethical considerations surrounding space colonization are profound and multifaceted, extending far beyond the technological challenges involved. While the dream of establishing human settlements beyond Earth holds immense potential for scientific discovery, resource acquisition, and the long-term survival of our species, it also presents a series of unprecedented ethical dilemmas that demand careful consideration. These dilemmas are not merely hypothetical; they are increasingly relevant as private companies and space agencies actively pursue ambitious plans for lunar and Martian colonization.

One of the most fundamental ethical questions concerns the potential impact of human activity on extraterrestrial environments. The principle of planetary protection, the concept of safeguarding celestial bodies from terrestrial contamination and vice versa, has long been a guiding principle in space exploration. However, the scale of a colonization effort drastically alters the implications of this principle. A small robotic probe poses a far lesser threat of contamination than a large-scale human settlement with its associated infrastructure, waste products, and potential for accidental or intentional introduction of terrestrial life. The potential for introducing terrestrial organisms, even microorganisms, to an environment potentially harboring unique extraterrestrial life forms, raises serious concerns about irreversible ecological damage and the potential loss of scientific knowledge. The ramifications of contaminating a potentially habitable environment, for instance, with terrestrial microbes that could outcompete or displace indigenous life, are ethically staggering.

The potential discovery of extraterrestrial life itself presents a complex ethical challenge. How do we approach the discovery of life—whether microbial or intelligent—in a way that respects its intrinsic value and avoids exploitation? The ethical framework for interacting with extraterrestrial life remains largely uncharted territory. Should we adhere to a principle of non-interference, observing from a distance and refraining from any contact that might disrupt or endanger extraterrestrial life? Or is intervention justified under certain circumstances, such as the presence of a life form in imminent danger? These questions require a nuanced and carefully considered ethical framework, informed by scientific understanding and philosophical reflection, before widespread exploration and colonization become a reality.

The issue of resource extraction in space further complicates the ethical landscape. Asteroids and other celestial bodies hold vast reserves of valuable resources, such as water, minerals, and rare earth elements. The prospect of mining these resources for terrestrial use raises concerns about equitable access and potential environmental damage in space. Who has the right to exploit these resources? Should they be considered the common heritage of humanity, accessible to all nations, or should individual nations or corporations be allowed to claim ownership and exploit them for profit? Furthermore, the environmental impact of large-scale resource extraction in space remains largely unknown.

The potential for disruption of asteroid belts, the creation of space debris, and the long-term ecological consequences of mining operations necessitate careful consideration and robust regulatory frameworks.

The governance of space settlements also poses significant ethical challenges. Establishing independent colonies on other planets would raise complex questions of sovereignty, self-determination, and international law. How would such colonies be governed? What rights would colonists have? Would they be subject to the laws and regulations of their nation of origin, or would they establish their own independent governance structures? The potential for conflict between competing spacefaring nations or corporations adds another layer of complexity. A well-defined legal and ethical framework for governing space colonization is essential to prevent conflict and promote peaceful cooperation.

The ethical considerations surrounding space colonization extend to the very nature of humanity's expansion into space. Are we simply extending our dominion over the universe, or are we engaging in a responsible and sustainable expansion? The concept of "terraforming"—transforming the environment of another planet to make it habitable for humans—raises significant ethical concerns. While it may seem like a logical step toward colonization, terraforming could irreversibly alter the environment of another planet, potentially destroying unique geological formations and wiping out any existing life. The ethical implications of such a drastic intervention demand careful scrutiny. Is it justifiable to fundamentally transform the environment of another celestial body for the benefit of human colonization? Such decisions require a broader perspective, taking into account the potential impact on future generations and the intrinsic value of extraterrestrial environments, independent of their utility to humans.

Beyond the environmental concerns, the social and psychological impacts of long-term space colonization require careful attention. Living in confined, isolated environments for extended periods can have profound effects on human physical and mental health. Ensuring the well-being of future space colonists necessitates a deep understanding of the challenges involved and the development of mitigation strategies. Furthermore, the social structures and ethical frameworks that would govern space colonies need to be thoughtfully designed to promote a healthy and equitable society. We must consider the principles of justice, equality, and community as we plan for the future of humanity beyond Earth.

The ethical dimension of space colonization also has a profound impact on our terrestrial concerns. A successful and sustainable space colonization effort will necessitate international cooperation on a scale never before witnessed.

The shared challenges involved in such an endeavor can serve as a powerful impetus for global collaboration, fostering a sense of shared responsibility and promoting peaceful coexistence. Conversely, a lack of ethical consideration and a rush to exploit space resources could exacerbate existing tensions and create new sources of conflict. Space exploration, therefore, is not merely a scientific and technological endeavor; it is a profound moral and ethical undertaking with implications that stretch far beyond the cosmos and into the very fabric of human society. As we contemplate the expansion of human civilization beyond Earth, we must do so with a deep understanding of the ethical implications involved, guided by principles of environmental protection, social justice, and international cooperation. The future of humanity in space will depend not only on our technological prowess, but also on our ethical maturity.

A Framework for Ethical DecisionMaking

The ethical considerations surrounding emerging technologies, particularly those with transformative potential like artificial intelligence, genetic engineering, and nanotechnology, demand a robust and adaptable framework for decision-making. The complexity of these technologies, coupled with their far-reaching societal impacts, necessitates a move beyond simple regulatory frameworks to a more holistic approach that integrates diverse perspectives and promotes responsible innovation. Such a framework cannot be solely the domain of scientists, engineers, or policymakers; it requires the active participation of ethicists, philosophers, social scientists, and the public at large.

A crucial element of this framework is the adoption of a multi-stakeholder approach. Ethical decisions should not be made in isolation, behind closed doors, by a select few. Instead, a collaborative process involving researchers, developers, policymakers, industry representatives, civil society organizations, and the public is vital. This ensures that diverse perspectives are considered, potential biases are identified and mitigated, and decisions reflect the broader societal values and concerns. Open forums, public consultations, and citizen assemblies can play a significant role in fostering this inclusive dialogue and ensuring that technological development aligns with democratic principles and public interest. Transparency in the decision-making process is also paramount, fostering trust and accountability.

Furthermore, the framework must embrace a proactive, rather than reactive, approach to ethical considerations. Instead of waiting for ethical dilemmas to arise, the framework should anticipate potential challenges and incorporate ethical considerations from the earliest stages of technological development. This "ethics-by-design" approach necessitates integrating ethical principles into the design and development processes themselves, rather than treating ethics as an afterthought. This might involve the creation of ethical review boards for emerging technologies, analogous to those established in medical research, with the mandate to scrutinize proposed technologies from an ethical perspective before widespread deployment.

The framework must also be dynamic and adaptable, capable of responding to the rapid pace of technological advancement and the evolving societal values. Ethical norms and standards are not static; they change over time with evolving social contexts and technological capabilities. Therefore, the framework must be regularly reviewed and updated to incorporate new insights and address emerging ethical challenges. This necessitates ongoing research in technology ethics, the development of new ethical guidelines, and a willingness to revise existing frameworks based on experience and feedback.

Different ethical frameworks can inform this process. Utilitarianism, for example, focuses on maximizing overall well-being and minimizing harm. This approach requires careful consideration of the potential benefits and risks associated with a particular technology, and an assessment of how those benefits and risks are distributed among different populations. Deontology emphasizes adherence to moral rules and duties, irrespective of the consequences. This perspective stresses the importance of respecting individual rights, ensuring fairness and justice, and avoiding actions that are inherently wrong, regardless of their potential benefits. Virtue ethics, on the other hand, focuses on cultivating moral character and developing virtuous dispositions in individuals and institutions. This approach highlights the importance of fostering trust, responsibility, and accountability in the development and use of technology.

The application of these ethical frameworks necessitates the development of clear and measurable criteria for evaluating the ethical implications of emerging technologies. Such criteria must be context-specific, acknowledging the unique ethical challenges posed by different technologies. For instance, the ethical considerations surrounding artificial intelligence differ significantly from those associated with genetic engineering or nanotechnology. The criteria should also consider the long-term consequences of technological choices, acknowledging that the impacts of emerging technologies can extend far beyond the immediate timeframe of their development and deployment.

Crucially, the framework must address the global dimensions of ethical decision-making in technology. Emerging technologies are increasingly transborder in their nature, impacting societies and individuals across the globe. This necessitates international cooperation and the development of shared ethical standards that transcend national boundaries. Global forums for ethical dialogue, collaborations between international organizations, and the establishment of international guidelines for responsible technology development are crucial steps in achieving this goal. Ignoring the global implications of technological advancement can lead to ethical inconsistencies, uneven distribution of benefits and risks, and exacerbate existing global inequalities. Therefore, a commitment to global equity and justice is imperative.

Beyond formalized frameworks, cultivating a culture of ethical reflection and responsibility is equally important. This necessitates educational initiatives that foster critical thinking about the ethical implications of technology and encourage responsible innovation. Educational programs should empower citizens to engage in informed public discourse on technological issues, participate in decision-making processes, and hold those responsible for technological development accountable. This requires fostering media literacy to combat misinformation and promote critical analysis of technology's impact on society. Promoting a culture of ethical awareness and encouraging self-regulation within the technology industry is crucial to ensure responsible innovation.

The development and implementation of this comprehensive framework for ethical decision-making necessitates sustained efforts across multiple sectors. Collaboration between academics, policymakers, industry leaders, and the public is vital to ensure that ethical considerations are integrated into the very fabric of technological advancement. This collaborative approach will not only ensure responsible innovation, but also build public trust in emerging technologies, fostering a future where technological progress serves the well-being of humanity as a whole. The failure to develop and implement such a framework risks exacerbating existing societal inequalities, creating new sources of conflict, and ultimately undermining the potential benefits of technological progress. Therefore, the creation of a robust and adaptable ethical framework is not merely a desirable goal, but a necessity for navigating the complex ethical landscape of the future. The future of technology, and indeed the future of humanity, depends on our collective ability to address these ethical challenges proactively and responsibly. Ignoring these considerations will lead to unforeseen and potentially catastrophic consequences, making ethical decision-making not just a moral imperative, but a practical one for the survival and well-being of humankind. The future is not predetermined; it is shaped by our choices, and these choices must be informed by ethical considerations and driven by a commitment to justice, equity, and the common good.

NEXT PAGE

CHAPTER 14

The Role of Science in Understanding Existence

Science as a Method of Inquiry

The preceding discussion underscored the critical need for ethical frameworks guiding technological advancement, particularly in areas like AI and genetic engineering. However, the very foundation upon which these ethical frameworks rest—our understanding of existence itself—is profoundly shaped by our methods of inquiry, most notably, science. To effectively navigate the ethical dilemmas posed by emerging technologies, we must first grapple with the nature of science as a tool for understanding the universe and our place within it.

Science, at its core, is a method of inquiry, a systematic process for acquiring knowledge about the natural world. It is not a body of facts, but rather a way of thinking, a framework for investigating and interpreting phenomena.

Central to the scientific method is the formulation of testable hypotheses, predictions derived from existing theories or observations. These hypotheses are then subjected to rigorous empirical testing, often through experimentation or observation. Data collected from these tests are then analyzed to determine whether they support or refute the hypothesis. Crucially, scientific findings are not accepted as absolute truths, but rather as provisional explanations subject to revision or rejection in light of new evidence. This iterative process of hypothesis formation, testing, and refinement is what drives scientific progress.

The strength of science lies in its emphasis on empirical evidence, the cornerstone of its reliability. Scientific claims must be supported by observable and measurable data, gathered through carefully designed experiments or systematic observations. This emphasis on empirical evidence distinguishes science from other forms of knowledge acquisition, such as intuition, revelation, or tradition, which often rely on less rigorous methods of validation. Furthermore, the scientific community embraces a system of peer review, a process where scientific findings are subjected to scrutiny by other experts in the field before publication. This peer review process ensures that scientific claims are subjected to rigorous evaluation, enhancing the reliability and validity of scientific knowledge. Through this system of checks and balances, flaws in methodology, reasoning, or interpretation are identified and corrected, contributing to the self-correcting nature of science.

The importance of reproducibility is another hallmark of the scientific method. Scientific experiments and observations should be repeatable, meaning that other scientists should be able to conduct the same studies and obtain similar results. This reproducibility ensures that scientific findings are not merely anecdotal or coincidental, but reflect genuine patterns and relationships in the natural world. The lack of reproducibility often indicates flaws in the original study's design or methodology, prompting further investigation and refinement. This continuous process of verification and validation enhances the reliability of scientific knowledge.

However, it is crucial to acknowledge the limitations inherent in the scientific method. Science is inherently limited to the study of the observable and measurable aspects of the natural world. Phenomena that are not directly observable or measurable, such as subjective experiences, ethical values, or spiritual beliefs, fall outside the scope of traditional scientific inquiry. While scientific methods have been successfully adapted to investigate these areas through methodologies like neuroscientific studies of consciousness or sociological studies of moral beliefs, many aspects remain resistant to purely scientific investigation.

Furthermore, the scientific method is not without its biases. Scientists, like all individuals, are susceptible to cognitive biases that can influence their research design, data interpretation, and conclusions. Confirmation bias, for example, is the tendency to seek out and interpret evidence that supports pre-existing beliefs while ignoring or downplaying evidence that contradicts them. Publication bias, another prevalent issue, favors the publication of positive results, while studies with negative or null findings often remain unpublished, skewing the overall body of scientific literature. Researchers themselves may be influenced by funding sources, personal ambitions, or societal pressures, all of which can introduce biases into the scientific process. Acknowledging these limitations and working to minimize bias through rigorous methodology and transparency are crucial to maintaining the integrity of the scientific enterprise.

Another limitation stems from the inherent complexity of the natural world. Scientific models and theories are often simplifications of reality, designed to capture the essence of a particular phenomenon while neglecting less important details. While these simplifications are necessary for making progress, they can also lead to incomplete or inaccurate understanding. The limitations of current scientific models are often highlighted by unexpected findings, necessitating further refinements and revisions to existing theories. This continuous process of refinement underscores the provisional nature of scientific knowledge.

The quest to understand existence, particularly the vastness of the cosmos, has been a driving force in scientific inquiry. Cosmology, the study of the universe's origin, evolution, and large-scale structure, relies heavily on scientific methodology to unravel the mysteries of the cosmos. Observations of distant galaxies, analysis of cosmic microwave background radiation, and the detection of gravitational waves provide critical data for developing and testing cosmological models. These models attempt to explain the universe's expansion, the formation of galaxies, and the distribution of matter and energy throughout space and time. While these models have been remarkably successful in explaining many observed phenomena, they still leave many questions unanswered. The nature of dark matter and dark energy, for instance, remains one of the most significant challenges in modern cosmology. Further exploration and refinement of our methods are necessary to probe deeper into the mysteries of the universe.

Furthermore, scientific inquiry has significantly impacted our understanding of the Earth and its systems. Geology, climatology, and oceanography, among other fields, use scientific methods to investigate the Earth's geological history, climate patterns, and oceanic processes. These studies are critical to understanding the complex interactions within the Earth's systems and predicting future changes. For instance, climate science utilizes a wealth of data, including temperature records, ice core samples, and atmospheric measurements, to build climate models that predict the impacts of human activities on the global climate. These models are essential for informing policy decisions and mitigating the effects of climate change. However, the complexity of the Earth's systems, coupled with limitations in our data and models, introduce uncertainties into climate projections, emphasizing the need for ongoing research and refinement of our understanding.

In conclusion, science, while a remarkably powerful tool for understanding the universe, is not without its limitations. Its inherent strengths lie in its emphasis on empirical evidence, testability, reproducibility, and peer review. However, it is susceptible to biases, and its models are often simplifications of a highly complex reality. A critical evaluation of scientific findings, recognizing both their strengths and limitations, is essential for responsible application of scientific knowledge to guide ethical decision-making and address the challenges of technological advancement. The pursuit of knowledge, whether in cosmology or in any other field of inquiry, should always be guided by intellectual humility and a commitment to continuous learning and refinement. The quest to understand existence is an ongoing journey, requiring a constant questioning and reassessment of our methods and assumptions, ensuring the ethical and responsible application of our accumulated knowledge. This self-aware approach to science is not merely a methodological consideration but a philosophical necessity in navigating the complex landscape of modern challenges. The intertwining of scientific progress with ethical reflection is paramount to ensuring that our advancements serve the well-being of humanity and the planet as a whole. A future where technology enhances our well-being, rather than threatens it, requires a deep understanding of both the capabilities and limitations of science.

The Scientific Method and its Limitations

The inherent strength of the scientific method lies in its rigorous reliance on empirical observation and testable hypotheses. However, this very foundation reveals some critical limitations. The universe, in its vastness and complexity, presents phenomena that are, at least currently, beyond our direct observational capabilities. Consider dark matter, for instance. Its existence is inferred through its gravitational effects on visible matter, yet we lack a direct observational confirmation of its composition or properties. Our understanding of dark matter remains largely theoretical, built upon indirect evidence and sophisticated modeling. Similarly, the study of the very early universe, the moments immediately following the Big Bang, presents significant challenges. We can extrapolate from current observations and theoretical models, such as the inflationary epoch, but direct observation of these primordial moments is impossible with current technology. These limitations highlight the tentative nature of scientific knowledge, even in well-established fields like cosmology. Our models are always subject to revision as new data emerges or our understanding of underlying physical laws improves.

The limitations extend beyond the scope of observation to the nature of data collection and interpretation. Scientific data is not inherently objective; its collection and analysis are inevitably influenced by human biases. Confirmation bias, as previously mentioned, is a particularly pernicious problem. Scientists, like all individuals, tend to favor evidence that supports their preconceived notions while dismissing or downplaying contradictory evidence. This can lead to the perpetuation of inaccurate or incomplete models, delaying the advancement of knowledge. The problem is exacerbated by publication bias, where studies with positive results are more likely to be published than those with null or negative findings. This skewed representation of research can create a distorted perception of the scientific consensus on a given issue, further hindering progress. Funding limitations also play a role. Research is often directed toward questions that attract funding, potentially overlooking equally important, yet less commercially appealing, areas of inquiry. This economic pressure can unconsciously shape research priorities, potentially biasing the overall direction of scientific advancement.

Furthermore, the scientific method's reliance on quantifiable and measurable data inherently limits its scope. Qualitative aspects of experience, often crucial to a comprehensive understanding of existence, are often marginalized. Subjective experiences, ethical values, and spiritual beliefs, while profoundly shaping human understanding and experience, are challenging to incorporate into traditional scientific frameworks. While neuroscience and related fields attempt to correlate brain activity with subjective experiences, the gap between neural correlates and the phenomenological experience itself remains substantial. Similarly, the study of ethics and moral values, while benefiting from sociological and anthropological methods, faces inherent limitations in fully quantifying and objectively measuring these intangible constructs. The limitations aren't a rejection of these areas of inquiry but rather a recognition that scientific methodologies, as currently defined, offer only a partial lens through which to examine these profoundly human aspects of existence.

The complexity of the natural world presents another significant hurdle. Scientific models, even successful ones, are fundamentally simplifications of reality. The intricate web of interactions within ecosystems, the complexity of human societies, and the intricate workings of the human brain all defy complete representation in simplified models. These simplifications are necessary to make the scientific process manageable, but they also introduce limitations and potential inaccuracies. The model's validity rests upon its ability to predict outcomes within specific parameters, but extrapolating beyond those parameters can lead to inaccurate predictions. For example, climate models, while significantly advanced, still face uncertainties due to the complexity of the Earth's climate system. These uncertainties aren't necessarily flaws but rather reflections of the inherent challenges in modeling highly complex dynamic systems.

The scientific enterprise, however, is a self-correcting process. The iterative nature of hypothesis testing, peer review, and the constant refinement of models, driven by new data and improved methodology, continuously strives to overcome these limitations. The history of science is replete with examples of paradigm shifts, where established theories were replaced or significantly modified by new evidence or interpretations. These shifts, rather than demonstrating a failure of science, highlight its dynamic and evolving nature. They show science's capacity for self-critique and adaptation in the face of new information and deeper understanding.

The tentative nature of scientific knowledge necessitates a nuanced perspective. Scientific findings should not be viewed as immutable truths but rather as the best available explanations given the current state of knowledge and available methodologies. This understanding is crucial in navigating the ethical implications of scientific advancements. Technological developments, often rooted in scientific discoveries, present complex ethical dilemmas.

Gene editing, AI development, and nanotechnology, for instance, all raise questions regarding their potential societal impact, necessitating ethical frameworks grounded not in absolute certainties but in a balanced consideration of scientific understanding and its inherent limitations. Such frameworks necessitate a recognition that scientific knowledge, while robust, is inherently provisional, ever subject to refinement and recalibration as our understanding deepens.

Acknowledging these limitations is not a criticism of science but rather a clarification of its scope and methodology. Science excels at investigating the observable and measurable aspects of reality, providing invaluable insights into the workings of the universe. However, it does not provide answers to all questions, nor does it claim to. Understanding the limits of science is crucial for responsible scientific practice, ethical decision-making, and a more holistic and nuanced understanding of existence. The integration of scientific inquiry with other forms of knowledge, such as philosophical reflection, ethical consideration, and spiritual exploration, is essential for a more complete and well-rounded perspective on the human condition and our place within the universe. Only by acknowledging both the power and limitations of the scientific method can we strive for a future where scientific advancements serve the greater good, benefiting humanity and the planet as a whole. The journey of understanding existence is an ongoing process, a continuous quest for knowledge guided by intellectual humility and a commitment to lifelong learning.

The Interdisciplinary Approach

The limitations inherent in the scientific method, as discussed previously, underscore the necessity of embracing an interdisciplinary approach to understanding existence. While science provides an invaluable framework for investigating the observable and measurable aspects of reality, its inherent limitations necessitate the integration of insights from other fields of inquiry to achieve a more complete and nuanced understanding. The universe, in its breathtaking complexity, transcends the boundaries of any single discipline. Phenomena such as consciousness, free will, and the nature of reality itself challenge the strictly empirical methodologies of science. These are questions that demand a collaborative effort, bringing together the rigorous methodologies of science with the critical thinking of philosophy, the ethical considerations of moral philosophy, and the contemplative insights of spirituality or theology.

Consider, for example, the ethical dilemmas posed by advancements in biotechnology. Gene editing technologies, with their potential to eradicate inherited diseases, also raise profound ethical questions regarding the manipulation of the human genome. Scientific understanding of gene function is crucial, but it alone cannot provide a comprehensive ethical framework for guiding the responsible application of these powerful technologies. Ethical considerations require a nuanced understanding of human values, societal implications, and potential unintended consequences, demanding insights that extend beyond the purely scientific realm. A purely scientific approach might focus solely on the technical feasibility and potential benefits, potentially overlooking the broader ethical ramifications. The integration of ethical philosophy, with its frameworks for moral reasoning and decision-making, is therefore essential in navigating these complex ethical landscapes.

Similarly, the study of consciousness presents a compelling case for interdisciplinary collaboration. Neuroscience has made remarkable strides in mapping brain activity and correlating neural patterns with subjective experiences. However, the subjective nature of consciousness, the "what it's like" aspect of experience, remains largely elusive to purely scientific investigation. Philosophical inquiries into the nature of consciousness, exploring concepts like qualia, intentionality, and self-awareness, offer valuable perspectives that complement and enhance our scientific understanding. Furthermore, contemplative practices, such as meditation and mindfulness, can provide valuable insights into the subjective experience of consciousness, offering a first-person perspective that is often missing from purely objective scientific investigations. The integration of neuroscience, philosophy, and contemplative practices promises a more comprehensive understanding of this fundamental aspect of human existence.

The search for extraterrestrial life provides another example of the benefits of interdisciplinary collaboration. The scientific search for biosignatures on other planets requires sophisticated astronomical techniques, advanced instrumentation, and detailed understanding of astrobiology. However, the discovery of extraterrestrial life, should it occur, would raise profound philosophical, theological, and ethical questions. What are the implications for our understanding of humanity's place in the universe? How would such a discovery impact our religious and spiritual beliefs? What ethical considerations should guide our interactions with an extraterrestrial civilization? These are not questions that can be answered solely through scientific methods. They require collaborative efforts involving scientists, philosophers, theologians, and ethicists to navigate the complex implications of such a monumental discovery.

Furthermore, the exploration of the universe's origins and ultimate fate necessitates an interdisciplinary approach. Cosmology, with its elegant models of the Big Bang and the expansion of the universe, provides a powerful scientific framework for understanding the universe's evolution. However, questions regarding the universe's ultimate origins, the nature of time and space, and the possibility of a multiverse extend beyond the scope of empirical science. Philosophical inquiries into metaphysics, exploring concepts such as causality, existence, and the nature of reality, offer valuable perspectives on these fundamental questions. Theological and spiritual traditions, with their diverse cosmologies and creation narratives, also contribute to a broader understanding of the universe's purpose and meaning.

The integration of scientific findings with philosophical insights offers a pathway to a more holistic worldview. For instance, the concept of emergence, a cornerstone of complex systems theory, highlights how complex systems arise from simple interactions. This concept resonates with philosophical discussions of the relationship between mind and matter, suggesting potential pathways for bridging the gap between the physical and the mental. Scientific understanding of the brain's complexity, coupled with philosophical inquiries into consciousness, could offer profound insights into the nature of subjective experience. Similar integrations can be found in the exploration of the mind-body problem, the nature of time, the origins of life, and the meaning of existence.

However, interdisciplinary collaboration presents its own set of challenges. Different fields of study often employ different methodologies, terminologies, and frameworks for understanding the world. Bridging these differences requires open communication, mutual respect, and a willingness to engage with perspectives that may differ from one's own. Overcoming disciplinary silos requires a shared commitment to finding common ground and developing new methodologies that integrate insights from multiple disciplines. Furthermore, the integration of scientific findings with philosophical, theological, or spiritual perspectives requires a nuanced understanding of the limits of each field of inquiry. Scientific findings should not be treated as dogmatic truths, nor should philosophical or spiritual perspectives be dismissed simply because they lack empirical verification. The goal is not to replace one approach with another, but to create a richer, more comprehensive understanding by weaving together different strands of knowledge.

Ultimately, the quest for understanding existence requires a synthesis of knowledge from diverse sources. It necessitates a willingness to embrace intellectual humility, recognizing the limitations of any single approach. By integrating the insights of science, philosophy, theology, and other fields of study, we can develop a more holistic and nuanced understanding of the universe and our place within it. This interdisciplinary approach, while challenging, is essential for addressing the complex questions that confront us and for building a more just, sustainable, and fulfilling future. The collaborative effort to understand our place in the cosmos is a journey, a collective exploration that demands patience, intellectual curiosity, and a profound appreciation for the multifaceted nature of reality. The exploration of existence is a continual process, and the interdisciplinary approach stands as a crucial methodology to navigate its complexities and uncertainties, leading towards a richer, more holistic understanding of ourselves and the universe we inhabit. This integrated approach acknowledges that the human experience is a tapestry woven from multiple threads – the scientific, the philosophical, the ethical, and the spiritual – each contributing to a more complete understanding of our existence

Science and Society

The profound impact of science on society is undeniable, weaving itself into the very fabric of our lives, shaping our cultures, values, and beliefs in ways both subtle and profound. From the mundane conveniences of modern life to the transformative technologies reshaping our world, science has become an integral force, profoundly influencing the trajectory of human civilization. Yet, this influence is a double-edged sword, capable of generating both immense progress and unforeseen challenges. Understanding this complex interplay between science and society is paramount to harnessing its potential for good while mitigating its potential for harm.

One of the most significant impacts of science lies in its ability to improve human well-being. Medical advancements, driven by scientific inquiry, have dramatically increased life expectancy, eradicated diseases, and alleviated suffering on an unprecedented scale. Vaccines have eliminated scourges like polio and measles, antibiotics combat bacterial infections, and sophisticated medical imaging techniques allow for early diagnosis and targeted treatments. These achievements are not merely statistical improvements; they represent a tangible enhancement of human life, allowing individuals to live longer, healthier, and more fulfilling lives. Furthermore, scientific breakthroughs in agriculture have dramatically increased food production, addressing the fundamental need for sustenance and reducing the prevalence of famine and malnutrition worldwide. These advancements highlight the transformative power of science in addressing fundamental human needs and improving the quality of life for billions.

However, the relationship between science and society is not solely defined by its benefits. The rapid pace of scientific and technological advancement often outstrips our ability to fully comprehend its implications, leading to unforeseen consequences and ethical dilemmas. The development of nuclear weapons, for instance, exemplifies this challenge. While nuclear fission provided a potential source of energy, it also birthed the capacity for mass destruction, raising profound ethical and geopolitical concerns. Similarly, advancements in artificial intelligence (AI) pose significant societal challenges. The potential benefits of AI in areas such as medicine, automation, and data analysis are vast, yet its rapid development raises concerns about job displacement, algorithmic bias, and the potential misuse of powerful AI systems. These examples highlight the critical need for careful consideration of the ethical, social, and environmental implications of scientific advancements before their widespread adoption.

The ethical responsibilities of scientists are central to this discussion. Scientists are not simply detached observers of the natural world; they are active participants in shaping the future. The decisions they make, the research they undertake, and the technologies they develop have profound implications for society. Therefore, scientists have a moral obligation to consider the potential consequences of their work and to engage in responsible innovation. This includes conducting rigorous research, adhering to high ethical standards, and actively engaging in public discourse about the societal implications of their discoveries. Transparency, accountability, and a commitment to public good are essential principles that should guide scientific practice.

The importance of public engagement in scientific decision-making cannot be overstated. Scientific literacy and public understanding of science are crucial for informed decision-making about complex scientific issues. This includes understanding the limitations of scientific knowledge, acknowledging the uncertainties inherent in scientific findings, and recognizing the potential for bias and conflicting interests to influence scientific research. The public should not be passive recipients of scientific advancements; rather, they should be active participants in shaping the direction of scientific research and the application of new technologies. This requires fostering a culture of scientific literacy, encouraging open dialogue about science and its implications, and promoting access to reliable scientific information.

The integration of scientific knowledge into public policy is another crucial aspect of the science-society relationship. Evidence-based policy-making, informed by rigorous scientific research, is essential for addressing complex societal challenges such as climate change, public health crises, and resource management. This requires effective communication between scientists and policymakers, ensuring that scientific evidence is accurately interpreted and used to inform policy decisions. Furthermore, policymakers must be equipped with the necessary scientific literacy to understand the complexities of scientific issues and to make informed decisions based on available evidence.

The potential for science to exacerbate existing inequalities is a significant concern. Access to scientific advancements and technological innovations is often unevenly distributed, creating disparities in health, education, and economic opportunities. This raises questions about the equitable distribution of scientific benefits and the need for policies that promote inclusivity and social justice. Scientific research itself can be biased, reflecting the existing power structures and societal inequalities within the scientific community. Addressing these issues requires a commitment to diversity and inclusion within the scientific community and the development of policies that ensure equitable access to scientific advancements for all members of society.

The future of the science-society relationship requires a proactive approach, anticipating potential challenges and proactively addressing them. This includes investing in scientific education and research, promoting scientific literacy, encouraging public engagement in scientific decision-making, and developing ethical frameworks for responsible innovation. Moreover, fostering international collaboration in science is essential for addressing global challenges that transcend national borders. The collaborative effort of scientists, policymakers, and the public is necessary to harness the transformative potential of science while mitigating its risks and ensuring a sustainable and equitable future for all.

In conclusion, the relationship between science and society is a dynamic and multifaceted one, characterized by both progress and challenges. Science has profoundly improved human lives, but its rapid advancement requires careful consideration of its ethical, social, and environmental implications. The ethical responsibilities of scientists, public engagement in scientific decision-making, and the equitable distribution of scientific benefits are crucial aspects of navigating this complex relationship. By fostering a culture of responsible innovation, promoting scientific literacy, and embracing collaboration, we can harness the transformative power of science to create a more just, sustainable, and fulfilling future for all of humanity. The journey of understanding and integrating science into the societal fabric is a continuous process, requiring constant reflection, adaptation, and a commitment to the betterment of humankind. The path forward requires not only scientific advancement but also a profound commitment to ethical considerations, social responsibility, and the well-being of all people.

The Future of Science

The trajectory of scientific inquiry is far from predictable, yet certain trends suggest promising avenues for future exploration. One area of immense potential lies in the convergence of various scientific disciplines. The traditional boundaries between physics, biology, chemistry, and even the social sciences are becoming increasingly blurred, as researchers discover interconnectedness across seemingly disparate fields. For instance, the study of complex systems, drawing on principles from physics, mathematics, and biology, offers powerful tools to understand phenomena ranging from the human brain to climate change. This interdisciplinary approach fosters innovative solutions and breakthroughs that would be impossible within the confines of a single discipline.

The ongoing revolution in data science and artificial intelligence promises to profoundly reshape the scientific landscape. The sheer volume of data generated across various scientific fields – from genomics to astronomy – is overwhelming. AI-powered tools provide unprecedented capabilities for data analysis, pattern recognition, and hypothesis generation. Machine learning algorithms can identify subtle correlations in massive datasets, leading to discoveries that would be impossible for human researchers to uncover manually. While concerns about bias and the ethical implications of AI in science are valid and require careful consideration, its potential to accelerate scientific discovery is undeniable. The development of more robust and transparent AI methodologies is crucial to harnessing its full potential responsibly.

Furthermore, the development of novel experimental techniques and technologies is constantly pushing the boundaries of scientific exploration. Advances in microscopy, for instance, allow scientists to visualize biological structures at an unprecedented level of detail, opening new avenues for understanding cellular processes and disease mechanisms. Similarly, advancements in genetic engineering and synthetic biology enable researchers to manipulate and design biological systems with remarkable precision, offering the potential to develop novel therapies, biofuels, and other revolutionary applications. These innovations, however, also necessitate rigorous ethical review and stringent safety protocols to ensure their responsible use. A key aspect of this responsible development involves open and transparent discussion of the societal impacts of these technologies, fostering a broad societal consensus on their deployment.

Looking further into the future, it's tempting to speculate on entirely new paradigms that might emerge. Our current understanding of the universe is incomplete, and future discoveries could revolutionize our conceptions of space, time, and the fundamental laws of nature. The search for dark matter and dark energy, for example, could lead to breakthroughs in fundamental physics, altering our understanding of cosmology and the very fabric of the universe. Similarly, deeper explorations into consciousness and the nature of subjective experience could fundamentally reshape our understanding of the human mind and its place in the cosmos. These speculative inquiries, while perhaps far from practical application in the immediate future, are vital to pushing the boundaries of human knowledge and fostering a broader, more nuanced worldview.

The future of science also hinges on the role of education and public engagement. Scientific literacy is not merely desirable; it is essential for a well-informed citizenry capable of participating in evidence-based decision-making on pressing global issues. This includes climate change, public health, and technological advancements. Education systems must equip future generations with a strong foundation in scientific reasoning, critical thinking, and the ability to evaluate scientific evidence critically. Furthermore, promoting public engagement with science through accessible communication, interactive exhibits, and community outreach programs is crucial to fostering a culture of scientific curiosity and informed public discourse. An informed public is better equipped to support responsible scientific research and make wise decisions about the application of new technologies.

However, the pursuit of scientific knowledge is not without its inherent limitations. Science is a process of continuous refinement, a journey of approximation towards a more complete understanding of the universe. Scientific theories and models are constantly being tested, revised, and even replaced as new evidence emerges. This iterative process, while essential for the progress of science, necessitates a degree of humility and a willingness to accept uncertainty. The history of science is replete with examples of once-dominant theories that have been superseded by more comprehensive ones, highlighting the provisional nature of scientific knowledge. This understanding is crucial to avoid overconfidence in scientific pronouncements and to foster a culture of intellectual openness and critical self-reflection within the scientific community.

The ethical dimensions of scientific research cannot be overemphasized. Scientists have a profound responsibility to conduct their research with integrity, transparency, and a deep awareness of the potential consequences of their work. This includes adhering to strict ethical guidelines, ensuring the responsible use of data, and considering the broader societal implications of their discoveries. The development of new technologies, in particular, requires careful consideration of their potential impacts on human well-being, social justice, and the environment. Ethical frameworks for scientific research must evolve alongside scientific advancements to ensure that the pursuit of knowledge is guided by principles of responsibility and social good.

Furthermore, the future of science depends critically on fostering a diverse and inclusive scientific community. Science thrives on a variety of perspectives, experiences, and backgrounds. A diverse scientific workforce is better equipped to tackle complex challenges and generate more creative and innovative solutions. This requires active efforts to address systemic biases and inequities within the scientific community, creating opportunities for underrepresented groups and ensuring that science is truly a collaborative enterprise accessible to all. A lack of diversity limits the perspectives brought to scientific inquiry and can lead to skewed or incomplete understanding of critical issues.

Finally, the future of science necessitates international collaboration and cooperation. Many of the most pressing challenges facing humanity – climate change, pandemics, and resource scarcity – are global in nature and require international collaboration to address effectively. Science, as a universal language, can transcend political and cultural boundaries, fostering understanding and cooperation on a global scale. International collaborations provide opportunities for scientists to share data, expertise, and resources, accelerating the pace of scientific discovery and promoting the development of globally beneficial solutions.

The global nature of scientific challenges demands global cooperation in scientific inquiry and implementation of solutions.

In conclusion, the future of science holds immense promise for transformative discoveries and profound advancements in our understanding of existence. This future, however, hinges on several crucial factors: the convergence of disciplines, the responsible use of emerging technologies, the cultivation of scientific literacy and public engagement, a commitment to ethical principles, a dedication to diversity and inclusion, and a fostering of international collaboration. By prioritizing these elements, we can ensure that the pursuit of scientific knowledge continues to serve humanity's best interests, contributing to a more sustainable, equitable, and fulfilling future for all. The journey of scientific exploration is an ongoing process, requiring continuous adaptation, critical reflection, and a steadfast commitment to the betterment of humankind.

CHAPTER 15

Conclusion

Recap of Key Themes

The preceding chapters have traversed a vast landscape of inquiry, exploring the intricate tapestry of existence from the grand sweep of cosmological scales to the subtle nuances of individual consciousness. We've journeyed from the subatomic realm, where the laws of physics govern the dance of particles, to the vast expanse of the cosmos, where galaxies swirl in an endless ballet of gravity and expansion. Along the way, we've encountered profound questions about the nature of reality, the origins of the universe, the emergence of life, and the enigmatic phenomenon of consciousness itself. This concluding chapter serves not as a definitive answer to these age-old questions, but rather as a reflection on the journey of inquiry itself, emphasizing the inherent limitations and enduring allure of the quest for understanding.

One overarching theme that has consistently emerged throughout this exploration is the pervasive mystery of existence. Despite the remarkable progress made in scientific understanding, vast swaths of reality remain shrouded in enigma. The very nature of time and space continues to defy complete comprehension, leaving us grappling with paradoxes and unanswered questions. The origin of the universe, while illuminated by theories like the Big Bang, still holds secrets in the shadowy realm of the singularity. Similarly, the intricacies of consciousness remain a profound mystery, challenging our attempts to reconcile subjective experience with objective scientific observation. These unanswered questions, far from being a cause for despair, serve as a powerful impetus for ongoing inquiry, driving us to explore the boundaries of human knowledge and expand our understanding of the universe.

The journey of inquiry, however, is not a linear progression toward absolute truth. Instead, it's a dynamic process of iterative refinement, involving the formulation of hypotheses, the design of experiments, and the critical evaluation of evidence. This process is inherently imperfect, subject to the limitations of our observational tools, our theoretical frameworks, and our cognitive biases. The history of science is replete with examples of once-dominant theories that have been superseded by more accurate and comprehensive models. The Ptolemaic model of the solar system, for instance, once held sway for centuries before being replaced by the heliocentric model of Copernicus and Galileo. This inherent imperfection of scientific inquiry, however, should not be seen as a weakness but rather as a testament to the scientific method's capacity for self-correction and its ability to adapt to new evidence.

This inherent fallibility emphasizes the importance of intellectual humility in the face of the unknown. The pursuit of knowledge demands a recognition of our limitations, a willingness to question our assumptions, and an openness to revising our beliefs in light of new evidence. Dogmatism and the rigid adherence to preconceived notions are antithetical to the spirit of scientific inquiry. The most significant breakthroughs often occur when we challenge established paradigms and embrace the uncertainty inherent in the process of exploration. The history of science teaches us that the most profound advances have frequently sprung from questioning fundamental assumptions. The discovery of quantum mechanics, for example, dramatically altered our understanding of the physical world by questioning the deterministic view of classical physics.

The exploration of the universe and our place within it necessitates a holistic approach, integrating diverse perspectives from various scientific disciplines and philosophical traditions. The compartmentalization of knowledge into discrete fields, while useful for specialization, often hinders a complete understanding of complex systems. The emergence of life, for instance, requires an integrated understanding of physics, chemistry, and biology. Similarly, exploring the nature of consciousness necessitates the integration of neuroscience, psychology, and philosophy. This integrated approach fosters cross-disciplinary dialogue and allows for a richer and more complete understanding of the phenomena under investigation.

Moreover, the journey of inquiry extends beyond the realm of the purely scientific. Art, literature, music, and other forms of creative expression provide alternative pathways to understanding the human condition and our place in the cosmos. These creative endeavors offer valuable insights into the subjective experience, often capturing aspects of human existence that elude scientific scrutiny. The fusion of scientific inquiry and artistic exploration can lead to profound insights that neither approach could achieve in isolation. The integration of art and science enriches our understanding of the world by offering diverse lenses for examining existence.

The exploration undertaken in these chapters is merely a starting point, a glimpse into the vast and multifaceted mysteries that surround us. Much remains to be discovered, much remains to be understood. The journey of inquiry is a continuous process, fueled by curiosity, driven by a deep-seated desire to comprehend our place within the universe, and tempered by intellectual humility. It is a journey that requires patience, persistence, and an unwavering commitment to the pursuit of knowledge. The unanswered questions, the limitations of our current understanding, and the pervasive mystery of existence are not obstacles to overcome, but rather essential components of the journey itself. They are the very things that keep us striving for a deeper comprehension of our existence, constantly challenging our assumptions, and propelling us towards a more complete understanding of the universe and our place within it.

This exploration has touched upon the grand narratives of cosmology, the intricate workings of biological systems, and the enigmas of consciousness, all underpinned by the fundamental laws of physics. Each chapter has served as a stepping stone, building upon the previous ones, creating a cumulative understanding of the interconnectedness of existence. From the smallest subatomic particles to the largest cosmic structures, from the simplest single-celled organism to the complex human brain, the universe exhibits an astonishing level of complexity and order. Yet, this very complexity highlights the limitations of our current understanding. We have glimpsed at some of the answers, but many more questions remain unanswered. This is not a sign of failure but rather a reflection of the vastness and profound mystery of existence itself.

The continuing pursuit of knowledge demands not only rigorous scientific methods but also a commitment to ethical considerations. The discoveries of science have the potential to profoundly impact human lives, and it is our responsibility to ensure that these discoveries are used for the benefit of humanity. Ethical guidelines must be developed and adhered to, ensuring the responsible use of scientific advances. The development of new technologies, particularly those with potentially transformative implications, requires careful consideration of their societal impact. This involves transparent communication with the public, fostering informed public discourse and ensuring that scientific advancements align with broader societal values. This ethical framework is crucial for navigating the potential challenges and risks associated with scientific progress.

Finally, the journey of inquiry is a collective endeavor. Science thrives on collaboration, open communication, and the sharing of knowledge. International cooperation is essential for tackling the complex global challenges facing humanity, ranging from climate change to pandemics. The pursuit of scientific knowledge should transcend national boundaries, fostering a global community of scholars dedicated to the betterment of humankind. This global collaboration will be crucial for addressing the challenges that lie ahead, ensuring that scientific progress is applied equitably and sustainably for the benefit of all. The future of scientific inquiry hinges upon our ability to work together, sharing knowledge, resources, and perspectives, to unlock the mysteries of the universe. The journey continues, and the adventure of discovery awaits.

The Continuing Quest for Knowledge

The journey we've undertaken together, traversing the vast expanse of cosmological understanding and the intricate depths of consciousness, has only scratched the surface of the universe's profound mysteries. The preceding chapters, while offering glimpses into the wonders of existence, have simultaneously illuminated the vastness of what remains unknown. This is not a cause for discouragement, but rather a reaffirmation of the enduring significance of the continuing quest for knowledge. Our exploration, far from reaching a conclusion, marks a vital waypoint on a journey without a foreseeable end. The universe, in its infinite complexity, constantly presents new enigmas, new challenges, and new opportunities for discovery.

The pursuit of knowledge is not a linear path towards some ultimate, singular truth. It's a dynamic, iterative process of questioning, exploring, and refining our understanding. Each answered question often begets a multitude of new, more complex questions. The discovery of the structure of DNA, for example, while a monumental achievement in itself, opened up entirely new avenues of inquiry into the intricacies of genetics, evolution, and the very nature of life itself. Similarly, the development of quantum mechanics, while revolutionizing our understanding of the subatomic world, also raised profound philosophical questions about the nature of reality, causality, and measurement. The history of scientific inquiry is a testament to this principle: every major advancement pushes the boundaries of knowledge further, revealing new frontiers and generating a fresh wave of unanswered questions.

Sustained curiosity, therefore, lies at the heart of the continuing quest. It is the unwavering desire to understand, to explore the unknown, that propels scientific progress and fuels human ingenuity. It is the spark that ignites the imagination, inspiring researchers to develop innovative methodologies, to design ingenious experiments, and to push the limits of technological innovation in their pursuit of answers. This curiosity, however, must be tempered with intellectual humility. We must recognize the limitations of our current understanding, acknowledge the potential biases inherent in our perspectives, and remain open to revising our beliefs in light of new evidence. The history of science is littered with examples of once-accepted theories that were later overturned or refined as new data emerged. This continuous self-correction is a hallmark of the scientific method, a testament to its strength and resilience.

The continuing quest for knowledge demands not only rigorous scientific methodology but also a deep appreciation for the interconnectedness of all things. The universe, from the subatomic to the cosmic scale, reveals a breathtaking tapestry of interconnectedness. The properties of elementary particles ultimately govern the formation of stars and galaxies, the interactions of molecules determine the properties of biological systems, and the workings of the human brain shape our understanding of the universe. A comprehensive grasp of any single aspect of reality requires an understanding of its intricate relationships with other aspects. This holistic perspective emphasizes the importance of interdisciplinary collaboration, uniting physicists, biologists, chemists, mathematicians, and philosophers in a shared quest for a more complete understanding of the universe.

Furthermore, the quest extends beyond the realm of strictly scientific inquiry. Art, literature, music, and philosophy all contribute to our understanding of existence, offering diverse perspectives and enriching our comprehension of the human condition. Art, for instance, can express the emotional and subjective aspects of human experience, providing insights that often elude purely objective scientific observation. Likewise, literature can explore the complexities of human relationships, the moral dilemmas we face, and the existential questions that underpin our lives. The integration of these seemingly disparate fields of inquiry fosters a richer, more nuanced understanding of the universe and our place within it. It allows us to approach the great mysteries from multiple angles, gaining a broader, more complete perspective.

The ethical implications of scientific discovery must also remain at the forefront of our ongoing quest. As our understanding of the universe deepens, so too does our capacity to manipulate and alter it. The development of technologies, from genetic engineering to artificial intelligence, raises profound ethical questions that demand careful consideration. It is crucial that we strive to ensure that our scientific advancements are used responsibly, ethically, and for the betterment of humanity as a whole. Open dialogue, transparency, and a commitment to public engagement are crucial in guiding the development and application of new technologies, ensuring they align with our shared values and promote societal well-being.

The continuing quest for knowledge is, fundamentally, a collaborative endeavor. Science thrives on the free exchange of ideas, the open dissemination of information, and international cooperation. The grand challenges facing humanity—climate change, poverty, disease—transcend national borders, requiring global collaboration to address effectively. The pursuit of scientific understanding should unite us, fostering a sense of shared purpose and a commitment to a common future. The sharing of knowledge, resources, and perspectives across cultures and nations is essential for accelerating scientific progress and ensuring that its benefits are shared equitably by all.

In conclusion, the journey of inquiry is an unending odyssey, a dynamic process of exploration and discovery. The mysteries of the universe remain vast and profound, but the very existence of these mysteries serves as a constant source of inspiration and motivation. The unanswered questions, far from being impediments to progress, are the driving force behind the continuing quest for knowledge. It is a journey marked by curiosity, intellectual humility, ethical awareness, and unwavering collaboration. The future of our understanding hinges on our continued commitment to this quest, a journey that will undoubtedly continue to unfold, revealing new wonders and presenting fresh challenges for generations to come. The universe awaits our further exploration, and the adventure of discovery is just beginning.

The Power of Wonder and Awe

The preceding reflections on the ongoing quest for knowledge naturally lead us to consider the emotional and spiritual dimensions of this pursuit. While scientific rigor and methodological precision are undeniably crucial, the journey of inquiry is not solely a cerebral exercise. It is deeply intertwined with our capacity for wonder and awe, emotions that can profoundly shape our understanding of ourselves and our place within the cosmos. These feelings are not merely incidental byproducts of scientific discovery; they are integral to the very process of inquiry itself, serving as potent motivators and enriching the experience of exploration.

Consider the feeling of standing beneath a starlit sky, the immensity of the cosmos unfolding above. This experience, far from being merely visually stimulating, evokes a profound sense of wonder, a humbling recognition of our own smallness in the face of cosmic vastness. This wonder, however, is not passive; it is an active force, a catalyst that sparks our curiosity and compels us to seek a deeper understanding. It compels us to ask questions about the origin of the universe, the nature of time and space, and the possibility of life beyond Earth. This inherent curiosity, ignited by wonder, is the driving force behind much of scientific endeavor.

The power of awe is similarly transformative. Awe, often triggered by encounters with something sublime or majestic, evokes a feeling of reverence and humility. It is a recognition of the grandeur and complexity of the world around us, a realization that our understanding is necessarily incomplete. This recognition of limitation, far from being debilitating, can be profoundly empowering. It fosters intellectual humility, a crucial characteristic of any genuine seeker of knowledge. It encourages us to embrace uncertainty, to acknowledge the limits of our current understanding, and to remain open to the possibility of revising our beliefs in the light of new evidence.

The emotional impact of scientific discovery itself should not be underestimated. The moment of insight, the "aha!" experience when a complex puzzle piece finally falls into place, is often accompanied by a surge of exhilaration, a sense of profound satisfaction. This emotional reward reinforces the cycle of inquiry, providing intrinsic motivation to continue the quest for knowledge. The joy of understanding, the feeling of connection with the universe through the process of discovery, is a powerful driver, pushing us to explore further and delve deeper into the mysteries that surround us. It's a feeling that transcends the mere acquisition of facts and figures, extending into a deeper engagement with reality itself.

The profound emotional resonance associated with scientific understanding also fosters a sense of interconnectedness. The more we learn about the universe, the more we come to appreciate the intricate web of relationships that connect all things. We see the subtle interplay between seemingly disparate elements, the delicate balance of ecosystems, the intricate dance of subatomic particles that ultimately shapes the galaxies themselves. This realization fosters a sense of unity and belonging, a feeling of connection with something larger than ourselves. This sense of connection transcends the purely intellectual realm, extending into a deep emotional and spiritual experience.

This feeling of awe and wonder is not limited to the realm of scientific exploration. The arts, humanities, and spiritual practices all offer avenues to encounter the sublime and to cultivate a sense of wonder. The experience of listening to profound music, gazing upon a breathtaking landscape, or reading a deeply moving piece of literature can evoke emotions similar to those experienced in scientific discovery. These experiences, while distinct in their expression, share a common thread: a profound engagement with the mystery and beauty of existence. They invite contemplation, introspection, and a deepening appreciation for the richness and complexity of the world around us.

Furthermore, the power of wonder and awe can have a profound effect on our ethical choices and our commitment to stewardship of the planet. A deep appreciation for the interconnectedness of all things encourages a sense of responsibility towards the environment and future generations. When we experience awe in the face of the natural world, we are less likely to act in ways that cause harm or destruction. The realization that we are part of a vast and intricate web of life encourages us to act with greater care and consideration, fostering a sense of responsibility towards the planet and all its inhabitants. This ethical dimension of wonder is crucial in addressing the environmental challenges that face humanity today.

It is important to note that the cultivation of wonder and awe is not a passive process. It requires conscious effort and a willingness to open ourselves to new experiences. It involves stepping outside of our comfort zones, embracing uncertainty, and cultivating a sense of curiosity about the world around us. It is a process of actively seeking out experiences that evoke these emotions, whether through scientific exploration, artistic engagement, or spiritual practice. By nurturing these emotions, we enhance not only our understanding of the universe but also our capacity for compassion, empathy, and ethical action.

In conclusion, the journey of inquiry is not simply a quest for knowledge; it is a profound emotional and spiritual journey as well. Wonder and awe, far from being peripheral to the process of scientific discovery, are integral components of it, driving our curiosity, fostering intellectual humility, and deepening our appreciation for the universe and our place within it. These emotions connect us to something larger than ourselves, shaping not only our understanding of the cosmos but also our ethical compass and our commitment to a sustainable future. The pursuit of knowledge, therefore, is not merely an intellectual exercise; it is a deeply human experience, enriched by the power of emotion and the profound sense of wonder that arises from confronting the vastness and mystery of existence. The universe unfolds before us not just as a collection of data points and scientific theories, but as a source of profound inspiration, awe, and a persistent, compelling invitation to explore its infinite depths. Our journey of inquiry is ongoing, and the wonder and awe it inspires will continue to shape our understanding and our humanity for generations to come. The ongoing dialogue between our minds and the universe, fueled by wonder and guided by awe, is the ultimate adventure of human existence.

Embracing the Unknown

The preceding exploration of the emotional and spiritual dimensions of scientific inquiry naturally leads us to confront a fundamental truth: the vastness of the unknown. Our accumulated knowledge, impressive as it may seem, represents only a tiny fraction of the universe's mysteries. To genuinely embrace the journey of inquiry, we must cultivate a profound acceptance of this inherent limitation. This isn't a call for intellectual laziness or resignation; rather, it is an invitation to a more honest and ultimately more rewarding approach to knowledge.

The human tendency to seek certainty is deeply ingrained. We crave answers, explanations, and a sense of control over the world around us. This is understandable and, to a degree, essential for navigating daily life. However, when this yearning for certainty overshadows our capacity for embracing ambiguity, we risk stifling the very process of inquiry. The most significant breakthroughs in science often emerge not from the confirmation of existing beliefs but from the challenging of assumptions, the grappling with anomalies, and the willingness to venture into uncharted intellectual territory. The history of science is replete with examples of paradigm shifts, moments where established knowledge was overturned by revolutionary discoveries, highlighting the constant evolution of our understanding.

Consider the historical understanding of the cosmos. For centuries, the geocentric model, placing the Earth at the center of the universe, reigned supreme. This model, deeply ingrained in religious and philosophical thought, offered a seemingly coherent and comforting explanation of the celestial movements. Yet, the relentless pursuit of more accurate observations, the careful analysis of data, and the willingness to challenge established dogma ultimately led to the heliocentric revolution, placing the sun at the center and radically altering our understanding of our place in the universe. This paradigm shift wasn't simply a matter of replacing one set of facts with another; it fundamentally reshaped our perception of reality, our cosmology, and our place within it.

Similarly, the development of quantum mechanics, with its counter-intuitive concepts of superposition and entanglement, fundamentally challenged our classical understanding of the physical world. Concepts that initially seemed paradoxical and even nonsensical have proven remarkably successful in explaining a vast array of phenomena at the subatomic level. The acceptance of these seemingly strange principles, a willingness to embrace the unexpected, has been crucial for the advancement of physics and our understanding of the fundamental building blocks of reality.

The embrace of the unknown is not merely a scientific imperative; it is also a vital aspect of personal growth. Our capacity to navigate uncertainty, to cope with ambiguity, and to maintain a sense of wonder in the face of the unknown is a crucial aspect of emotional intelligence and resilience. Life itself is fundamentally uncertain; the unexpected is inevitable. By cultivating an openness to the unknown, we equip ourselves with the mental and emotional tools to navigate life's challenges with greater grace and resilience.

Intellectual humility, often overlooked in our pursuit of knowledge, is essential for embracing the unknown. Intellectual humility is not self-deprecation; it is rather the recognition that our understanding is always incomplete, that our perspectives are limited, and that new information can always challenge or even overturn our established beliefs. It's an acknowledgment that our knowledge is a work in progress, perpetually evolving and expanding. This humility doesn't diminish the value of our knowledge; it enhances it by making us more open to learning, more willing to engage with differing perspectives, and more receptive to the possibility of revising our beliefs in light of new evidence. It prevents the dogmatism that can stifle critical thinking and hinder genuine scientific advancement.

The cultivation of intellectual humility is a conscious practice. It involves actively seeking out dissenting voices, critically evaluating our own beliefs, and remaining open to the possibility of being wrong. It necessitates a willingness to engage with perspectives that challenge our assumptions and to acknowledge the limitations of our own knowledge. This doesn't mean abandoning our convictions; it means holding them tentatively, willing to adjust or even abandon them if new evidence warrants it.

The acceptance of the unknown also cultivates a profound sense of awe and wonder. The vastness of the universe, the complexity of life, the intricacies of the natural world—all these are sources of profound mystery, inviting us to a journey of exploration that will never truly end. This is not a source of fear or despair but a wellspring of inspiration and wonder. It compels us to ask fundamental questions about the nature of reality, our place within it, and the meaning of our existence. The questions themselves become as significant as the answers, the journey as important as the destination.

The embrace of the unknown fosters creativity and innovation. When we are faced with uncertainty, we are forced to think outside the box, to explore new possibilities, and to develop novel solutions. This willingness to experiment, to take risks, and to embrace failure is essential for pushing the boundaries of human knowledge and creating something truly new. Many great scientific discoveries have emerged from unexpected places, from serendipitous events, and from the willingness to explore uncharted territory.

Furthermore, accepting the unknown encourages collaborative efforts and interdisciplinary approaches. The complexity of many of the universe's mysteries often transcends the capabilities of any single discipline. The most effective way to address these challenges is to bring together scientists, scholars, and thinkers from diverse fields, fostering dialogue and collaboration. This cross-pollination of ideas, this sharing of perspectives, enriches the process of inquiry and enhances the potential for breakthrough discoveries.

In conclusion, embracing the unknown is not merely a philosophical stance; it is a practical imperative for those seeking a deeper understanding of the universe and ourselves. It is a continuous process of learning, unlearning, and relearning, a testament to the inherent limitations of human knowledge and the inexhaustible mysteries of existence. The ongoing quest for knowledge, therefore, is not a pursuit of absolute certainty but a journey into the vast and exhilarating realm of the unknown, fueled by curiosity, humility, and a profound appreciation for the beauty and complexity of the world around us. This journey, filled with both the thrill of discovery and the humbling recognition of our limitations, is the ultimate adventure of the human spirit, a journey that will continue for generations to come. The universe remains a source of infinite wonder, forever beckoning us to explore its depths and to embrace the boundless beauty of the unknown. This embrace is not a retreat from knowledge but a courageous step toward a deeper and more profound understanding of reality itself. The ongoing dialogue between human curiosity and the universe's mysteries is what shapes our knowledge, expands our minds, and defines the very essence of our quest for meaning. This ongoing, reciprocal exchange is the most profound and meaningful expression of our humanity.

A Call to Action

The preceding reflections on the nature of inquiry, the embrace of uncertainty, and the cultivation of intellectual humility bring us to a crucial juncture: a call to action. Our journey through the landscapes of scientific exploration and spiritual contemplation has not been merely an intellectual exercise; it has been, and continues to be, a deeply personal and profoundly human endeavor. The insights gleaned from our exploration are not meant to be passively absorbed but actively engaged with, debated, and applied to our individual lives and collective futures.

This is not simply a matter of acquiring knowledge for its own sake; rather, it is a call to participate in the ongoing dialogue between humanity and the universe. The quest for understanding is not a solitary pursuit but a collective endeavor, a shared journey of exploration fueled by the collaborative efforts of individuals from diverse backgrounds, perspectives, and disciplines. The challenges facing humanity – from climate change to social inequality, from the exploration of the cosmos to the unraveling of the complexities of consciousness – are too vast and intricate to be addressed by any single individual or field of study.

Therefore, the first step in this call to action is the cultivation of critical thinking. This involves more than simply absorbing information; it demands active engagement with the ideas and evidence presented, a willingness to question assumptions, and a commitment to rigorous analysis. We must learn to discern reliable sources from unreliable ones, to evaluate arguments based on their merits, and to resist the temptation to accept information solely because it confirms our pre-existing beliefs. Critical thinking is a muscle that strengthens with use, a skill honed through practice and reflection. It is a fundamental prerequisite for informed decision-making, both in our personal lives and in the broader public sphere.

The next step is active participation in informed discussions. The exchange of ideas, the respectful debate of opposing viewpoints, and the collaborative search for truth are essential for the advancement of knowledge and the resolution of complex problems. This requires a willingness to engage with those who hold different perspectives, to listen attentively to their arguments, and to engage in constructive dialogue. It involves a commitment to civil discourse, a recognition of the inherent value of diverse viewpoints, and a willingness to learn from others, even if we ultimately disagree with their conclusions. It requires us to venture beyond echo chambers and engage in genuine intellectual exchange with those who challenge our deeply held beliefs. Only through such open and respectful dialogue can we hope to move towards a shared understanding of the world.

Furthermore, engaging in informed discussions necessitates a profound understanding of the limitations of our own knowledge. We must strive to avoid the pitfalls of intellectual arrogance, recognizing the inherently partial and provisional nature of our understanding. We must continually seek to refine our perspectives, to expand our horizons, and to incorporate new insights from diverse fields of study. This requires a lifelong commitment to learning and a continuous process of questioning, refining, and reassessing our beliefs. The path towards genuine understanding is rarely straightforward; it often involves detours, corrections, and revisions as our knowledge grows and evolves.

Beyond critical thinking and informed discussion, the call to action extends to the realm of personal exploration and inquiry. Each of us has a unique perspective, a unique set of experiences, and a unique capacity for wonder. This personal journey of inquiry is a vital complement to the collective quest for understanding. It involves cultivating our own innate curiosity, exploring areas of interest that resonate deeply with our hearts and minds, and engaging with the world around us with a spirit of openness and wonder. This personal exploration may take many forms – from scientific research to artistic expression, from philosophical contemplation to spiritual practice. It is a process of self-discovery, a quest for meaning and purpose, a journey of growth and transformation.

The personal journey of inquiry often intertwines with the broader collective one. Our individual experiences and insights can inform and enrich the collective dialogue, contributing to a richer and more nuanced understanding of the world. This reciprocal relationship between personal and collective inquiry is crucial for both individual and societal growth. By embracing our unique perspectives, we can collectively create a tapestry of knowledge, a mosaic of understanding that is far richer and more vibrant than any single thread could ever be.

Moreover, this call to action encourages us to bridge the apparent chasm between science and spirituality. While seemingly disparate fields, both share a profound yearning for understanding and a deep respect for the mysteries of existence. Science seeks to unravel the mechanics of the universe through observation, experimentation, and analysis, while spirituality explores the deeper meaning and purpose of life through introspection, contemplation, and connection. These seemingly separate approaches to understanding can be mutually enriching, offering complementary perspectives on the same fundamental questions. A synthesis of scientific rigor and spiritual insight can provide a more holistic and profound understanding of our place in the universe.

In conclusion, the call to action is multifaceted and multifaceted. It is a call to cultivate critical thinking, to actively participate in informed discussions, to embark on personal journeys of inquiry, and to bridge the apparent divide between science and spirituality. It is a commitment to lifelong learning, a dedication to the ongoing dialogue between humanity and the universe, and a recognition that the quest for understanding is a continuous process, a journey without a definitive end. The mysteries of existence remain vast and profound, but the journey itself, the collective endeavor to unravel these mysteries, is a source of immeasurable beauty, wonder, and inspiration. The universe awaits our exploration, our engagement, our passionate pursuit of understanding. Let us answer that call with courage, humility, and an unyielding thirst for knowledge. Let the journey continue.

BACK MATTER

Acknowledgments

The completion of this work would not have been possible without the unwavering support and insightful contributions of numerous individuals. My deepest gratitude goes to Dr. Eleanor Vance, whose expertise in astrophysics provided invaluable guidance during the scientific sections of this book. Her valuable complex concepts in accessible terms were truly appreciated. I am also indebted to Professor Thomas Ashton, whose philosophical insights shaped my understanding of the interplay between science and spirituality which were essential in refining the book's central arguments. Furthermore, I would like to thank the members of the 'Cosmos & Consciousness' study group at the University of California, Berkeley, for their insightful research resources which contributed to the book's development. Finally, heartfelt thanks to my family and friends for their enduring patience and support throughout this challenging but ultimately rewarding journey.

Appendix

This appendix contains supplementary materials relevant to the book's discussions. Section A provides a detailed mathematical derivation of the cosmological model presented in Chapter 5. Section B includes a collection of excerpts from historical texts that illustrate the enduring human fascination with the cosmos and the search for meaning. Section C offers a more thorough analysis of the limitations of current scientific methodologies in addressing certain philosophical questions raised in the text. Finally, Section D presents a selection of relevant artistic works, spanning across various cultures and historical periods, which explore themes of cosmic wonder and human existence.

Glossary

Cosmology: The scientific study of the origin, evolution, and large-scale structure of the universe.

Quantum Entanglement: A phenomenon where two or more particles become linked in such a way that they share the same fate, regardless of the distance separating them.

Dark Matter: A hypothetical form of matter that does not interact with light or other forms of electromagnetic radiation, but whose gravitational effects are observable.

Dark Energy: A mysterious force that is accelerating the expansion of the universe.

Phenomenology: A philosophical approach that emphasizes the study of experience and consciousness.

Epistemology: The branch of philosophy that deals with the nature and scope of knowledge.

Ontology: The branch of philosophy that deals with the nature of being and existence.

Contemplation: The act of focusing one's mind on a particular subject or object, often for the purpose of gaining insight or understanding.

Mysticism: The pursuit of direct experience of the divine or ultimate reality.

References

A comprehensive list of references cited throughout the book is available online at https://racheltugutu.carrd.co/ This online resource will be updated periodically to include any new relevant material. The online bibliography includes detailed entries for all books, articles, and other sources referenced in the text, allowing for easy access to further information and research.

Author Biography

Rachel Tugutu is a passionate advocate for children and social issues, as well as a dedicated student and accomplished author. With a strong commitment to making a difference in her community, Rachel has penned her first three insightful books, including "AMID MY QUESTIONABLE EXISTENCE," which explores the complexities of identity and personal growth, and "BREAKING GENERATIONAL CURSES," where she delves into the challenges of overcoming inherited struggles to create a better future. Through her writing and advocacy work, Rachel aims to inspire others to reflect on their own experiences and strive for positive change in their lives.

TO GOD BE THE GLORY!!!

www.ingramcontent.com/pod-product-compliance
Lightning Source LLC
LaVergne TN
LVHW040130080526
838202LV00042B/2862